16⁹⁵

D0952055

THE HOLY USE OF MONEY

THE
HOLY USE
OF MONEY

Personal Finance in
Light of Christian Faith

✼✼

John C. Haughey, S.J.

DOUBLEDAY & COMPANY, INC.
GARDEN CITY, NEW YORK 1986

Library of Congress Cataloging-in-Publication Data

Haughey, John C.
The holy use of money.

Includes index.
1. Economics—Religious aspects—Christianity.
2. Stewardship, Christian. I. Title.
BR115.E3H34 1986   261.8′5   85–29213
ISBN 0-385-23448-1

Contents

	Introduction	vii
I	Naming and Healing the Illness	1
II	The Sublation of the Economy	50
III	Inclusion, the Second Function of Faith	69
IV	Obedient Hearing—The Third Function of Faith	105
V	Extending the Tent Poles	140
VI	Discipleship and Today's Economy	177
VII	Hope and Economic Activity	200
VIII	That Christ May Be My Wealth	234
	Notes	247
	Index	267

Introduction

Putting a title on this book was a more difficult task than writing it. The editors and I were able to come up with a number of suggestions but we couldn't agree on which was the best. They cherished: "The Currency of God or The Wealth of Christians." I preferred "Money Changers: The Christian Transubstantiation of Wealth or Reminting Mammon: A Faith Audit of Personal Finances." The final and present choice of the title, *The Holy Use of Money*, accurately captures the spirit and import of the volume and the subtitle confines the area of the volume's reflections.

The most difficult concept to yield on was that of transubstantiation. I yielded because I believe the editors were correct in seeing it as a very old category that would make sense only to middle-aged and older Roman Catholics. Conceding to their misgivings does not diminish my desire to explain why I was slow to surrender the metaphor. The book is about the change religious faith can bring to our use of money, our capital, our assets—in a word, our wealth. At the Eucharist, the intentions of priest and congregation as well as their sacramental powers are key to the action that has been traditionally described as transubstantiation. In a similar way, the intentions as also the powers of Christians, who because of baptism participate in the priesthood of Christ, are key to the substantial change that can be wrought in our material and financial resources. This volume spells out in detail what is required in order for people of faith to exercise their powers so that they are substantially affecting the assets over which they have some disposition.

Transubstantiation is a metaphor. In the case of the Eucharist, the bread and wine do not physically become Christ. They remain bread and wine while they mediate the real presence of Christ to us. He really becomes food and drink for us but we don't drink and eat the Son of God. What we drink and eat mediates him to us. The marvel in this is not the change that comes over the bread and wine but the change that comes over a people God chooses to be his own when they choose to exercise the faith with which God has embued them. The Eucharist cannot be explained except that the believers believe bread and wine into being what Christ wills it to be for them. He wills it to be him for them. But he's not confined only to this mode of being present to them. More than bread and wine should mediate him to us. Money can and should, which is one reason for the volume.

If faith can see Christ giving himself to us in bread and wine, it can also see him giving himself to us in more than these. In Roman Catholicism's understanding of the matter, there are sacraments and sacramentals that are outward signs by which God's graciousness is concretized and extended to us. While these outward signs are stable, authoritative means for the flow of God's goodness to us, they are not exhaustive of it. Our faith can be made sensitive to seeing even the medium of exchange, which is what money is, as God's graciousness concretizing itself to us. Even more importantly, faith can direct its use. This is a second reason for the volume, which is also a meditation on the holy use of money. It will specify what is entailed in the permeation and direction of money by faith.

The analogy with the Eucharist can be carried too far, of course. Banks are not tabernacles, for example, holding our sacred species, except for those people who are hopelessly addicted to the accumulation of wealth or psychotic. Ordinary people assign considerably more importance to the tangible and intangible goods that their money can procure than they do to money itself. This is as it should be since it is primarily a medium of exchange. Even as a medium of exchange, however, it is essential to see money in a theological light. No less important is seeing our assets in the same light. Otherwise our wealth operates too much like a sovereign in us, with wealth being subject to no one and us subject to it. Most of us live in a state of ambivalence about this "filthy lucre" or of permanent concern about it or of inexplicable attraction to it which exacts from us a price we don't freely choose to pay, namely, peace or community or the freedom to be compassionate to others.

For those who are helped by situating theology in its many branches, this study will be for the most part an exercise in Christology. It is in part inspired by a volume published in 1977 by the Dutch Jesuit theologian Franz Jozef van Beeck. His *Christ Proclaimed* (Paulist Press) furnished me with an insight into the ways in which faithful Christians of each generation grow Christ freshly, so to speak, by the way they handle their everyday concerns. Unlike van Beeck, I concentrated on the monetary, financial, and material concerns we all have every day. These need not be fugitive but can be brought into the mystery of Christ and transformed there. A drastic change in the way we handle these concerns awaits a change in our perception of Christ. In turn, the role Christ plays in this world will be seen in a new light. These changes are not simply in our consciousness. They are also in the objects and subjects themselves. These changes are not superficial, a fact that adds merit to the metaphor transubstantiation to describe them.

One way of explaining a book is to say what it is not. This book is not a commentary on the American Catholic Bishops' Pastoral on the Economy. I began my work roughly at the same time the Bishops' committee began its work. I completed my work, for the most part, before their first draft was published. I have taken a quite different approach than their document does, as anyone familiar with it will see immediately. Second, this is not an ethical treatise as one that is ordinarily understood. Its "shoulds" are few; its "musts" are nonexistent. It stays in the "is" mode of theological discourse, attempting to explain what it is about our Christian faith that pertains to life in this economically fueled American culture. It is more of a Christological meditation, in a word, than an ethical treatise.

Nor is it an economic or social analysis of the American economic system. It is a faith analysis because it begins and ends in faith, but a faith mediated by wealth, however slight or monumental that might be for anyone of us. Its reasoning will not appeal to those Christians who are unaccustomed to reasoning from their hearts. If I have done my task well, I hope that hearts will concur with this faith analysis; if poorly I am sure they will withhold their assent. Neither will it appeal to those Christians who have learned to so interiorize their faith that it disappears from the grid of people and systems and institutions, leaving no evidence by which it can be traced and verified. Finally, it is not a subtle exhortation to Christians to give their money to the poor. If anything it is more of an exhortation, first of all to myself, to be faithful to God in using the few things over which we have been placed. God would free us so that our material and financial resources become means for our discerning purposes. By each of us being faithful to the flow of the life of faith in us, together we can be Christ in time. By growing in Christ, we grow to be Christ in our culture and generation.

There is hardly a person alive who doesn't see the need for drastic systemic changes in our economic patterns of behavior both domestically and internationally. The ordinary way of trying to bring these about is by systemic analyses, for example, of our budget or trade deficits, plus strategy followed by action. This volume is also interested in systemic change but doesn't believe that it can come about only in the way cited. One reason for this is that the dichotomy usually posed between individual change or systemic change breaks down when the starting point of the hoped for change is religious faith. As a response to God's action in us faith is already action in the human order. Faith acted upon in our everyday lives is already social action, the beginning of social change. Individuals acting on faith make waves within the smallest social units of which they are a part, their interpersonal relationships, and in the largest of these units, the organizations with which they are associated, and on all the units in between. A disembodied faith, meaning a deficient faith that does not have action as part of it, would not be mediated by the goods of earth and, therefore, would not be system-affecting. This volume, however, does not reflect on a disembodied, but an embodied faith. "Every child of God overcomes the world. And this is the victory that has overcome the world—our faith." (1 John 5:4)

The Gospel is, among other things, a route, a way. It is a way of living in the world, with the things of the world. This route can be traced and the things of the world can be read in terms of this journey. The route, in chapter form, will begin a description of the primary action God in Christ would take in us who are consumers and producers in today's economy. The second chapter then seeks to know what Christ's own perspective is about the economic order, both how he saw this dimension in his own historical life and how he sees this dimension of our lives. After this initial perspective and appreciation of his healing intentions, the third chapter sees the primary response that takes place at the intersection, so to speak, at which the human spirit touches on the economic order. This is the activity of inclusion as this chapter calls it. This ongoing action is followed by an ongoing process of valuing, which is an obedience of the heart, a subject developed in several ways in Chapters IV, V, and VI. The seventh chapter deals with the great hope to which we are called and how this might permeate our everyday financial activities. The last chapter takes the thesis of the volume and shows how it was Paul's experience.

I am particularly indebted to the members of the Woodstock Theological Center of which I had been a member since its founding in 1974. They chose to undertake a project beginning in 1982 on religious values and the American economy. This volume got going with that decision and impetus. In particular, Fr. James Hug, S.J., director of that project, was a source of encouragement throughout. Sally Walsh was a godsend in its first stages. Jude Howard and Eileen Phillips who staff Woodstock's offices were indefatigable in their efforts to see this manuscript through. Joan-Marie Freitag and Joy Williams also manifested infinite patience and generosity, while it took its final shape during the year I was at Seton Hall University as visiting professor.

THE HOLY USE OF MONEY

✦✦

CHAPTER I

Naming and Healing the Illness

A complaint inspires this volume. The complaint is that in our American culture money talks all the day long and faith is virtually silent. It's not like faith to be silent, but in the presence of money it has learned to accept a monologue. This volume will try to help faith talk as effectively to money as money talks to faith.

There are several reasons why faith needs to talk to money. Some would say it should because they are concerned about injustice, or with maldistribution and the inequities that need to be overcome locally and internationally. Others because they are concerned about their own impoverished financial condition and wonder what, if anything, God can or would do about it. Others are unsure about their plenty and wonder about their obligations to those who have precious little. While this volume will be sensitive to all of these interests, it is even more concerned with the condition of those who have neither plenty nor too little and who find themselves caught up in what seems to be an expenditure of excessive amounts of time and energy "making ends meet," as they say. Meanwhile their deepest values, such as love, justice, community, compassion, are attended to poorly. Money doesn't do our bidding; we do its bidding. It doesn't embody our values. We find ourselves its minions.

By money here I mean something untechnical and all-embracing, both the out-there economic system and our own in-house financial condition, meaning that small part of the economic system of which each of us has a piece. This financial condition includes our capital, our liquidity, and our assets, such as they are.[1] These are the proxy stand-ins in our lives for the economic system and its financial structures. Our own in-house capital, and our need for more of same, link us inalienably to out-there money and the economic system. Our use of money affects the system. Money, therefore, is like a two-way courier. We use it to meet our needs and express our interiority insofar as we use it to embody what we value and pursue our purposes. But out-there money makes inroads into our interiority, indiscriminatingly communicating notions and values, which trigger off in us a number of desires, for better or worse.

Ideally, this courier works for both sides, bringing messages from out-there money to us and from us to out-there money. But it doesn't do this latter part of its job very well. By our economic behavior the economic system knows our wants. How much these wants are conditioned by the system is something we have to ask ourselves. Even more important is the matter of our values and whether our economic behavior registers these. If the only evidence the economic system has from us is the wants the system itself has induced in us, then the courier is working for one side even though it is carrying messages both ways.

For this chapter to be successfully launched, the reader needs to concur with three of the assumptions underlying it: first, that the deeper values most of us would pursue in our better moments are justice, love, community, and compassion; second, that in those of us with a religious background these values are related to our religious faith, probably even generated by our faith;[2] and third, that in most of us faith is weak, even defective.

The subject matter of this chapter is faith, faith that has grown defective because of money and faith that can be freed to release its power. If it is whole, clear, and acted on, faith will speak clearly to money. It will carry messages to the system. The system will register our deeper values by the use we make of our in-house money. But if we who believe are compromised by money, confused by it, and accommodated to it, then we need first of all to see our condition, repent of it, and be made whole. Hear the paradox here: your faith will make you whole if you can see that your faith is defective. But its deficiency can become more evident by reflection on our relationship to money than it can by any abstract reflection on our relationship to God as such.

What keeps these observations from being a vicious circle is the character of faith in God. God who can heal, can heal our faith. A faith that isn't releasing its power is a faith that needs to be made whole. These observations will probably seem too religious to some, too privatized to others, especially those who are concerned about the economic system and making it just. I am no less concerned about the system and its health. The key difference is that the approach I am taking places much more stock in the power of faith than we are accustomed to expect from it. Faith made whole is powerful, even for public life. Defective faith, compromised faith is not powerful, as public life and our American economy can testify. The American economy doesn't suspect the power of faith. Nor will it if we who are religious citizens do not see our need to be healed.

When Faith Is Sick

So far all we have are assertions, and assertions of a rather abstract character at that. The First Book of Kings will begin to flesh out and ground some of the connections we are trying to establish. This ancient text, Chapters 1–11 in particular, can enlighten our contemporary relationship to our culture and its economy. The text covers the era of King Solomon's reign. An excellent exegetical reading of the spiritual condition of the people has been done by Walter Brueggemann.[3]

The people have faith in Yahweh, certainly, but it is a peculiar kind of faith. It knows affluence. It is conscious of its past victories and is attempting to pursue an order promoted by Solomon. The people's consciousness is affected by Solomon's vision of social reality. This consciousness was a betrayal of the radical vision of Moses. The royal consciousness of Solomon and the people was consolidated by several devices.⁴ First, a system of tax districts virtually eradicated the pluralism of the tribes in favor of state control. Second, a bureaucracy that imitated the larger empires began to develop. It helped to immunize the people to questions of justice and compassion. A standing, well-equipped army, furthermore, protected Israel but it was not supple to "the rush of God's spirit."⁵ And, finally, the fabled gift of wisdom with which Solomon was imbued turned into "an effort to rationalize reality, i.e. packaging it in manageable portions."⁶

The royal consciousness of Solomon's era tended to co-opt the stark transcendence of Yahweh. Their Yahweh is no longer over-against royal power as He was in the Moses era when He was on the side of the poor. Solomon's God is domiciled in the temple Solomon built for Him. He functions as a legitimator, so to speak, of the politics and economic arrangements of Solomon's court. The king is at peace and at ease with his own version of God. And the "order" that ensues makes any who are not happy with this arrangement malcontents, even religiously suspect. "For those who regulate and benefit from the order a truly free god is not necessary, desirable or perhaps even possible."⁷

In imitation of the king, consumption and production become the preoccupation of the community. As consumption looms large, covenant lessens in importance. Yahweh's embrace of His people and theirs of Him does not have to be quite so total as it was when Israel's plight was great since now "you have plenty of good things laid by for many years to come" like the man with the bumper crop of grain in Luke. (Luke 12:19) Along with this slackening of need of Yahweh comes a lessening of concern for one another. Once people's image of God is of One who does not have deep feelings for those in need, this affects their "fellow feeling." A God who would sustain them in the life they had become accustomed to is the new image of God the people buy into. "Achievable satiation," which is the description Brueggemann gives to the imperial program, numbs them to God and one another.⁸ Their religion becomes a subtle form of legitimation of their own political and economic way of life. God's people become like the God they began to conjure rather than the One they had previously obeyed. They become listless, numb, without passion, without compassion. Not until new political circumstances and the prophets break into this numbness do the people come to an awareness of their subtle revisionism and glimpse anew the alternative way of life Moses had led them into.

Thus, a combination of three different dimensions of Israel's life, the political, the economic, and the religious, explain Israel's unfaithful form of order. There is the economics of affluence (1 Kings 4:20–23; 10:14–29) coupled with the politics of marginalization even of oppression (1 Kings 9:15–22) reinforced by the religion of immanence. (1 Kings 8:12–13) "There is no notion that God may act apart from and even against this regime . . . He is 'on call' and access to him is controlled by the royal court."⁹

Each of these three dimensions feeds the other two for a culture to become sick and for its illness to be terminal. An economics of affluence enables a population to ignore others' pain as well as its own. "We can eat our way around it."¹⁰ But this in turn requires a political system that marginalizes those whose pain is the greatest. These arrangements are consolidated by a religious system that has figured God out and made Him so accessible "that his abrasiveness, his absence, his banishment are not noticed."¹¹ Together these systems redefine the meaning of being human and religious. Before the sickness could be healed, there had to be a recognition that it had lodged in them. They had to differentiate between themselves as determined by their economic culture and their true humanity before God. If this was the condition they were in, how much more is this the case with us in our culture.

From this one example much can be learned. First, clearly the Scriptures have much to tell us about ourselves and our own culture. Second, a scriptural paradigm does not solve a problem in the culture or the system, but it discloses the source of the problem, the human heart, and the right order it is meant to live in and generate as well as the wrong order it lives in and reinforces. Thus the starting point for changing the system need not be the system itself. Third, it discloses what those who have heard the word have going for them, namely, faith, but faith that needs to be purified and strengthened.

And last, the numbness of Solomon's era is an example of how important it is to begin with an awareness of how deranged, disordered, and sick we are individually and collectively. The sickness is both cultural and religious, personal and collective, systemic and individual, economic and of the heart. It will not be healed or cured till it is seen. This is why I began with Scripture, a particular paradigm, and the need to have the word of God pierce our consciousness with an awareness of the spiritual condition of each of us and our culture so that our faith might be purified and God might heal us. For faith to function it must first be well.

Luke

It's all very well and good to seek to have "faith" speak to "money" but where will this faith that is going to do the talking come from? Faith doesn't exist apart from human beings and visit the human enterprise as if it had a life of its own; rather, it is always historical and inculturated. It is accessible through a faithful people who live or lived in a particular culture or moment of history. Ideally this faith would be contemporary and American. But to whose faith would we have recourse to teach us the language we need to speak to money? How would we know that the lessons of our contemporaries were not an accommodation or compromise of faith to the economic system? An accommodated faith cannot speak to money since money has taught it what to say, which is not much, and what not to say, which is to be quiet and learn what "reality" is.

This doubt about a viable faith paradigm that is contemporary doesn't come from a cynicism about the religious condition of Americans or because of some ideological brief against our economic system. Nor does it occur because I think there is some inner necessity that money will inevitably dictate to faith. The doubt comes because even the most faithful among us do not have the needed distance from the economic system that permeates our lives to put money in its place. Money's omnipresence and complexity make it virtually impossible for us to stand apart from it and take the measure of it.

There is, however, an incarnated faith that can serve as an example for us to take the measure of our economic culture and teach us how to operate within it with greater integrity, fidelity, and power. The Gospel of Luke/Acts is peculiarly suited to fill this need. It is a Jesus story, more precisely an interpretation of the Jesus story. It both reflects the community's beliefs about Jesus and instructs about the conditions of following him. It is explicitly concerned with the issue of money and possessions.[12] Luke saw that some of his contemporaries had not allowed their Christian faith to take the measure of their material and financial needs and resources. As a result, money was taking the measure of their faith and weakening it.[13] As an Evangelist Luke announces to his hearers and readers who Jesus is and what faith in Jesus entails. As a member of the faithful he communicates the faith of his community both as it is being lived and as it might be lived in the economic culture contemporary with him. And as a pastoral leader of the community he selects those aspects of the life, words, and deeds of Jesus that address his own community's faith needs.

Luke was probably a Gentile from Antioch who wrote the Gospel around A.D. 80–85 for a Gentile readership.[14] He was concerned about the retention of the initial fervor of the first believers. While Jesus apparently had in his lifetime invited many to sell all they had to follow him and his understanding of the imminent coming of the Kingdom of God, Luke and the community contemporary with him had to deal with the delay in the coming of the Kingdom.[15] Luke was eager to spell out the way of life that Christians had necessarily to settle down in and live while they awaited the return of Jesus and the fullness of the Kingdom of God his second coming would bring.

It is most unlikely, of course, that either Jesus or Luke would have made either their culture or the economy a distinct object of consciousness.[16] This kind of perception and act of abstraction would have been foreign to the consciousness of their age. What was not foreign to Jesus or, therefore, to Luke was insight into the condition of the hearts of the populace in general and in individual cases. What he saw and how he responded to that condition is what the Gospels give us.

A core issue in both Jesus' and Luke's time was that of assets. It was all well and good for Jesus to invite some of his followers to give all to the poor and come follow him, but if Luke's contemporaries were to give all they owned to the poor or to the leadership and if the delay in Jesus' second coming continued, how could their dispossession be prudent? But, on the other hand, if people did not express their trust in God and love of neighbor in concrete, material terms, then Christianity was certain to grow into an interior, disembodied kind of arcane knowledge transmitted by ideas rather than by the flesh and blood acts of sharing, compassion, and love by which it had been communicated since the time of Jesus.[17] What was at stake, therefore, was the possibility of the very character of Christianity itself changing if a clearer vision for the dispensing and retaining of wealth such as it was with Luke's contemporaries could not be brought forward. The fact is the material resources of the community's members, especially the wealthier members, were being used insufficiently as means for the expression of their faith and of their care for one another.[18] Accordingly, Luke selects many of the materials he has at his disposal to address this concern.

Much of the message of Jesus in Luke and the import of his mission centered on the reign of God. He announced it. He lived in such a way that he was a sign of its inauguration. He trusted in God and entrusted himself to God. His hearers had to decide whether they could trust his trust in God and place themselves in God's hands the way Jesus exhorted them to or whether they should hold to a prior sense of themselves and God, a sense that made more of self-provision. Jesus' God was aware of every least detail and need in people's lives. This awareness was matched by His power to affect every least detail and to do so with the care of a father for His children, according to Jesus. This benign, proximate, powerful, compassionate, fully alert relationship of God to His people was the reign of God, according to Jesus. This symbol already familiar to his hearers, was given enormous weight by Jesus.[19]

The antithesis of the way of life Jesus lived and proclaimed was characterized by an anxiety that acted like a fever of varying degrees robbing those afflicted with it of a desire to listen to any ideas about how close God was and how much He saw and provided for our needs. People had to get on with their concerns. But those who trusted Jesus' characterization of God as Father and the proximity of God's reign began to be healed. Their faith in God as it was mediated by Jesus' words and deeds began to change their attitude about self-provision. Their fever began to lift as they took his word into their hearts. (Luke 8:15) Those who weren't sure had to make a decision. Either Jesus was right and they must reimage their attitude toward God, their own needs, and possessions or Jesus was wrong and they could continue to worry about tomorrow and hope in their own ability to provide for themselves while believing in a more remote God than his, one who expected them in effect to retain their own sovereignty, to some extent at least. They could throw their lot in with him and like him name God as Father and expect that He would not leave them without their daily bread. Or they could continue with the operational image of God they had developed which made concern for this bread one of many priority items on their scale of anxieties. Oddly enough, it seems that those who had the least reason to be concerned about their daily bread because they were well enough off were the most dubious about Jesus and the proximity of the God he preached. And many of those who had the most reason to be concerned about their daily bread, the poor, were among the most responsive to Jesus' words.

Luke's Jesus, like Matthew's, Mark's, and John's, preaches salvation. Salvation in Luke is human well-being which derives from being rooted in God.[20] This well-being was at all levels—relational, social, physical, and spiritual—of people's existence. For Luke, the physician, Jesus was like a physician who addressed those who needed to be well. The absence of well-being was sickness. His hearers' sicknesses were social, physical, moral, and spiritual. Jesus splits the house. Some take his word to heart and begin to come to health at all levels of their lives. Some prefer their present condition, not seeing it as sickness compared to the kind of health he would bring them. The moral state of his hearers, it should be noted, would not be sufficient explanation for the acceptance or rejection of him. If only the good heard him and the evil rejected him, his mission would have been a saving of the saved, which is not what he thought he was about. The deeper reason for the division of the house, therefore, seems to come down to: some knew they were "in need of a physician" and some admitted no such need. They were doing fine, thank you. Those who knew they were not well, the sick, he could heal.

There were two very different kinds of sickness with respect to possessions that Jesus, the physician, diagnosed. One was moral. If the sickness was moral, Jesus' words attempted to sting his hearers into compunction and repentance. (Luke 16:13–31) Whenever he discerned avarice, covetousness, and greed, he dealt with these as sins, naming them such and attempting to call the sinners to repentance. But there was a more pervasive illness than just a moral one that Jesus sensed among his hearers, one that caused them to intercept and trivialize the word he spoke to them. His hearers were preoccupied, their "spirits" had been preempted. Their illness distracted them from the degree of attention needed to hear the Word of God, receive it, and have it unfold in the soil of their souls.

> As for the part that fell into thorns, this is people who
> have heard, but as they go on their way they are choked
> by the worries and riches and pleasures of life and never
> produce any crops. (Luke 8:14)

In other words, among the sick were not only lepers but those disfigured with anxieties; not only the blind but those who had no vision of the place of possessions and money in their lives; not only the crippled but those who were in bondage about their future and its solvency.

Mammon Illness

What I will contend here is that with regard to the illnesses Jesus perceived, there was major illness of the spirit that pervaded the ranks of his hearers, one that I will call generically "mammon illness." It had different symptoms. The illness has different strains, if you will. Each of these is in some way or other related to mammon. Mammon is not simply a neutral term in Luke. It is not simply money. It connotes disorder. It means "that in which one puts one's trust," from its root meaning.[21] Mammon becomes then a source of disorder because people allow it to make a claim on them that only God can make. Judging from the many references Jesus made about money and possessions, Jesus must have discerned this mammon illness to be widespread. Concerns about money and possessions constituted a major obstacle to his hearers being able to accept his words about the character of God and his kingdom.

There were three symptoms that indicated to the physician that mammon illness, a sickness more of the spirit than of the will, was afflicting his hearers. The first symptom was running after things. (Luke 12:30) It is as if he were saying: "To provide yourself and yours with what you want and with what you need to live, eat, drink, wear, you think you have to run." He connects running with unbelieving. He invites his hearers to connect slowing down and walking with believing. He doesn't deride any and all self-provision, just self-provision that is done from anxiety, from disbelieving, from believing there is a part of reality that is beyond the pale of God's sovereignty, or the reign of God. Luke's Jesus links running with anxiety and anxiety with futility.

He proposes several simple scenes for the afflicted to contemplate. They are humorous and ironic. (Luke 12:22–34) He points to a wisdom in birds that don't sow or store or starve that his listeners will be well advised to reflect upon and emulate. He suggests there is something that wild lilies whose beauty exceeds the splendor of Solomon at his best have to say too. Like the ravens and the lilies, his hearers will also find the food and dress they need. "Your Father well knows you need them." (Luke 12:30) He invites them to live within the ambit of God's knowing, caring, and providing for them. "Set your hearts on his kingdom, and these other things will be given you as well." (Luke 12:31) This was an invitation to imagine a different way of being. It is an invitation to stop running and allow God to have the concerns that they were harboring.

The Kingdom was the most emotionally comforting symbol Jesus could have evoked for his hearers. To Israel it had always represented a future that would be the completion of desires, of wants, and of needs. It represented plenitude, abundance, freedom from fear, and an everlasting joy. He added other images that evoked different aspects of living in the reign of God such as the image of the purse. (Luke 12:33) Put your money in a different purse, a different treasury, a different bank account, one that moths can't get at and that cannot be stolen from you by anyone. One who wanted to see things this way and believe this about God had to ask for it, seek it, knock, so to speak. (Luke 11:9–13) One could not come into this new way of seeing, this new release from anxiety, this seeking first His kingship by one's own efforts. Like the bread one needed and the clothing one needed, even this new way of living would be provided by Jesus' God who as Father would give "the Holy Spirit to those who ask him!" (Luke 11:13)

A second symptom indicating that the culturally mediated mammon illness was caught was numbness. It happens slowly, without one being aware of what is happening or fully choosing the condition. One begins to serve mammon rather than mammon serving one's chosen purposes and values. This allegiance induces the state of numbness. Unlike the first symptom, which shows up in one's relationship to material resources, this second symptom shows up in one's relationship to others. One is not present to people. One's own economically related concerns make others remote, even invisible. Compassion takes a lesser and lesser place at least operationally for one who has caught from one's economic culture this sick relationship to others. The economic culture of Jesus' and Luke's day was considerably simpler and less determining of Israel's ethos than it is in modern life; nonetheless, Jesus saw the numbness that it "induced."

There are two parables in Luke that touch directly on this symptom of numbness and relate it to salvation. The one is about "a rich man who used to dress in purple and fine linen and feast magnificently every day. And at his gate there used to lie a poor man called Lazarus, covered with sores, who longed to fill himself with what fell from the rich man's table." (Luke 16:19–21) The rich man is depicted as aware of Lazarus but he chooses to allow the abyss between them brought on by their different circumstances, opportunities, and material wealth to remain unbridged.

His numbness has eternal consequences. God ratifies the abyss, the chosen nonrelationship. The rich man's wealth inured him against being moved by compassion.

The surprises of the parable are the way God and God's spokesman, Abraham, view wealth and poverty, the dignity of the poor man, and the need for the rich man to come forth to be healed. Had the poor man's sores, which are licked by the dogs, been touched by the rich man, they would have been his salvation. It is not until he is in flames that the rich man becomes aware of the importance of the touch of Lazarus:

> Father Abraham . . . send Lazarus to dip the tip of his
> finger in water and cool my tongue, for I am in agony in
> these flames. (Luke 16:24)

Because of his chosen inactivity in time, the rich man is deprived of what could have saved him, the sacrament of the poor man's touch. Without it he was inured within the reign of material wealth and all that it had procured for him. His comfort and wealth numbed him to the discomfort and grave need of the other which he could have alleviated. The hearers of Luke's Gospel are being told: make sure you see "the others" the way God sees them. Their need may be instrumental for your healing. Make sure your own wealth does not blind you to God's identification with them and their importance for your salvation. What is also hinted at here is the character of salvation. It is a now thing at least for starters. It is not extrinsic to what two people do or fail to do, or many for that matter, but intrinsic to their interaction. That interaction, furthermore, has material goods, food, clothing, shelter, health care as an essential part of it. Finally, salvation is not a reward for doing good. The good being done is already the salvation begun.

The other parable that highlights the Lucan Jesus' insight into numbness and compassion is that of the Good Samaritan. (Luke 10:25–37) A lawyer had posed two questions to Jesus: What had he to do to inherit eternal life and who was his neighbor? (Luke 10:25; 10:29) A very Jewish Jesus made the two into one and gave them a startlingly concrete answer. The two religious figures in the story, the priest and the Levite, exhibit both symptoms of mammon illness. They are both in a hurry, on the run, and they proved to be quite numb. The implication is that it was their peculiar form of wealth, their religiosity, that sealed them within their numbness. It enabled them to misperceive their condition, justifying it in fact. While they chose to be uninvolved with the sufferer who was stripped, beaten, and left on the side of the road half dead, the Samaritan "was moved with compassion when he saw him." (Luke 10:33) In this he was like God and Jesus himself, both of whom Luke is concerned to depict as capable of "being moved with compassion." (Luke 7:13; 15:30) All three are emphatically not numb. Healthy are those who are capable of being so moved. The surprise in the parable is that it is the religiously despicable one (in his hearer's assessment) who is most like Jesus and God. The violated person is worthy of his time, his care, his money. (Luke 10:35) The Samaritan was free to be compassionate. He was free enough of himself to love his neighbor. He was free from the need to be about the task of being religious or righteous which the other two weren't. Religion can be a cause of numbness Jesus informs his hearers.

In each of these parables Jesus hints at one of the ways by which this numbness can be pierced. Those who are in pain (who cannot be numb because of their pain) can reveal to those who are not their actual condition that the numb do not see themselves to be in. Solidarity with those who grieve can be salvific for those who do not. Jesus may have learned this lesson by the responses given to his proclamation of the reign of God. Those who were attracted to Jesus were the grievers, by and large, those who ranked very low on Israel's acceptability scale. Those who were most content, on the other hand, with their society's arrangements were frequently the numbest. "Only grievers can experience their experiences and move on to hope for something other than what they have and see as attainable," namely, the reign of God in their midst.[22]

There was a third symptom of mammon illness. It was a split consciousness. This illness developed in people who had two masters and tried to serve each. These were "God and money [mammon]." (Luke 16:13) Since each claimed a total loyalty, the price of trying to be in both worlds was the splitting of one's consciousness into two parts. Jesus named the phenomenon and denied the split would work. "No servant can be the slave of two masters; he will either hate the first and love the second, or be attached to the first and despise the second. You cannot be the slave both of God and of money." (Luke 16:13) It is the character of each of these two (incomparable) realities that each seeks to be served, and trusted. Each would be a master making a claim on one's allegiance. Whosoever attempts to serve both of them has to create separate spheres of meaning. The separation seriously weakens the person. With the split, faith becomes less and less capable of making sense of or affecting anything in the sphere of "the world."

A good case could be made that Jesus hit upon the split consciousness symptom by trying to figure out the Pharisees. Here they were patently religious yet at the same time they were avaricious people. (Luke 16:14) Their piety could coexist with avarice because their consciousness was split. Yet it is informative how their image of God was contorted by their avarice. Their God, for example, rewards by observance measured by amounts, by quantity rather than by the condition of the heart. (Luke 16:15; 18:9–14) But the evidence that their religious game was not even being played with much faith in God was the need for the players to be seen, noticed, honored when they were acting religiously. Even their religious faith had been mammonized. With their example to remind him, Jesus could assure his hearers that the split doesn't work.

As was the case in Jesus' day so also is it in our own. We do not create the split in ourselves. We are taught it. We have inherited it. The culture teaches, engenders, and reinforces this separation of the economic sphere from the sphere of human valuing and religious believing. Notwithstanding its genesis, its cure must be pursued. A cure is pursued only if the condition is perceived and perceived as a sickness. The way a split consciousness works is that one spiritualizes or transcendentalizes God above this pedestrian world, especially the world of filthy lucre. Having located Him in a sacred site, such as heaven, Church, liturgy, spirituality, intimate union with God, one can know, love, and serve the One who has been sanitized. That done, one can then get on with the other cordoned off sphere of this world which usually has much to occupy this other side of one's consciousness. There is no end to learning its ropes; especially complicated are its economic operations.

The laws, processes, procedures, and disciplines of the economic system, all are important to know. It is a world of fact, science, objectivity, and theory. But the world of economics and finances, if it is separated in our consciousness from the world of faith, has its own sphere of "values" which it communicates along with the monies and possessions that are the stuff of its "life." This sphere of goods can become a sphere of meaning with its own canons to teach on how to "make it," what making it entails, and even who you are who would make it.

The cost of retaining each of these spheres in their separateness is that by trying to serve each, one "makes it" in neither. One becomes too concerned with this world to know the consolation of faith yet too hesitant to subscribe totally to its forms to "succeed." They don't remain in tension for long. One becomes less important than the other, unfortunately usually the sphere inhabited by the sanitized version of God. Not that we then cease to believe in Him but His sovereignty becomes more honorific than operational. He is found in the gaps. Looking for Him is the exception, then. And finding Him is even more exceptional. The long history of a split consciousness is the main reason why faith is not wise or comfortable operating in the sphere of business, finance, commerce, trade, taxes, securities, insurance, and so forth.[23]

Economic matters whether micro or macro are not intrinsically disordered but they easily become so once human transcendentality subjugates itself to what should remain a means for attaining human ends. If the world of mammon is not mastered by human purposes freely chosen and commensurate with human dignity, then the person loses his or her way and becomes the mastered. If, on the other hand, the world of one's finances is kept in an instrumental status and not allowed to have its own way or be unintegrated in the person's immediate or ultimate purposes it is an invaluable, essential servant. It need not dictate its terms to those with possessions and finances. But trying to have two separate treasures, two different purses—God and a nest egg unattached to God—one finds oneself taking orders from each for a while and eventually from only one because "You cannot be the slave both of God and of money." (Luke 16:13)

The Diagnosis

What Jesus had uncovered was more than an illness. It was a whole way of life that was being lived by those who had learned to put their trust in God and in money at the same time. He excoriated those who took the lead in legitimating this both/and way of life and he sought to heal those who had succumbed to it. It is worth noting that Jesus does not excoriate the tax collectors, since as a group it seems they did not live in a both/and way of life. They were up front with their fraud and extortion. But he was not so gentle with the religious leadership who tried and in many cases succeeded in having the best of both the world of material security and religion. Honors were avidly sought by many of those who were religion's professional class.[24] Although their words communicated a message of trust in Yahweh, their lives were a lesson in trying to have God, material security, and honor all at the same time. In this regard, recall the etymology of mammon. It derives from the Aramaic root which means "to trust in."

It seems, therefore, that there were four possible stances that Israelites took toward money in Jesus' day. The first was cupidity, avarice, or outright greed. This was mammonolatry and a moral problem; if a person repented of it, he or she could come into a right relationship with God. The second stance which is what we are concentrating on here, was a both/and kind of trust in God and in money. These God-and-mammon Israelites kept two purses, so to speak. In the one they stored up heavenly treasure by their good works. In the other purse they had earthly treasure. This consisted of honor, if they were among its professional religious classes, material security, possessions, and money "which they loved." (Luke 11:43; 16:13–15) Those who were in this group had two masters each of whom vied to be the only one served. The third stance was to master money using it for one's own purposes.

In this case money was instrumental and therefore neutral in and of itself. The purposes for which it was used determined the quality of the actions which made use of it. When money was subordinated to good purposes, it was in the position proper to it. Sometimes these purposes, of course, were evil, which harks back to the first stance—an outright use of money for the chosen purpose of greed, gain, acquisition. There were good purposes which kept money a means by which these purposes were pursued, although significantly it is hard to think of any New Testament instances of such a use. The fourth stance toward money, the one Jesus encouraged, subordinated money's use to human purposes, purposes that in turn were subordinated to God. Placed under the reign of God, money then lost its actual or potential mammonolatry; it ceased to be mammon; it did not operate as a competing object of trust. There was left then only one object of trust—"Abba."

Seeing mammon operating in Israel is probably as close as Jesus came to what we today would call social analysis. Luke's Gospel contains many hints of his growing perception about how mammon was weakening the power of Israel's faith. The extensive journey motif, for example, at the core of how Luke structures his Gospel (Luke 9:51 to 19:27), terminates with Jesus arriving at Jerusalem and cleaning out the temple which had become "a den of thieves" rather than a house of prayer. (Luke 19:45–46) Mammon, in other words, was more than an illness that individuals fell victim of, it was a way of life that entwined itself throughout the social life of Israel. Its institutions, especially its central institution, the temple, were symbols to Jesus of the spiritual condition of Israel, which had come to have a both/and way of life in which mammon was given its due and God was given His. God's due, however, was in fact being subjected to the demands that mammon made on those who had charge of the temple. Mammon's agents were, of course, the Romans who required that Israel be heavily taxed, perhaps as much as 40 percent of its revenues.[25] But the temple had become the financial epicenter of Israel. It was there the money changers exchanged foreign currencies, at a profit. It was there the animals were sold for the temple sacrifices and the temple tax was collected. In Jesus' day this whole enterprise was under the supervision of the Sadducees who at the be-

hest of Rome were the middlemen who delivered to Rome what
Rome required, to their own advantage according to some com-
mentators.[26] They operated, albeit unawares, as mammon's more
proximate agents.

The point here is that trusting in money was a way of life which
coexisted with a religious way of life because it was not seen as an
accommodation of faith to money or as a contradiction of a faith
that claimed to trust Yahweh alone. This way of life was embed-
ded in most of Israel's structures, even in its most sacred one, the
temple. These served as seemingly innocuous carriers of mammon
illness to the people. The group that should have recognized this
for what it was were the religious professionals, but since they
enjoyed the best of both worlds they were either unable or unwilling to see their own compromised position. But also when it was
exposed, they were adamant to eradicate any one whose words
skewered their ambivalence.

It should be obvious, therefore, that money not placed under
the reign of God does not stay neutral very long. It soon becomes
mammon and develops a reign that is antithetical to the reign of
God. It is in competition then as an object to be trusted and a
source of security. Those who have it soon become its minions. It
has them, though they are only aware of having it. In procuring
and acquiring it, they come to serve it. To complete this scriptural
picture of our compromised humanity, it should be pointed out
that mammon, in turn, has a master, though he is off the stage.
Satan is the master of mammon.[27]

Christologists trace Jesus' insight into the religiously compromised situation of religious Israel as something he himself had to
discover and deal with in himself. Israel's both/and way of life
constituted an ongoing temptation in his life.[28] What is beyond a
doubt is that trusting God was an ongoing choice for him. Hence
he was always free to not trust God. Or probably what is closer to
the mark is that he was tempted both to trust God and at the
same time to open a second account, one in which he had a way
out if his project failed. The three temptations might be seen as
different ways Jesus was tempted against a total trust in God or
against putting all his denarii in the Abba basket. Hence he was
tempted to use his gifts to provide for himself (bread). (Luke 4:2–

4) Or to concede the kingdoms of the world as the devil's own as
the tempter boasted they were. This would have acknowledged
the tempter was their master and done him homage. (Luke 4:7)
And finally he was tempted to test whether his trust was warranted, by getting ahead of himself, so to speak, by, for example,
throwing himself from the parapet of the pulpit. Would I then be
borne up, as Scripture has it? (Luke 4:9–12)

The three responses given by Jesus to the three different temptations against trust of God are an example of a unitary consciousness. He chooses to stick with the one purse rather than
open a just-in-case account. He will not allow himself any lapse of
trust in God or concede any sovereignty to mammon anywhere or
to Satan, who was behind mammon's tenuous and supercilious
reign. And finally, he trusts God with himself as he is and with his
future without putting God to tests He had to pass to warrant
Jesus' continuing trust of Him. Perhaps the ascription of the
temptations to the devil is a post-factum clarity. The temptations
would have been fairly easy to overcome if the figure of the devil
was in evidence when Jesus was subject to them as the Synoptics
depict. The temptations, however, would have been much more
tempting if the tempter had been off the stage and only the human
consciousness of Jesus was front and center. He would have had
to continually deal with the objective insecurity of his situation.
There was nothing automatic or easy about trusting God for him
who was "put to the test in exactly the same way as ourselves" in
the matter of trust. (Heb. 4:15) Surely reasons for not trusting
God only grew in the course of his ministry. They did not diminish.

The desert setting of the temptations, scholars contend, was
probably selected by the Synoptics to contrast Israel's infidelity to
Jesus' fidelity. Certainly it recalls the temptations that overpow-
ered the first messianic people in the desert when they lost confidence in Yahweh and preferred to make a god of gold.[29] Certainly
a golden calf in whom divinity could be invested was a lot more
tangible and easy to trust than the invisible, intangible Yahweh. In
fact wasn't it trusting Him that led them to the wretched desert in
the first place? The new Israel, in the person of Jesus, retraces the
steps of Israel, by being conducted into the desert by the Spirit

there to learn trust, trusting in one God with the unitary consciousness which preceded and followed his three choices. He would emerge from the desert and from the temptations against trust (which probably stalked his whole ministry) and began to assault the disease of half-trust that permeated Israel. This disease of the spirit with its dual sources of trust was infidelity structured into a religious way of life. The mission of the Lucan Jesus was taken up with exposing its existence and curing those who had fallen victim to it. We will now examine how he went about this.

The Cure

To cure, Jesus needed the sick to have faith, some faith which he tried to stir up to great faith. He needed their imagination which he tried to fire. But first of all he needed them to need to be changed, cured, made whole. What made a cure virtually impossible was the absence of need, blindness about one's condition of spirit, and dullness and doubt especially about Jesus.

Faith is only power when it functions. It functioned when what Jesus' hearers believed in was acted upon. They believed in God. They didn't always act on their belief. They had learned to actively believe at some times and to not believe at others. They had learned to actively believe about some matters and to not believe about others. Jesus' mission was to have them actively believe about all matters. He sought to stir up their faith in God. Their faith admitted to degrees of functioning and to selective functioning. He tried to teach them to include all of the matters that concerned them including what they were to eat, what they were to drink, what they were to wear. (Luke 12:22–29) If their meager faith could begin to function more vigorously over matters and in areas in which they had been trying to be their own sources of providence, a healing could begin in individuals and in all of Israel, Jesus was sure.

Since the specific thing that interests us here is the increase of power that religious faith can generate over economic/financial matters, the question is, How did Jesus generate faith power to function more forcefully in persons of faith and thus heal them of their unfree ways of relating to possessions, money, and material resources? First of all, those who thought of themselves as well or, more accurately perhaps, those who were sure they were dealing with that part of reality as it intractably is were invited to see themselves and reality in a different light. Jesus proffered to their imaginations pictures of an alternative way of viewing reality. These alternative ways of viewing things, themselves, God, and God's proximity to them were, in a word, kingdom pictures. If they found their spirits resonating to these kingdom vignettes Jesus held out to them, they could begin to move from anxiety to trust, numbness to passion and compassion, a split consciousness to a unitary consciousness, self-providence to childlike trust.

The role played by the imagination is a key to the healing process inaugurated by Jesus. (I say inaugurated because Jesus evidently did not reserve the healing portion of his ministry to himself but sent the twelve and the seventy-two forth to proclaim the reign of God and cure the sick.) (Luke 10:1–20) Believing in the God of the kingdom of God Jesus preached was itself the beginning of a healing of the attitudinal, emotional sickness of the type we are examining here. Although the use of money and possessions is the point we are interested in, one's self-perception, God-image, and perception of others are closely tied in with that aspect of a person's worldview. These four different realities are inextricable.

A generalization seems possible from Jesus' success or lack of success in having his images of the kingdom of God accepted or ignored by his hearers. Those who needed to imagine reality in a new way were prepared to listen to him and let his way of perceiving the kingdom speak to their imaginations and hearts. But those who were "making it" in the religious, social, political, economic conditions of Jesus' day did not need a new way of envisioning reality. They were the beneficiaries of things as they were. This need or its absence, therefore, appears to have conditioned the attraction or nonattraction Jesus' hearers felt about his person and message about the character of the kingdom of God. This is simply another way of saying the beatitudes. Those who were secure, or powerful, or accepted, or rich, those who could laugh did not need the kingdom of God. Their counterparts did. (Luke 6:20-26)

How did the imagination work in those who were attracted to his message, namely, those who needed to be in the world differently? Samuel Taylor Coleridge observed that the imagination "dissolves, diffuses, dissipates in order to recreate."[30] By their words the prophets shattered old worlds "bringing them to the end" in order "to form and evoke new worlds (causing them to be)."[31] Taking his cue from Paul Ricoeur's insight into the subversive character of an imagination that can see social realities in a wholly new way, Brueggemann observes that the prophets' redescription of their own world and that of the hearers made their preaching "subversive activity, and indeed maybe the primal act of subversion" because it discredited and delegitimated "the conventional modes of perception, the conventional slogans, the ideological coverups that could no longer claim allegiance."[32]

The imagination is a key not only to a change in consciousness but also to conversion. Imagination has been well described as "a cognitive power that knows personal, psychic truth, grasping it in a holistic way and with feeling, a feeling that can lead toward conversion and commitment."[33] The whole person is invited into a new way of seeing reality and relating to it with a different spirit and from a new angle of vision. William Lynch's observation is apposite here: "It is not too much but too little imagination that causes illness."[34] Once the imagination is sparked, a migration can begin from one's known and familiar world to a new world, a new arrangement of parts, a new order of persons and things, a bursting out from the ordinary bound-in way one perceives oneself, one's possessions, others, God. The kingdom is the old world seen new, transformed, not rearranged, or more of same. Conversion is turning toward and acting from this new arrangement, leaving the old as no longer real or true or beautiful. Every real conversion is first a revolution at the level of our directive images. By changing our imagining, we see ourselves and the world in an entirely new light.[35]

This can sound very abstract. In fact, with Jesus it was very concrete. He never proclaimed the reign of God abstractly. He was concrete—disconcertingly so. For example: "The kingdom of

Heaven is like a merchant looking for fine pearls; when he finds one of great value he goes and sells everything he owns and buys it." (Matt. 13:45–46) Here is the familiar and unfamiliar in continuity with each other. The merchant moves from pedestrian routine activity to passionate, all-consuming activity. He moves from a plethora of humdrum aims to one all-out purpose. The merchant's life is rearranged because in the midst of all he had, he found one pearl of such spellbinding beauty that it would cost him his whole collection to acquire it. His eye is single as he follows through with the leaving and the losing for the gaining. Notice, he could not add the new pearl to those he already had. It was either/or, not both/and. What he had had to be transformed. His monies and pearls then had a clear purpose; they were all reduced to the status of means for the pursuit of an end. The cost was clear. The means were clear. Divestment and dispossession for acquisition of the incomparable pearl.

The kingdom of God, for Jesus, was not a spacey, spiritualized other world. It was composed of the things of this world, but focused differently, seen in their relationship to the immediate, compassionate, powerful presence of the Father of Jesus. He was the wealth Jesus sought. He was the pearl of great price for Jesus. He was the treasure hidden in the field of Jesus' vision which had him continually transfigure every other detail in his field of vision. Once a person took on Jesus' field of vision, he was susceptible to the transvaluation of every single coin he would ever again possess. All would have a finality now they didn't have before.

This parable shows the function imagination plays in conversion by bringing the hearer to see new possibilities in familiar scenes. A new image of self, the possibility of a seizure of one's heart that gives life an overriding purpose and, therefore, a change in how one sees and uses material and financial resources—these become possibilities if one hears Jesus' few words. The parables were the favorite device Jesus used to portray the kingdom to his hearers' imaginations. A parable is not weighed or analyzed. It is to be entered so that one's world is seen in a new light.[36] One no sooner enters into its panorama, which is full of the familiar, than one is conscious of the disparity between the way one is accustomed to view these familiar items and the way they are arranged in the parable. The further into the parable one goes the more likely it is that the parable will take the measure of one's most inveterate biases and dispositions. There is also a sense of an invitation to not go back to one's habitual ways of perceiving but to take on this new mode of perception. To choose this new way is the beginning of healing. One is exorcised of the demons of disordered affections or dysfunctional values or misplaced priorities that the previous worldview carried. The kingdom pictures Jesus gives reveal what constitutes health or more concretely the attitudes that make for a health in the use of one's material resources, possessions, and money.

The following parables and stories about healing can be entered by those who would be healed today. They are not only about past events and long ago words; they are also for today's world and the reign of God which lies before those who would be healed, the entrance into which can transfigure the world one lives in. This reign of God, this world transfigured is possible through the Word of God. Or perhaps better, a whole new way of seeing the world I now live in and perceive is a possibility. One's healing is contingent on leaving the one and entering the other. God's Word heard with faith and expectancy can jar the numbness, thwart the running, and unify the split in consciousness. God's word is "alive and active: it cuts more incisively than any two-edged sword: it can seek out the place where soul is divided from spirit, or joints from marrow; it can pass judgment on secret emotions and thoughts." (Heb. 4:12)

Parables That Would Heal

The first parable to be entered into is found in Luke 16:1-8.

"There was a rich man and he had a steward who was denounced to him for being wasteful with his property. He called for the man and said, 'What is this I hear about you? Draw me up an account of your stewardship because you are not to be my steward any longer.' Then the steward said to himself, 'Now that my master is taking the stewardship from me, what am I to do? Dig? I am not strong enough. Go begging? I should be too ashamed. Ah, I know what I will do to make sure that when I am dismissed from office there will be some to welcome me into their homes.'

"Then he called his master's debtors one by one. To the first he said, 'How much do you owe my master?' 'One hundred measures of oil,' he said. The steward said, 'Here, take your bond; sit down and quickly write fifty.' To another he said, 'And you, sir, how much do you owe?' 'One hundred measures of wheat,' he said. 'Here, take your bond and write eighty.'

"The master praised the dishonest steward for his astuteness. For the children of this world are more astute in dealing with their own kind than are the children of light."

This parable is not found in the other Gospels. It reflects the pastoral concerns of Luke. As with the Gospels and the parables in particular a number of readings are possible. The following reading of this parable is only one. First of all "the wily manager" is faced with a wholly new situation. His bridges have been burned, his job is over. The assessment of his past is that he has dissipated the master's property and is being forced to face the future with physical limitations and repugnances. "Dig? I am not strong enough. Go begging? I should be too ashamed." (Luke 16:3) By dint of the new circumstances within which he finds himself he is forced to reassess his relationship to people with whom he had previously related only in terms of his own agenda and profit. His trust, therefore, is forced away from mammon.

A radical transformation or transvaluation takes place. The manager has then to place himself in the hands of people. He must trust them in order to have any future at all. When the owner "praised the dishonest steward for his astuteness" (Luke 16:8), in effect, it is Jesus who is commending a move from at least a self-centered use of money and possessions to one that, though perhaps short on altruism, at least is vulnerable and other-oriented. The manager begins to use money with a sense of community and his own real needs rather than using human beings for himself and in fact mammon's reign. Hence the owner's commendation.

But Luke's Jesus goes even further by way of comment: "Use money, tainted as it is, to win you friends, and thus make sure that when it fails you, they will welcome you into eternal dwellings." (Luke 16:9) While the wily manager had only his immediate future in view, by seeking to win the favor of people who would take him into their homes, Luke goes another step and intimates a connection between their homes and the manager's eternal dwelling place. From the context of Luke's Gospel one can surmise that the reception of the manager by the community whom he has first bilked and then needed probaby refers to the acceptance of pagans into the Christian community. Those who have wealth within the community are being told: Your wealth is in the members of the community now rather than in your money. You must see yourselves, your money, and others with wholly new eyes, eyes that see the eternal significance of being in this relationship to one another in Christ. Your money and possessions now have a purpose. Make friends for yourselves by sharing your goods with others. Luke is here articulating a discipleship of communality that grows by the use of monies and of possessions reduced to means to an end, an end that takes into account the members of the community and their needs. The value of money now is in its transformability into treasure that can last. Perceiving the community and relationship to its members via one's material and financial resources is the new way of being, one that means in fact salvation or damnation, as the parable of the rich man and Lazarus brings out even more clearly.

Previous readings of the wily manager parable tended to focus on the moral flaw of the manager. But it is not the profit in itself that the manager had calculated on making that either Jesus who tells the story or the rich man whose property it is took to be wrong. Recent evidence indicates that personal profit for the middleman was an accepted custom even though it added to the debt that each of the servants owed their master.[37] The Lucan Jesus seems unbothered by this early form of usury. "Use money, tainted as it is, to win you friends" (Luke 16:9) was advice particularly needed for Luke's contemporaries. They needed to be wholly disengaged from a God-and-mammon way of life. Wealth is "tainted"; (Luke 16:11) it "fails you," (Luke 16:9) they are warned. By the right use of their elusive wealth, the rich Christians would come to know lasting wealth. But Luke's Jesus says that your brothers and sisters in Christ are capable of being "eternal dwellings" and your bonds with them lasting bonds. (Luke 16:9–11)

This parable touches each of the three forms of mammon illness. The manager was so accustomed to running he never stopped long enough to see the people with whom he trafficked in any other light than as objects of the transactions he had made with them. Nor did he show any respect for the master or owner. Toward both the owner and the owner's debtors he was crass. Or even better, numb. The new development, being fired, forces him to look at himself, the master, and the debtors in a new light.

And the split consciousness is also directly addressed in the corollary that warns, "No servant can be the slave of two masters: he will either hate the first and love the second, or be attached to the first and despise the second. You cannot be the slave both of God and of money." (Luke 16:13) It is clear who the one master is. The second master was money. "He will either hate the first and love the second, or be attached to the first and despise the second." (Luke 16:13) And lest there be any doubt what he means, Jesus exclaims, "You cannot be the slave both of God and of money," (Luke 16:13) as the manager had attempted. A unitary consciousness is what the Lucan Jesus is holding before his hearers as the way he would have his followers be.

The parable will be given very different responses depending on where the hearer is with money, relationships, community, Christ, salvation. One reaction to the parable is furnished within the text immediately following the parable and Jesus' explanations of it. "The Pharisees, who loved money, heard all this and jeered at him." (Luke 16:14) They did not let his word into their hearts. They turned it back and derided the one who spoke it. They hardened their hearts against it, disavowed their guilt, were shielding themselves from seeing their behavior pointed to in Jesus' words. They refused to be aware that the God they purported to believe in and obey had become one of their possessions who obeyed them while they obeyed mammon. God was one of several pearls in their keep. Jesus' words are chilling. "You are the very ones who pass yourselves off as upright in people's sight, but God knows your hearts." (Luke 16:15) The wily manager was a hustler with a characterological flaw that could be healed, but the

Pharisee was a sinner with a moral flaw of which he would have to repent before he could be healed. (Luke 19:11–27)

A second parable to be considered is in Luke 19:12–26.

"A man of noble birth went to a distant country to be appointed king and then return. He summoned ten of his servants and gave them ten pounds, telling them, 'Trade with these, until I get back.'

"Now it happened that on his return, having received his appointment as king, he sent for those servants to whom he had given the money, to find out what profit each had made by trading. The first came in, 'Sir,' he said, 'your one pound has brought in ten.' He replied, 'Well done, my good servant! Since you have proved yourself trustworthy in a very small thing, you shall have the government of ten cities.' Then came the second, 'Sir,' he said, 'your one pound has made five.' To this one also he said, 'And you shall be in charge of five cities.' Next came the other, 'Sir,' he said, 'here is your pound. I put it away safely wrapped up in a cloth because I was afraid of you; for you are an exacting man: you gather in what you have not laid out and reap what you have not sown.' He said to him, 'You wicked servant! Out of your own mouth I condemn you. So you knew that I was an exacting man, gathering in what I have not laid out and reaping what I have not sown? Then why did you not put my money in the bank? On my return I could have drawn it out with interest.' And he said to those standing by, 'Take the pound from him and give it to the man who has ten pounds.' And they said to him, 'But, sir, he has ten pounds . . .' 'I tell you, to everyone who has will be given more; but anyone who has not will be deprived even of what he has.' "

(I am omitting verses 14 and 27 on the assumption that exegetes are correct in saying that these are from another parable or context.[38] They obscure the point of the primary parable.)

This second parable is as enlightening on the subject of money and possessions as is the first. This parable is told by Jesus "because he was near Jerusalem and they thought that the kingdom of God was going to show itself then and there." (Luke 19:11) He was going away but the new epoch was to come after his death and resurrection and the outpouring of the Spirit. During this new

epoch his followers' attitudes toward material resources, possessions, and money were crucial. Hence the parable's servants know
that the resources over which they have control are not their own.
They belong to the one in a faraway country. Since they cannot
pronounce "mine" of them, they are mere stewards of the master's goods. They please him furthermore by the creativity and
energy they bring to the use of the goods. The resources are not
meant to remain inert but can turn a profit by shrewd investment.
It is not enough, according to the parable, simply to see oneself as
a steward of the good things God has given, one must be industri-
ous in the way one uses them. For any of the Lucan hearers of the
Gospel who were at a loss about how they were to make use of
their time while they awaited the continually delayed second coming of Jesus who was in a faraway country, the parable suggested
there was much to be done. They show a resourcefulness and
sense of responsibility about the goods over which they had control. Control, but not ownership. There is only one owner. When
the owner-king returned they would be humiliated if their time
had been spent idly or by merely preserving what they had been
given. The owner-king is not gentle. He is passionate and adamant. His passion is about his kingdom. He sets up over its vil-
lages the servants who obeyed his command to invest what they
were given. He takes all from the servant who did not live his days
bringing an increase to the wherewithal he had at his disposal.

The central issue of the parable is that a reflective, creative, and
resourceful use of one's resources is the ever-present way those
who are awaiting the fullness of the reign of God have of growing
in Christ and pleasing God.

Jesus' purpose here was undoubtedly to supply a vision of the
source and purpose of the goods, resources, and powers he and his
hearers enjoy. This in turn developed into a vision of stewardship
of goods. Thus they could see themselves as the stewards of God
who would serve Him by bringing an increase of thirty-, sixty-, or
a hundredfold to that which has been given them.

A third parable to be considered is in Luke 18:10–14.

"Two men went up to the Temple to pray, one a Pharisee, the
other a tax collector. The Pharisee stood there and said this
prayer to himself, 'I thank you, God, that I am not grasping,

unjust, adulterous like everyone else, and particularly that I am not like this tax collector here. I fast twice a week; I pay tithes on all I get.' The tax collector stood some distance away, not daring even to raise his eyes to heaven; but he beat his breast and said, 'God, be merciful to me, a sinner.' This man, I tell you, went home again justified; the other did not. For everyone who raises himself up will be humbled, but anyone who humbles himself will be raised up.''

This parable is addressed to some people who prided themselves on being upright and despised everyone else. (Luke 18:9) (It should be noted that this material is peculiar to Luke. No such parable is found in the other Gospels.) On the face of it the Pharisee's thankfulness to God seems to be an act of faith. But it soon becomes clear that his gratitude is more self-congratulatory born of judgment of others with whom he compares himself favorably. His eye, furthermore, is on himself and his own performance, not on God or on his need of God or on God's largesse on his behalf for that matter. The tax collector's reputation for having a nefarious relationship to money is an occasion for the Pharisee to reinforce his own self-righteousness. Not only does he not defraud people as the tax collector does, but he lives a life of supererogation. "I pay tithes on all I get." (Luke 18:12) By tithing his goods, possessions, and money he inured himself against the judgment of God and certainly was in need of no physician. Religiously he was healthy, he assured himself.

One can begin to sense Jesus' exasperation at what passed for religion and for what counted as religious. Lips that thanked God concealed hearts that judged and hands that doled out a tithe on everything owned were clenched against neighbor. Religious acts such as thanksgiving and tithing in Jesus' perception often served only to delay self-knowledge and obscure the need for conversion in many. They substituted the ritualization of belief for belief. They did not see that their trust was in themselves and in their own abilities to perform acts of religion, not to mention in sufficient wealth to have the luxury and the leisure to be able even to consider tithing. The irreligious person or religiously impoverished person was in a better position to approach the God Jesus preached. They could approach God needy, contrite, emptied of self-justifying behaviors. The tax collector brought a cavernous heart to the temple which was filled with God's own justice when he left. He could be healed because he knew he needed to be.

The connection between faith and finances has been too often reduced to two religious activities—thanksgiving and steward-ship. While these are undoubtedly key junctures between faith and finances, these two parables indicate how easily even these seemingly religious actions can conceal much that remains un-healed and unconverted. Some of the robber barons, for example, have claimed that the inspiration behind their amassing wealth has been Christian stewardship.[39] This does not discredit the cate-gory of stewardship, of course, but it does indicate the need to bring a cautious and critical attitude to the way it is employed because of its ability to coexist with a ruthless competitiveness or an unsuspected avarice. In other words, an explicit stewardship consciousness can conceal a God-and-mammon accommodation of faith or even a mammonolatry.[40]

The same caution and critical pause should accompany the rit-ual of thanksgiving, the giving of thanks to God for what we have of material well-being. It can aid one's self-assurance that one is right with God, something that might or might not be the case. Certainly a facility in offering thanks to God for what one has and owns in a culture such as our own, which is characterized by "conspicuous consumption," must be examined, especially if it is the only mode of prayer practiced and hence the only dimension of awareness Christians bring to the relationship between Christ and their financial condition.[41] Thanksgiving as prayer is beyond cavil, of course. Thanksgiving as a ritual needs to be continually examined to remain fresh prayer. Unexamined religious rituals can conceal most of all to those practicing them the truth of the relationship one has to God.

Before completing this section on Jesus' healing power over people in their relationship to their economic culture, several other words of Jesus should be noted. I will call them sting words because they are meant to do just that. They are aimed at a type of spiritual condition that has duped a person and a whole popula-tion into misreading God, themselves, and religion.

Again the type in question is the Pharisee.[42] The situation is a dinner to which Jesus is invited. (Luke 11:37–42) The Pharisee is surprised that Jesus does not perform the prescribed ritual of washing his hands before eating. Jesus' words "cut more incisively than any two-edged sword." (Heb. 4:12) On this occasion he observed their concern to wipe clean their surface selves, "the outside of cup and plate," while leaving the insides impermeable to God's grace, thus remaining "filled with extortion and wickedness." (Luke 11:39) Since in their consciousness they were religious, as their rituals assured them, they would never have arrived themselves at the assessment that Jesus had of them. They might have been more open to God and Jesus, without such rituals as thanksgiving and ablutions.

His forceful, brutally direct words could have brought Jesus' hearers to remorse and to repentance if they saw their sin in his description. He insisted on their going deeper than their religiosity to examine their hearts, the insides of the cup finding there both their poverty and need for God's mercy as also of the fact of God's love. Jesus makes two suggestions for those who could let his word cut into them and repent of their ways. The first is to give alms. "Instead, give alms from what you have and, look, everything will be clean for you." (Luke 11:41) Perhaps the giving of alms here is a recommendation that they do so in sufficient measure to become aware of the degree of trust they had in their mammon which was the root cause of the rapaciousness they were living in. Then, voluntarily poorer, they could come to an awareness of their need for God and God's mercy. Their disposition would then be similar to the tax collector's who went up to the temple to pray.

Almsgiving can be important for achieving and expressing a unitary consciousness. But almsgiving, too, can be a ritual that is performed to be seen and one that adds to the performer's self-blindness. Furthermore, one can continue to trust in mammon and give alms. One can give alms "from one's surplus," as Jesus observed, and remain in the God-and-mammon posture of spirit, or one can give and grow in trust of God in doing so. A pericope in Luke 21:1–4 explains this difference; it also mirrors the parable of the two who went up to the temple to pray. "He glanced up and saw the rich putting their offerings into the treasury, and also a poor widow putting in two copper coins. At that he said: 'I assure you, this poor widow has put in more than all the rest. They make contributions out of their surplus, but she from her want has given what she could not afford—every penny she had to live on.' "

Jesus suggests something else to the Pharisees at the dinner at which the hand-washing controversy arose. Jesus tells them to get their eyes off small things and themselves and focus on "justice and the love of God!" (Luke 11:42) Justice, His justice, is what God would have them receive. And His love of His people was why He would do so. He sought to confer on them his justice out of love of them. They had maneuvered themselves into the foolish position of conferring justice on themselves by their observance of religious rituals and laws. As a result, their attention was on minutiae—tithing, giving 10 percent of the value of the "mint and rue and all sorts of garden herbs" they owned. (Luke 11:42) They had missed the proverbial forest by their attention to these minute stems. Jesus tried to force them from self-concentration and minutiae fixations so that they could exhibit the largesse and compassion of God to their neighbors, their students, and the needy of Israel.

A fourth parable to be considered is in Luke 12:16–21.

"Then he told them a parable, 'There was once a rich man who, having had a good harvest from his land, thought to himself, "What am I to do? I have not enough room to store my crops." Then he said, "This is what I will do: I will pull down my barns and build bigger ones, and store all my grain and my goods in them, and I will say to my soul: My soul, you have plenty of good things laid by for many years to come; take things easy, eat, drink, have a good time." But God said to him, "Fool! This very night the demand will be made for your soul; and this hoard of yours, whose will it be then?" So it is when someone stores up treasure for himself instead of becoming rich in the sight of God.' "

In this parable Jesus is saying, "Watch, and be on your guard against avarice of any kind, for life does not consist in possessions, even when someone has more than he needs." (Luke 12:15) He takes the major activity of those whose energy goes into mammon and holds it up to ridicule. This activity is accumulation. Jesus illustrates this with an imaginary person who makes elusive and illusory mammon his object of trust. He pronounces the chilling "fool" over his life because his accumulation will go for naught. On the face of it this seems a bit harsh since he didn't do anything morally wrong. Wasn't he, after all, just being a good steward of his bumper crop? Not in Jesus' perspective. Perhaps "fool" is more of a description of what one is being made by wealth than it is a name. The fact is he makes the fundamental error of confusing the length of his life with the amount of time it would take to make use of his material possessions. They lulled him into believing his life came from what he had. For life does not consist in possessions, even when someone has more than he needs. (Luke 12:15) He is not a fool because he is well off, he is a fool because he identifies his very existence with the security he thinks comes from having grain stored in barns. The attempt to win life from possessions is folly.[43]

He is being made a fool of by possessions because of his optic. Jesus, in this material that is peculiar to the Gospel of Luke, is concerned with the interpretation one brings to one's possessions since it affects one's sense of oneself, others, God, and life's purpose. In this parable the fool's basic mistake is confusing his life with his possessions. "Fool! This very night the demand will be made for your soul; and this hoard of yours, whose will it be then?" (Luke 12:20) The fool's favorite adjective was "my"; he begins to look pathetically myopic: "my harvest, my grain, my grain bins, my goods." His relationships to others and to God do not enter into his decisions about his resources. The gain in grain only heightened his self-immersion. Two different optics are held up by Jesus: the world of "me" in which you reach for yourself or the world of "us" in which one also "grow[s] rich in the sight of God." (Luke 12:21) The hearers of this word were being invited to handle their gains and their possessions in the sight of God and others. This was how Jesus would have them deal with these and come to health or remain healthy. Or they could handle their wealth from within the confines of their self-immersion, thus showing or reinforcing their sickness by that mode of operation. The fool goes this latter route. Others' needs, the fragility of life, the elusiveness of wealth and what it can purchase—all of these facts, or truths, this whole perspective, eludes him.

To sum up this section on healing, it seems that from these four simple parables one can conclude that there are several perceptual dimensions to the healings Jesus performed (and would still perform) on those who were sick with this mammon illness. One was to see the meaning of others, especially community members, in and for themselves in contrast to seeing people in terms of oneself or one's agenda or gain. The second dimension was to see one's resources as the owner's who has given them to be developed and developed as His. The third was to approach God, keenly aware of our poverty and need of Him rather than of our wealth, spiritual or financial. To approach God, needing His fullness, gains His attention. To approach God with our own fullness does not. And finally the role of alms, justice, and love of God fills out the dimension of health in the relationship of people of faith to their material/financial resources.

Jesus cured his hearers of this illness by giving them a different worldview they could enter. They were free to do so or not. A cure would not be affected if they insisted on retaining the worldview that trusting in mammon or mammon-and-God had engendered in them.

Healing Actions

Jesus had another way of healing mammon illness. He not only spoke about the disease, he acted on it in a direct, personal way. This second kind of healing took place when Jesus jarred the affectivity of the sick people, their loves, fears, and resentments by initiating a personal relationship. Sometimes, he succeeded; sometimes he failed.

The story of Zacchaeus (Luke 19:1–10) is an example of a healing of disease when Jesus came into contact with wealth and a wealthy person. The diseased man was "one of the senior tax collectors" of Jericho. Not surprisingly, he was a wealthy man. Not all tax collectors were wealthy.[44] Chief tax collectors, of course, were wealthier than those they employed. (Tax collector here is probably a toll collector who paid set revenues to Rome for the district for which he was given responsibility.)[45]

Zacchaeus, then, exacted toll fees from people passing through his district, Jericho, a key junction for those traveling to and from Jerusalem, up and down the Jordan, to and from Arabia. He and his employees collected tariffs and acted as customs officers, taxing goods being transported through Jericho and, of course, adding in their own profits to the amount. As a group they were despised because of the exorbitant amounts they exacted from the people. They were associated in the mind of the public with greed and extortion.[46] Their necessary relationship with the Roman authorities did nothing to add to their lovability either. When John the Baptizer sought to bring tax collectors to repentance, they asked him what they ought to do to show their change of heart and life. He told them: "Exact no more than the appointed rate." (Luke 3:13)

The story of Zacchaeus is an important one in the Gospel of Luke. It would be fair to say that it is to Luke's Gospel what the raising of Lazarus is to John's Gospel, since each is the last episode or act of ministry before Jesus' entrance into Jerusalem.[47] Also it is a story peculiar to Luke as the raising of Lazarus is to the Fourth Gospel. It is probably meant to be juxtaposed to the story of the rich member of the ruling class who could not respond to Jesus' invitation to disengage from his wealth. (Luke 18:18–27) Zacchaeus was similar to that figure in his wealth, but dissimilar in his power since he was not a member of the ruling class. He was a member of a despised class. Hence he is an interesting crossroad personality—one side of him represented the group who were least likely to enter the kingdom, the wealthy. (Luke 18:24–25) At the same time many of his "profession" in other places where Jesus had already ministered joined Jesus with alacrity, for example, Levi. Jesus, showing "things that are impossible by human resources, are possible for God" (Luke 18:27) heals Zacchaeus by doing what no one else in the town had done and what no one else in the town expected a holy man would do: accept him, single him out, choose him.

"Zacchaeus, come down. Hurry, because I am to stay at your

house today." (Luke 19:5) Jesus doesn't mention his riches; if anything, he avails himself of them. Zacchaeus "hurried down and welcomed him joyfully." (Luke 19:6) Zacchaeus' heart broke open. He was accepted. He was accepted by a holy man. This broke the impasse of heart between himself and God, an impasse presumably born of his awareness of wrongdoing and guilt with respect to money. He had also been immobilized because of the resentment that he had incurred with the population, the towns-folk. They did not disguise their disdain for him before or then. (Luke 19:7) He resented their judgment of him and their self-righteousness. He had been in a kind of catch-22 bondage, a bond-age that was brought on more by money than it was a bondage to money as such.

With one stroke, Jesus frees him from his prison. The experi-ence is so freeing for him that Zacchaeus acts as if he has a new identity, as if he had been born anew. He manifests this by his joy and by the fruits of a change of heart, a metanoia. He strips himself of his camel-sized wealth by announcing that his almsgiv-ing will involve "half of my belongings" which he gives to the poor. (Luke 19:8) And the allegations of fraud that had caused his marginalization by the people if verified will be subject to a four-fold restitution by him. (Luke 19:8)

This story has several overtones that are enlightening. One is the stress on today. "Today salvation has come to this house." (Luke 19:9) "Zacchaeus, come down. Hurry because I am to stay at your house today." (Luke 19:5) Today he promises to give half his belongings and make restitution. This is a peculiarly Lucan emphasis about salvation.[48] The delay in the Parousia heightened Luke's and the community's awareness that salvation was not something that was being awaited. It is operative now. Hence the fruits of salvation must be evident now also. The sharing of one's belongings and the proper use of money *now* would be the evi-dence that salvation was taking place. The evidence that this sal-vation is being enjoyed and lived now is made concrete by Zacchaeus' largesse, by his breaking open what had presumably constituted his "salvation" before, namely, his wealth. He did not "sell all"; nor was he asked to. He showed his inner disposition about being accepted and chosen by Jesus by the way he disposed of his wealth. His was a now discipleship that was shown by his largesse toward the poor and by his meticulous care that he be exonerated of fraud or extortion or any of the abuses associated with the misuse of monies.

Zacchaeus is saved not because of what he does with his wealth. Rather what he does with his wealth shows that he has been healed of mammon illness. As a result of his healing he can be counted as a son of Abraham who had been lost but was searched out and found by Jesus and brought into his real heritage, namely, a life of union with God and neighbor. (Luke 19:9–10)

Luke was eager to show the linkage between the use of material resources and salvation. His Zacchaeus story underscores the foundational character of having been chosen by Christ. Luke's Gentile readers or hearers would have been so many Zacchaeuses who had been searched out by Jesus who desired to stay at their house. It was not their righteousness that had him choose them. Why they were chosen was largely indecipherable as was the case with Zacchaeus. Love and Jesus' refusal to see merits or demerits in the usual ways of measurement helped them explain the mystery. Lucan readers/hearers realized that salvation for each of them entailed being chosen by Jesus to come into their houses. The subsequent use of their monies was the evidence they had welcomed him. Faith enabled and entailed their reassessment of their resources. The story of Zacchaeus was now available to them to ponder. He who was lost in his resentment, in his wealth, and in his guilt was found. From a heart that had been penetrated there began a new relationship not only to God but also to the other Jerichoans, one that was just and generous today. If Jesus had already selected them and had come to their houses, evidence of their salvation would be a discipleship that showed itself by their use of their resources.

There is another story in Luke that doesn't turn out as well. It describes a man who suffers from the same malady we are examining, namely, a deep disorder of spirit incited by his wealth. Again Jesus sees the illness and would heal it but the victim does not see himself in the same light and refuses, at least at that moment, the means Jesus held out to him to come to wholeness. (Luke 18:18–25)

The sick person is described by Luke as a member of the ruling class and very rich. He knew something about power and independence, and therefore is contrasted to children who know nothing about either. I mention this because the occasion of his approaching Jesus was the welcome Jesus gave to children who wanted to be touched by him. "It is to such as these that the kingdom of God belongs." (Luke 18:16) On the other hand, "Anyone who does not welcome the kingdom of God like a little child will never enter it." (Luke 18:17) This very rich member of the ruling class then questioned Jesus what he had to do to enter into this reign of God or "inherit eternal life." (Luke 18:18) He had known and kept the commandments since his youth, so he was not a spiritually ignorant or coarse person. Jesus chooses a drastic solution to meet the need the man's question implies. The solution is a wholesale conversion at the level of his affections. For this to come about he had to leave where his affections were and what his affections were wrapped around. The text makes clear that this was control and wealth. The second half of Jesus' solution is most revealing about this new way of life. Jesus invites him to join him, to follow him, to be with him as he journeys to Jerusalem and the reign of God it symbolized for which Jesus would give up what he possessed, surrendering even his life. (Luke 18:32–33)

It is essential to consider the two comments within which this episode is enclosed. The first comment has already been noted, namely, the need for an attitude of childlikeness. The child was the symbol Jesus used for the "anawim," the poor in spirit or lowly in the Christian community.[49] They could trust in God alone because He was all they had or knew to trust in. The second, which comes at the end of the episode, records Jesus' prediction about the manner of his own leaving of all things: mockery, scourging, and execution to be followed by resurrection on the third day. (Luke 18:32–33)

But the more poignant and central issue here is the affections of the man's spirit and heart. Jesus forthrightly sought to capture those. The healing would have to take place at the level of love because the sickness was a love attachment. The sickness would not be cast off if there were nothing to take its place. That which would take its place, by Jesus' invitation, was trust in him, allegiance to him, loyalty to him, love of him, in a word, following him. He teetered, declined, and grew melancholy. What he was attached to had a stronger pull than what he was invited to attach himself, and his future, and his heart to. He was unfree because he had assigned such a great value to what he possessed that even his desire for God was conditioned by his retaining what he associated with his very well-being. He sought God but on his own terms. Jesus spelled out the two steps by which he could have come to freedom and to an attachment commensurate with his desire and need. He probably would have been willing to enter Jesus' version of the Kingdom if he had been able to perform his way into it, or do something more because of a new knowledge of the law. But having less, in fact only Jesus, was not an acceptable prospect for him and so he goes off starkly solitary, "for he was very rich." (Luke 18:23)

Jesus' listeners' anxiety level rose sharply apparently when he linked having wealth with the impossibility of entering into the reign of God. (Luke 18:14–15) But when they ask, "Who then can be saved?" they are told that "things that are impossible by human resources, are possible for God." (Luke 18:27) What is possible for God is to become human. What is possible for God is to have His love for us and His lovability become evident to a human being. What is possible, then, is that they leave what they loved before Him out of love of Him.

Purses That Do Not Wear Out

Although the period of Christianity in which the instant dispossession of all one's possessions to follow Jesus was past for reasons already mentioned, and the mode of discipleship for Luke's generation would not have been one of instantaneous dispossession, what did continue as a constant through both periods was the issue of where one really lived, what one really clung to, whom one really loved. About this there was to be no mistake. What Peter observed, "We left all we had to follow you," (Luke 18:28)

describes what all the followers of Jesus have to do in all generations. The following of Jesus is not to be juxtaposed, added to, or
accommodated to what one owns. The following of Jesus is not to
be undertaken in the minutes left over after one has attended to
what one owns. Nor is the following of Jesus simply a figure of
speech. Making it so can obscure a deep illness. For some Christians, Jesus follows them, he is one of their possessions.[50] Rather,
the single-mindedness comes from having one purse, one goal, one
pearl, one love. Jesus was inviting the rich ruler into this possibility. Luke was inviting his readers to reflect on where their hearts
were with respect to Jesus. If they were incapable of being free of
their possessions, then they had either reverted to their condition
of sickness before they knew him or they had never really given
themselves to follow the way he had forged, the truth he was, and
the life he would be for them. Their use of their possessions was to
express their deepest loyalty and love. They were also in fact to be
free to renounce their possessions should "the kingdom of God"
beckon them to do so. (Luke 18:29) The power to do this, of
course, was beyond them, but this way of living was not for that
reason impossible.

What was this power that was beyond them but that could be in
them, but whose presence did not diminish their freedom? It was
the power of love, the power to love, the power to love Jesus, the
love of Jesus. He could and did become the place in which the
heart of his closest followers abided. "Wherever your treasure is,
that is where your heart will be too." (Luke 12:34) He became the
purse in which they invested their hearts, and their treasured possessions. When Jesus cured those whose hearts were sick with this
disease, he did not intend to leave them in a neutral place, simply
having swept their place clean of the "unclean spirit" of money-
become-mammon which demanded attention, loyalty, service.
(Luke 11:24–26)

In short, to understand Jesus' healings of mammon illness, the
two main features cited in this chapter must be kept in mind. The
first has to do with a perspective change. It was seen in the parables. The second has to do with the new object of trust which/
who was also loved. This object in the beginning of the Gospel of
Luke is clearly God and the reign of God. But it begins to become

even more personal and specified as the Gospel unfolds, without, of course, the reign of God ever being withdrawn or superseded. That new object of trust and love was, of course, Jesus. Love of him was the new "spirit" that was to occupy the house swept clean of illness.

The story of the demoniac also belongs here. While a disordered relationship to material possessions and finances (either financial resources one has or would have) operates in individuals, it will also be found in communities and cultures. In fact, it is unlikely that it will be found in individuals without also being in their communities. This is a way of reading the story of the demoniac in the country of the Gerasenes. The demon in the story (Luke 8:26–39) has so taken over the man that it (or maybe even "they," since its name is "legion") speaks for him; he does their bidding. When Jesus exorcises the man, they enter into two thousand swine (this number is Mark's) who are convulsed and charge over the bluff only to be drowned in the abyss. (Luke 8:33) In the myth world of Jesus' time, as also in Old Testament cosmology, the coming of the kingdom was to have the demons consigned to the watery deep, which was a symbol of the chaos conquered by the creator in the beginning.[51] Hence they plead with Jesus to be allowed to wander the earth and not to be consigned to this watery chaos which is their final destination. Jesus rebukes and overwhelms them by using a power that further reveals his relationship to the long-awaited kingdom of God.

For our purposes, the important part of the story is not the demons in the man but the sickness in the townspeople. Rather than rejoicing that one of their own has been disinfested and restored to health, they give no sign of joy that his long anguish is over. They do, however, give clear evidence that they want Jesus to depart from their midst. The possessed person who becomes well in this incident turns out to be merely the first instance of what the whole town needed to have happen to it. But its population resists. In fact, it acts in the same way as the demons in the possessed man acted. They accord Jesus a negative kind of homage by pleading to be left alone. (Luke 8:37) They see there is something special about him and rather than invite him, and his power into their midst, they ask him to depart. In effect they are saying, "We are not ill. We prefer 'the order' we knew before you came into our countryside." But notice the order they preferred and who they were willing to "sacrifice" in order that it continue. There had been a man in anguish so long that they were numb to his anguish much as Israel was to that of her marginal ones in Solomon's reign. The possessed man's demons were so much a part of the townspeople's order that the demons' disappearance was disorienting. The absence of the large herd of swine was the bottom-line evidence of their disappearance. The economics of the pagan town was much tied up with the raising of pigs. But the town had grown used to a kind of order that placed such a priority on economic pursuits that the well-being of one of their most tortured citizens was not cause for rejoicing since the price of his healing gutted their resources. This is the sign of their collective sickness. Their reaction to Jesus, it should be noted, also presages Israel's decision about Jesus: You must go. The Sanhedrin decreed, "If we let him go on in this way [e.g., calling Lazarus from the tomb], everybody will believe in him, and the Romans will come and suppress the Holy Place and our nation." (John 11:48) The devil that the Gerasenes knew before Jesus came into their midst was preferable to the unpredictable order this man with his numinous power would unleash if they accorded him welcome.

Like his Father's own compassion, Jesus' compassion is not turned off by the illness of the town. Hence he decides to leave in their midst a minister, a witness who by dint of his hard-won competence could also remind the townsfolk what they were unable to see at that moment, that a healer had come among them who acted with power. The cured demoniac who wanted to accompany Jesus into an unknown land was sent back by Jesus into his own town. As a result, he "went off and proclaimed throughout the city all that Jesus had done for him." (Luke 8:38)

Something more needs to be said about this possessed man and the sickness that afflicts the town's culture and that the culture mediates to the townspeople. There is a naïveté about mammon illness if the only conception we have of it is that it inheres in individuals. At the same time, the capacity for thinking about systems, or mediating structures or social analysis would not have been possible for Jesus, for the culture in which Jesus lived, or for the cultures from which our Scriptures come. In other words, the idea that the town was as ill as the demoniac or even the possibility that the demoniac's demon was mediated to him through the town's value confusion and exacerbated by its inhuman ways of dealing with its individual victims—these would have been impossible lines of thought in those times. That we can and do think in terms of social systems today makes it all the more necessary that the historical-critical method of scriptural exegesis not be the sole moment in the process of interpretation or use of the Scriptures. To make this the only moment or process of interpretation results in a positivism that reduces the value of the text to a mere trickle of the power it could unleash.[52]

Historical-critical exegesis is needed for the community of believers to interpret what the Word of God might say to them. But gathering this exegetical information is only one moment in a whole process of hearing that word. Rather than one, two fidelities must be operative. One is fidelity to the text *cum* exegesis; the other is fidelity to one's consciousness. While the one runs the danger of a crass subjectivism, the other approach has any number of dangers: objectivism, archaism, irrelevance, elitism, sterility, pedantry—in a word, the subjection of the word of God to scientific positivism. Eisegesis is a reading into the text what is not there. Exegesis on the other hand derives its information from the text. It seeks to locate the literal meaning of the text as intended by the writer. When that is done, there can be a coming together of the unique consciousness or preunderstanding of the reader and the text.[53]

Applied to the text on the demoniac, this would mean that Luke would not have said that the town was ill but the perception of systemic illness has warrant from the text. What happens between the text and the reader/prayer is dialogical. What results is not exactly what the author had in mind in his original writing. Yet what the author wrote is why the reader/prayer can see how a culture that is ill makes ill people. And ill people make a culture ill. This meaning isn't deposited in the text but the text and the reader/prayer together have actualized this meaning. As Schneiders puts it: "The real meaning does not pre-exist the understanding of the interpreter. The understanding of the reader is

constitutive (although not exclusively so) of the meaning of the
text as the interpretation of the artist is constitutive of the music.
The score by itself is a normative possibility of music. The text, by
itself, is a normative possibility of meaning. It must be actualized
by the interpreter."[54]

A Healthy Economic Anthropology

Jesus can be a healer in many ways of the kind of illness incurred by a disordered relationship to money or possessions. One
of the surest of these ways is the use of these healing stories and
parables by those who see their need to be healed of this sickness.
Those who would be cured must be predisposed to allow God's
healing word be spoken to them through the Scriptures. Jesus'
power to heal is no less operative today than it was the day the
Gospel events took place or the parables were spoken to the persons possessed by the illness. Mammon illness is no less real, we
are no less sick today than the people were the day Jesus healed
them. The healer is Christ. He is the same yesterday, today, and
forever.

Healing as we have talked about it in this chapter begins a
process of conversion. The conversion involves a change of the
worldview through which we perceive. It also involves an emotional change in one's effective response to the situations and realities one looks upon and is involved in. The optimum conditions
for this healing and conversion to take place are explicitly religious ones. Specifically, this would mean one really knows one is
sick (or that we are sick); that we needn't be; that one is seeking to
be healed and is expectantly having recourse to God in Christ (if
one is Christian) for this to take place; and that one is capable of
prayer in pursuing this objective. But more than all of these, conviction that Jesus can and would make us well is what will make
the difference. Since healing and conversion are ordinarily a gradual process, persistence is needed. This is also because the degree
of change necessary for the healing process and the longer-term
conversion process to take place is so discontinuous from the hab-

its and worldviews learned previously that the presence of the Spirit will be needed for that which is impossible for us to pull off with our own powers. "Things that are impossible by human resources are possible for God." (Luke 18:27)

Finally, it seems necessary to be explicit about what would constitute the kind of health that shows itself in people's relationship to their finances and possessions. The first characteristic of health in this area would be that our assets serve us, not the other way around. We are not money's minions. It must do our bidding, not us its bidding. A second characteristic of health is that, assuming some degree of solvency and therefore discretion, what I do with what I have expresses my values, pursues my purposes, conveys who I am, and my sense of what I'm for—in a word, me. Anyone could take an instant inventory and see, for example, that I have life insurance because I intend to provide for other members of my family should I die. I have a car because I need transportation. It is a small car because something more expensive or pretentious I do not regard as important. It would not be me. And so on, through the myriad things over which I have some disposition. What I have (as also what I don't choose to have) enfleshes my interiority and communicates my sense of myself to others. A third characteristic of health, one that is implicit in the first two, is that a person has developed a unitary consciousness to deal with his or her world.

Three further comments need to be added to this presumably incontrovertible description of a healthy economic anthropology. The first has to do with freedom. It is not necessarily unhealthy or unfree to be operating within very definite constraints. There is always a reciprocity between what I have, have saved, own, how I spend my money, and all the "givens" that face me and are over against me. It is in terms of these givens that I make my choices. These givens, for example, include the prices of things, the amount of money I have, the demand there is for the things I want, and so forth. Less personally, the givens also include such things as the existing systems of banking, commerce, taxation, consumption, and production. We are not free to remove ourselves from them or from the overall, complex system of supply and demand within which economic interaction takes place in our

modern American world. Nor are we free to use as a means of
currency, stones or denarii. Even though there are, always have
been, and always will be givens, this fact of itself is not coercive.
The point is, I do not exercise my freedom or my purchasing,
selling, or investing in a world of my own devising, or in a world
of unlimited possibility, but within social givens, within structures
and systems that constrain but do not eradicate my freedom.

The second comment is that individuals and groups can arrive
at some degree of health in their relationship to their economic
culture, but their culture with its financial structures and economic system can be quite unhealthy, in fact, very ill. Can be and
at present is. The proof of this is not hard to find. If we allow our
imaginations a brief foray into the third world, it is obvious that
the relationship between what most human beings have and what
is humanly necessary for them is one of deficiency. Less globally,
it is obvious that our culture reacts the way the Gerasene town
reacted to Jesus. We prefer our order, notwithstanding its victims,
to the price healings cost. The myriad structural problems of un-
employment, unfair wages and prices, resource maldistribution,
destitution, hunger, famine, and so forth must be solved, of
course, if the system is to be healthy. But we cannot wait till this
happens before we become healthy as individuals and communities. In fact, healthy systems are more likely to develop via people
who have a healthy relationship to money and possessions than
via people who are not only in an unhealthy economic culture but
are sick with one of the illnesses it carries. A healthy few are more
likely to affect many than are many who have caught the disease
likely to change the structures while neglecting their own need to
change.

A third comment about this area of personal finances and material resources is that although I believe, in the abstract, that a
person who is not religious can have a unitary consciousness,
those who are much more likely to possess such a quality will be
religious people because presumably their faith could come to see
as one both worlds that otherwise remain apart in the person's
consciousness. The opposite is also true, namely, that those with
the deepest fissure of consciousness will often consider themselves
religious people for reasons already mentioned. In the matter we

are examining in this volume, a split consciousness deals with financial and material resource issues with one part of its consciousness. The economy and the financial structures that are subsets of it have a life of their own only because they are given this by the split consciousness of us who deal with them. The fact is, most of us are working both sides of the street and doing so as if each of us were more than one person. It is as if each side of me were a whole, thus making that to which I conform its own whole thereby choosing to ignore the inconsistencies, the epistemological schizophrenia, or even the hypocrisy in this kind of behavior. Split consciousness is partly explained by the secularization that developed in modern times. It is also explained by the failure of the churches to come to grips with secularization with a theology and spirituality of secularity.

A unitary conscious does not develop by trying to have one object of consciousness. The affections are the key to developing a unitary consciousness. To have a unitary consciousness one must have learned to live in his or her heart, choosing from there, thinking from there, acting from there. Our consciousness is rooted in our love(s). Healing does not in the final analysis start by changing attitudes but by a transformation at the point of desires, with loves and hates, attractions and repugnances. A conversion is, finally, a change at the level of one's loves. The Gospels' call is to have all our loves come from and lead to One. To be healed fully we must love fully. A tall order, but what is impossible for us is possible for God to do in us.

CHAPTER II

✦✦

The Sublation
of the Economy

The healing process described in the first chapter should be complemented with a perception of what God's intentions are for our economic systems. In the first chapter we were attempting to have the light of faith shine on our "in-house money." In this chapter we will attempt to have this same light of faith play on "out-there money," the economic and financial structures that constitute our economic system. If we were to see what God would do with these, and is doing with these, we could align our own economic behavior more closely to these intentions. This should both affect the structures to some degree and consolidate our own healing over against them. The transubstantiation of wealth presumes not only a change in our own economic behavior but a change in our perception of the structures within which we operate.

God reveals Himself and His intentions. For Christians and Jews the privileged locus of these disclosures are the Scriptures. Catholic Christians would also see tradition as a further source for understanding such matters.[1] Is there anything in Scripture and tradition that would illumine our understanding of God's intentions for our own economic system? I believe there is. This chapter will claim that these sources can be read as saying that God in and through Christ would sublate the economy.

Something is sublated when it is brought to a higher condition than it previously enjoyed.[2] The notion of sublation gained attention because of Hegel, but one doesn't have to be an Hegelian philosopher to benefit from what is implied by it.[3] For me, the many insights that Scripture and tradition contain about Christ's actions in and posture toward the economy can be encapsuled in this notion of sublation, a notion that is contained in neither Scripture nor tradition.

Our Images of Christ

Pedagogically it would be better to begin by first surfacing some of the inchoate images we might have about Christ's attitude toward the economy than it would at this point to explain more about this notion of sublation. We almost certainly have impressions about God's attitudes and perception of our economy and its structures if we actively believe in God. We image the Christ we follow and follow the Christ we image. We also have an image of his relationship to things. What is our image of Christ's relationship to out-there money? There surely was an economy in Israel in his day. Presumably he would not have looked at it as a separate phenomenon any more than he would have viewed politics that way. Nevertheless, buying and selling, producing and consuming, need and superfluity were constantly in his consciousness since his words often allude to these. And beyond the question of his attitude toward the economy of his day, what is his will about it now, insofar as we can find out? Can he be said to have an intention about our American economy, and if so, what is it? It would seem superficial for us to claim to follow him and not seek to know what his stance toward the economy was in his day and is in our day.

It seems there are six possible images one can have of Christ and the economy, each with some warrant both within scriptural sources and from Christian history. Each of these ways of imaging Christ can also be found among contemporary Christians. Very briefly here the first of these would be that he was and, therefore, still is basically indifferent to the economy. He was and is interested in the hearts of people, this image would "argue." Neither what goes into our mouths, that is to say, patterns of consumption, nor what is produced by us, our patterns of productivity, is what interests Christ, but rather where our hearts are with God and one another. He lived in this world with its structures, its political and economic structures, as if he were not in it. It was as if he were following Paul's advice to the Corinthians even before Paul wrote it: ". . . those who have been buying property [should live] as though they had no possessions; and those who are involved with the world [should live] as though they were people not engrossed in it. Because this world as we know it is passing away." (1 Cor. 7:30–31) The world's transiency and his interest in our interiority are two of the fonts that generate the image of a Christ with this indifferent attitude.

A second image of Christ's posture toward the economy, one that was entertained by Christians from the earliest days till now, is one of hostility. There is always the scene of Jesus turning over the tables of the money changers to fuel this image. And there is also the intimate connection between following him and renouncing all of one's possessions. (Luke 14:33) There must be, therefore, something basically incompatible between Christ and wealth of any kind. The New Testament seems to say this. It is either/or— either you serve, love, give yourself to God or to money. (Luke 16:13) This is how he was in his historical years and he hasn't changed. Money hasn't either.

A third image Christians have of Christ vis-à-vis the economic system is one of co-optation. He makes use of it for his purposes but doesn't sanction any of its purposes. He had a mission and still does, and in the pursuit of it, money is needed to establish and maintain the institutions which further this mission. There were, for example, women who appear to have helped "finance" him and his disciples in his ministry. So also he, through his Church, makes use of the economic system to develop the mission of the Church in the world and the people of God who are the agency for the execution of this mission. He doesn't take the economic system on; he uses it now as he did in his day. One practice of the

Church that serves to reinforce this image is the omnipresent collection at its liturgical services.

A fourth image some Christians project onto Christ's relationship to the economy is one of conquest. He is at present subduing it and bringing it into subjection to his reign. To this end he is even now in the process of destroying "every principality, every ruling force, and power." (1 Cor. 15:24) But a large portion of these errant powers are in economic systems. Their frequent injustices and indifference to human beings makes their conquest urgent. This posture isn't exactly in the Gospels, since Jesus did not exercise this degree of power till his resurrection. But he is Lord now and he will succeed in this task so that when he hands all that has become subject to him over to God the Father, God will be all in all.

A fifth image is one of a Christ who fades into his people in each of their cultures. To find out, therefore, how to be Christian in a given economy one must observe or consult the fervent Christian people in that culture. This is what Incarnation requires. It is far too abstract to inquire about Christ's will for an abstract economy. Or it is too late, maybe. The Christ who would answer the question cannot be retrieved. How sincere Christians behave in the economy of their own culture is the best way to answer this question.

We must go from image to judgment. Once the operative image has surfaced, we must judge the accuracy of the image. I judge all five of these images to be adequate on occasion, but inadequate as a predominant image. The first image of indifference comes close to a spiritualized faith, a faith that refuses the works or deeds that embody it. The second image of hostility appeals to those who are alienated from society. The third image of a co-opting Christ disowns responsibility for the world and seems opportunistic. Faith in a subduing Christ breeds or reflects a triumphalism or a superiority to the limitations we all have to live with. And finally a faith that would get its norms from the way the faithful interact with the economic system of their culture will almost certainly discover an enculturated faith, one that accommodates itself to culture rather than leavens it.

There is an element of truth in all five of these images. But as the basic posture of Christ, they lead us off the track, I submit. If our faith is going to succeed in speaking to money, if the courier is to take clear messages from us to the system, if our following of Christ is really following his way and will about the economic systems (to mix three metaphors), then this question about how Christ relates to these systems and would relate to them through us must be given a better focus.

I believe a more accurate reading, though admittedly it will take some doing to make it an image, would see Christ's relationship to the economic system as one of sublation as I have already indicated. The etymology of the word "sublation" is *sublatus,* the past participle of the verb *tollo,* which means to lift up, to carry, to bear something beyond its former condition.[4] I use "sublation" here to mean that a given economic system would be sustained and transformed by Christ without its being ignored, loathed, overrun, or tolerated by him. (For Christ to be sublating it, of course, presumes that the system is not radically flawed, a presumption that grows in likelihood if the continuance of the system is due to the willing participation of the citizen consumers and producers.)

To say that sublation is the best overall description of Jesus' relationship to the economy says something ancient and something new, as an earnest scribe should. The ancient thing sublation says in this matter of the economy and Jesus relates to what the Council of Chalcedon said in 451 about the metaphysical constitution of the person of Christ. It decreed that in him there were two natures "without confusion, without change, without separation."[5] These two natures were not homogenized as a result of their union in the person we call Jesus. His humanity was in a relationship of sublation to his divinity, in our words. Before Chalcedon the Cappadocian Gregorys were at pains to affirm the fact that Christ was totally a man because if he were not, our humanity would not have been redeemed.[6] They developed what is called the soteriological principle of Christology which reads: "What is not assumed is not redeemed."[7] Because every aspect of his humanity had been assumed by the second Person of the Trinity, we are saved in our total humanity. Sublation, therefore, is in some respects an ancient idea because these very early Christological controversies and insights were in effect seeing Jesus' own humanity retaining its integrity notwithstanding the condition of glory it enjoyed from the Incarnation onward.

Suggesting that Jesus' relationship to the economy should be seen in terms of sublation is also a new idea since the Incarnation was just the beginning of a process. Christ's humanity is now in a relationship both to humanity as it has developed in the world and to the world as humanity has developed it. The most recent Council, Vatican II, observed these developments and did so in terms of Christ. It saw Christ as intending "to appropriate the whole universe into the new creation, initially here on earth, fully on the last day."[8] More specifically, he intends "to restore and develop unceasingly the temporal sphere of things" of which economic systems are an essential part.[9] He intends to do this in such a way that the temporal order in each of its elements is not deprived of "its independence, its proper goals, laws, resources and significance for human welfare."[10] Rather, he would "perfect the temporal order in its own intrinsic strength and excellence."[11] But each of these intentions envisions Christ extending his relationship to "the whole universe" and it structures through humanity.[12] The structures that make up the temporal order "possess their own intrinsic value." This value has been implanted in them by God.[13] But God's intentions for the temporal order would include bringing its structures to the degree of perfection of which they are capable.

Notice, therefore, how the notion of sublation begins with the relationship of Jesus' divinity to his humanity and is then extended to and through our humanity to the social structures by which human beings organize themselves. God's intentions are glimpsed in all of these differing realities. These intentions can be reduced to one, to bring that which He has made to the perfection for which it was made. It should also be evident that God would do this through not despite human beings.

The particular instrument of sublation that Vatican II concentrated on was the Church.[14] Just as the historical Christ expressed himself and related to the people and systems of his own society by means of his body, as any human being does, so the instrumentality ordinarily used at present by the Risen Christ to relate to the world are the people-members of his body. (1 Cor. 12:12) These members are citizens of two cities. They belong to their particular societies, each of which is structured with particular social, political, and economic institutions. They also belong to Christ. But Christ would sublate all structures and societies to himself. He would do so in large measure through the members of his body who function in the world with its structures.

The process of sublation, therefore, is not miraculous in the sense that it takes place outside of what we might call the ordinary laws of social interaction and institutional development. Nor is it suprahuman in the sense that it takes place despite people. The members of the Body of Christ are the ordinary instrumentality used by the Risen Lord "to draw all [both people and their structures] to myself." (John 12:32)[15] Members of the Body of Christ are not the only ones he uses, of course, since he has other human instrumentalities who are not of this fold. (John 10:16) Nonetheless, it is the part his own members can play in his sublation of the economy that interests us most in this volume. This chapter wants to establish that Christians can speak to money more effectively if they have their economic behavior attuned to the purposes of Christ. By seeing Christ's intention for the economy in terms of sublation they will be more instrumental in assisting his sublation of the economy.

If it were taking place now, what would sublation look like and what steps should we be taking to have it come about? The Vatican Council gives us the beginnings of an answer to this question. If we take the measure of the systems rather than their taking the measure of us, if they express our humanity, are stamped with our freedom, and values, are sensitive to our common humanity, human values, rights, and needs, then sublation is taking place. If our economic activities and arrangements are "under the control of mankind," if the human dignity of people is respected and enhanced by the workings of our economic system in general and by the particular ways in which it attempts to work out its never-wholly-solved problems, then Christ's sublation of the macroeconomic system has at least begun. When social systems, particularly the economic and financial structures of a society, serve human beings, they are doing what they exist to do because "the human person is the source, the center and the purpose of all socio-economic life."[16] Today's complex structures are not unlike the simple structure of Sabbath in Jesus' day. It was "made for man, not man for the sabbath." (Mark 2:27) These structures were made for us, not we for these structures.

The Blue Crab

Since I began this excursus with images, I'd like to illustrate sublation with a metaphor drawn from nature. The scene is of blue crabs swimming across the vast expanse of the Chesapeake Bay.[17] It is autumn. There are thousands of these crabs once your eye becomes accustomed to the sight. On closer inspection, a smaller crab has climbed onto a larger one and is being carried or borne across the choppy waters. This is the female of the species, maybe not more dangerous, but certainly smaller than the male. The two have mated on the bottom of the bay, and part of the commitment, so to speak, includes this somewhat unexpected, touching ritual. The lesser is carried by the greater to a destination from which the next generation of blue crabs will be born.

This scene recalled to my mind sublation. It furnished an image of Christ's relationship to the economy, preposterous as that may seem, since in this scene I saw a strength that was not at the same time a takeover; a hospitality that was at the same time an identification; a passionate commitment that carried the otherwise helpless one; an embrace that affected the one embracing quite as much as the one embraced.[18] The similitude should be obvious.

"The rightful autonomy of the creature," "the legitimate autonomy of human culture," "the autonomy of earthly affairs," "the rightful independence of science" are some of the Vatican Council's summary phrases for indicating the respect religious people are asked to have for the disciplines and structures by which the world has developed itself.[19] Secular reality has become considerably more autonomous since the days when God so loved the world that He sent His only Son into it. God's love of the world is now inextricably linked with Jesus, and therefore history, and the developments of the human enterprise which have come about in the course of history.

As a result of his self-emptying, taking on even "the form of a slave," Jesus became Lord of the enterprise he had served to the point of death. As its Lord now, Jesus sublates the human enterprise. He does this as one who is part of the enterprise because he is eternally one of us. But as its Lord, he draws all to himself. "And when I am lifted up from the earth I shall draw all people to myself." (John 12:32) This is a pregnant suggestion from John. Lifting Jesus up from the earth on the Cross was systemic evil's finest hour, its zenith moment. God, however, lifted Jesus above its momentary success, thus breaking the sway in which the world was held by systemic evil, personified as "the prince of this world." (John 12:31) With the raising of Jesus in the Resurrection the prince of this world began to lose his hegemony. (John 12:31)

There is a third sense in which Jesus is lifted up. That is by those who acknowledge that he is Lord. He draws all, both people and the structures within which they live, to himself by the many ways in which people acknowledge that there is a Lord of the structures, a point toward which every created reality converges.[20] This acknowledgment can run the gamut from explicit awareness and praise to implicit awareness and integrity of conscience in human affairs, depending on the proximity of the individual to the Good News.

I am obviously taking liberty with the texts of Scripture here. The notions of systems, systemic evil, and social structures would have been foreign to the New Testament authors. The texts, however, have a "surplus of meaning" that can be evoked when a modern consciousness meets the ancient text.[21]

There are other passages that are particularly apt to convey this image of Christ. One of these passages would locate our understanding of sublation under the image of headship. "He has let us know the mystery of his purpose, according to his good pleasure which he determined beforehand in Christ, for him to act upon when the times had run their course." (Eph. 1:9–10) This plan is to "bring everything together under Christ, as head, everything in the heavens and everything on earth." (Eph. 1:10) Here the plan is the sublation of all things by Christ and he is even now hard at work carrying out his mission.[22]

Another passage has several images that fill out the notion of sublation. One envisions Christ in the context of precreation. He was "the first-born of all creation . . . he exists before all things." (Col. 1:15–17) Then it goes on to claim that "in him were created all things in heaven and on earth," including "everything visible and everything invisible, thrones, ruling forces, sovereignties, powers—and in him all things hold together." (Col. 1:16–17) Finally, it is sure that "all fullness [is] to be found in him": by God's pleasure and by means of him God will "reconcile all things to him, everything in heaven and everything on earth, by making peace through his death on the cross." (Col. 1:19–20)[23]

The Colossians and Ephesians letters have what is usually referred to as a high Christology, one that is focused on the divinity of Christ and, therefore, is very compatible, for example, with the idea of the preexistence of the Son of God.[24] My own preference, as well as the preference of most modern Christologists, is for a low Christology, one that begins with the humanity of the historical person Jesus.[25] What this human being said and did, his own human relationship to God, what happened to him in the course of his brief history, his limitations—these are the things that interest "low" Christology, even though what is conveyed by the New Testament authors has elements of both. A low Christology is a better vehicle for appreciating that Jesus was an instrument of sublation used by the Godhead during his earthly sojourn just as we are used now by the Risen Christ during our earthly sojourn. Not only his and our individuated humanity but his and our humanity in its social units, our communities, with all their ways of determining the quality of our life together, are meant to be instruments of sublation.

It should begin to be evident that there is a very close connection between the notions of sublation and redemption but that they are not identical. First of all, redemption is requisite because we are fallen human beings. The historical Jesus was not being redeemed by God, yet his humanity was in a posture of being sublated by the Godhead, as were the social wholes of which he was a part and by extension the structures that supported his life.

Obviously sublation is an analogous concept. It is analogous to redemption insofar as God perfects that which is sublated. Sublation is necessary because fallen human beings make sinful structures. But structures are not redeemed whereas they can be perfected, meaning aligned to and instrumental of valid human purposes. I would locate both the activity of perfecting structures and of using them to pursue moral goals under the aegis of sublation. Both our humanity and the structures it establishes would then be operating under the Lordship of Christ, notwithstanding our awareness of this.

If Jesus' relationship to the everyday life of Israel, including its economic arrangements, and in turn the Risen Lord's relationship to the present life of the world, including its structures and systems, can be seen in terms of sublation, then Christians should be able to relate to the world and its structures more perceptively. We can make this more specific and will do this in two ways. One by a closer look at justice, the other by examining the grid of self-appropriation supplied by Bernard Lonergan.

Bringing economic and financial structures to the degree of perfection of which they are capable is a consummation devoutly to be wished. Its well-wishers are legion; those who have succeeded at it are few. The usual way of attempting to realize this goal is by being just and developing just structures. Justice is a much more familiar idiom to both world and Church than sublation is. That very familiarity, however, carries some negative freight along with it. Feelings of helplessness, frustration, exasperation, uncertainty, conflict stalk many who would pursue or have pursued justice in the myriad forms in which it is sought and desired.

While justice can become exceedingly abstract as a subject, I will simply sketch the overall topography of justice that the Roman Catholic church has mapped out especially these last ninety years in its social teachings. It is necessary to at least broach this complex subject in this chapter because the more we know about justice the better agents of sublation we will be since the pursuit of justice is the ordinary intentionality by which sublation takes place.

There are three kinds of justice according to traditional Catholic social teaching: commutative, distributive, and social. Commutative justice is concerned with the realization of the equal dignity of people in their interpersonal transactions with one another.[26] The basis of commutative justice is that all people are equal as people in their "unmediated relations" with one another.[27] The most frequent forms of commutative justice are contracts and promises. These "bind individual to individual in the sphere of private transactions."[28]

Distributive justice is even more germane to Christ's sublation of our economic system since it focuses on the relationships between society and its citizens or its subgroups. The structures of a given society will be just if its public goods are allocated justly. Citizens have rights to the public goods of society that are essential to their dignity. Distributive justice is achieved "when social patterns are so organized that they meet the minimum needs of all persons and permit an equal opportunity to participate in the public activities which meet these needs."[29] Access to the social, political, and economic life of the community is an essential component of distributive justice. Rights such as the right to work, the right to vote, the right to adequate medical care, the right to shelter are some of the specific forms of distributive justice.[30]

Social justice complements distributive justice because it "demands from each individual all that is necessary for the common good."[31] It also makes claims on governments because they are responsible for "the creation of those social, economic and political conditions which are necessary to assure that the minimum human needs of all will be met."[32] The goods that members of a community have in common must be generated by the efforts of each. Social justice stresses the need for each to create these goods, services, and wealth and for society's authorities to create the conditions for upbuilding this commonweal.

The social teaching of the Roman Catholic church has also developed a number of ethical principles by which conflicts of justice can be adjudicated. The recent drafts of the U.S. Catholic Bishops, entitled "Catholic Social Teaching and the U.S. Economy," is a good example of the applicability of this tradition to some of the country's more urgent economic issues like employment, poverty, agribusiness, and so forth.[33] These drafts could be seen as efforts to bring the specific economic structures to the degree of perfection of which they are capable. They could also be seen as part of the growing evidence that the Roman Catholic church along with many other Christian churches is making justice an intrinsic part of its agenda and institutional self-understanding. One of the more celebrated instances of the church's articulation of this development comes from the International Synod of Bishops' statement entitled "Justice in the World." It states: "Action on behalf of justice and participation in the transformation of the world fully appears to us as a constitutive dimension of the preaching of the Gospel or, in other words, of the Church's mission for the redemption of the human race and its liberation from every oppressive situation."[34] Seeing justice as internal to the church's agenda and mission didn't begin with the 1971 Synod, but its statement summed up a century of development.

Sublation and the Realms of Meaning

There is another way of reading God's intentions for the economy. This second way is to examine the changes in human consciousness that have enabled human beings both to develop their economies and use them to serve their purposes. My contention here will be that the development of human consciousness with its four realms of meaning is a necessary precondition for people to become agents of Christ's sublational intentions for the economy. Lonergan's grid enables us to root sublation in what is often referred to as an economic anthropology.[35]

Lonergan divides the history of human consciousness in three stages.[36] In the first period, consciousness was undifferentiated and in the second and third periods it is differentiated. Undifferentiated consciousness derives the meanings it generates from two sources, one is common sense, the other is the sense of the transcendent. Common sense perceived and dealt with people and things concretely. These particulars of our everyday experience were taken simply as they presented themselves. Relating to one another, eating and drinking, providing food and drink, producing what was necessary for shelter and well-being—these activities were done with common sense and without much abstraction from the particulars. Undifferentiated consciousness also derived meaning from a sense of the transcendent. Particulars were read in terms of the gods or God. Thus: God has provided what we have or God will provide what we need. Meaning, therefore, for centuries derived from common sense or transcendence or, more frequently, a combination of the two.

A quantum leap occurred in human consciousness when it was able to abstract from particulars and develop "theories" about how the particulars were in themselves and in their interrelationships and hence, how they could be manipulated to better meet people's needs and serve their purposes.[37] Theory becomes a whole new source of meaning. It makes use of the data of common sense to systematize meaning and direct activity. The need to develop theories, learn theories, follow theories came about because common sense could not answer all our questions or meet our needs. This systematic exigency for theory is a leap forward in the capacity of consciousness to affect reality. While the realm of common sense reads particulars in their relation to us, the realm of theory reads particulars by their "internal relations, their congruences and differences, and the functions they fulfill in their interactions."[38] It creates the conditions of possibility that human beings can become more actively involved in shaping their social systems. Those who would be participants in God's activity of perfecting the social systems have to operate from a differentiated consciousness. Insofar as we employ theories as sources of meaning, our consciousness is differentiated.

It doesn't need to be argued that economic theory, which is only one of innumerable instances of theory, has done much to shape modern civilization. Although Adam Smith and his *Wealth of Nations* (1776) had forerunners, he put forth the most influential economic theory of the eighteenth century.[39] Since then many theories in the myriad matters relating to finances and the economy, not to mention theory about every other aspect of human endeavor, have never ceased to develop. What could be argued is whether economic theory necessarily aids the human condition and inevitably betters the structures of society. Obviously that will depend on how good the theory is or what it purports to do, namely, know and interpret the data. It will also depend on the development of a fourth font of meaning.

Interiority is this fourth font of meaning. This font's meaning comes from the self that has developed a capacity to become conscious of itself while it is intending or apprehending its object.[40] Interiority develops the capacity to judge and make choices about these objects with greater freedom and deliberation. The more the other realms develop the more necessary is a grounding of the self in this fourth realm. Certainly theory can reconstrue reality in small ways and large, but interiority is the capacity both to reflect on the implications of theories' employment and to act on the basis of these judgments. We can reconstrue our world via theory but we reconstruct it more humanly via interiority. Two synonyms for this fourth font of meaning are self-appropriation or individuation.

The development of this capacity for self-appropriation frees individuals from the limitations of being mere parts of social wholes or from the confining role identities that are peculiar to those who live in the world of undifferentiated consciousness. Theory and individuation, as Jung would call it, are the reason we have a modern world with its ingenuity, enterprise, creativity, pluralism, and diversity.

Lonergan's four realms of meaning sketch out the anthropological developments that are necessary for human beings to actively shape their lives and society's structures. This scheme shows the rich capacities of consciousness. It does not purport to give norms for the betterment of our structures as ethics, ethical theory, laws, justice, and social theory attempt to do.

A differentiated consciousness, because it is freer, more knowledgeable and self-aware is, all things being equal, more a reflection of God. The more we construct our world through theory and self-appropriation, the more we show ourselves to be made in the image and likeness of God. With God we become co-creators of the reality we find ourselves in. By the same token, the theory could be in error; the interiority could be mistaken. The fact that a more fully human act takes place from a differentiated consciousness is not a guarantee it is a more moral act or that it conforms to God's sublational activity in Christ.

Proof abounds that actions taken from a differentiated consciousness do not guarantee that our systems are better or that we are better off. While differentiated consciousness has enabled us to develop all the extraordinary features of modern life, it has also given us urban blight, acid rain, technological horrors, the nuclear weapons impasse, and the increasing concentration of wealth in the hands of a few. The conclusion to this negative evidence is not that we should hanker for the good old days of undifferentiated consciousness. We should not try to shut down the twin engines that have brought us into the modern world, namely, theory and interiority in Lonergan's scheme. We couldn't do so even if we were to come to such an inviable and ignorant conclusion that such a shutdown was called for.

A better conclusion could be drawn by going back to Lonergan's scheme about consciousness where I pointed out his division into three stages. I have mentioned only two, from undifferentiated to differentiated. In the history of the development of consciousness, a further differentiation has taken place. "In a third stage the modes of common sense and theory remain, but science asserts its autonomy from philosophy and there occur philosophies that leave theory to science and take their stand on interiority."[41] In the third stage of consciousness, "science gives up any claim to necessity and truth. It settles for verifiable possibilities."[42] While much good comes from this, the worst feature of the differentiation is the effect it can have on consciousness. It splits it. The glories of a differentiated consciousness do not inevitably nor inexorably lead us to a split consciousness, but this is the direction most modern consciousness moves toward, I submit. The split between philosophy and science is only one reason for the split consciousness. There is another more pervasive reason for our split consciousness. It is a fact that theory in its myriad forms has enabled us to develop what we need to know to have more, but we are insufficiently grounded in interiority and transcendence as realms of meaning to ensure that this more adds to the quality of human life.

The most pervasive symptom of a split consciousness is the fact that what we have and what we value tend to be out of sync with each other. What we have (or might have or need to have or want to have) tends to receive much more attention than who we are. Insofar as having preempts our attention, our deeper values get short shrift. Personally and collectively we can harness our unrelieved differentiation and move toward values such as justice, community, compassion. If they are not pursued they will lessen in their importance to us, in which case differentiation will proliferate into greater fragmentation and even more chaos than we presently experience.

Values will not be a passion with those who are preoccupied with what they have. The prefix is germane. *Pre*occupied would mean one's consciousness is crowded with things and the "theories" needed to acquire them, so that awareness of another, the other's needs, others, the community, become remote. Occupied is another matter. Presumably we're all occupied with making a living, financing our purposes, making ends meet. Doing these universal activities in such a way that a split consciousness does not develop is what interests us here.

A split obviously has developed in the world itself between the functioning of the economy and the good of people and human values. This split has deepened considerably since the eighteenth century and the development of economics.[43] The economy has increasingly developed a life of its own. The fissure between economic and financial structures on the one hand and values and human needs is widening, it would appear. We even find ourselves being invited into a perverted form of consciousness because an undirected differentiation would make us into the economy's pawns who acquiesce in being used for its well-being rather than demand that it serve our humanity.

The role of faith in the perception and pursuit of values, the role of faith in the direction of differentiation, the role of faith in the attainment of interiority all deserve commentary. Suffice it to say here that faith is perverted if it is used to reinforce the split consciousness. This is done when matters of faith are separated from matters of the world, in particular the world of the economy. This cordoning off of religion and economics into separate realms leaves us content to avail ourselves of the commodities, so to speak, of both worlds. We then seek to have the best of both worlds, in other words. A differentiated consciousness, on the other hand, that is healthy seeks to see the world of economics and finance, at least those parts of them that touch our lives, within the frame of reference populated by God, Christ, Gospel, faith. Faith seeks to give an account of money and our economic exigencies and to have our behavior in the economic and financial structures that touch our lives penetrated by faith, hope, and love of Christ and one another.

Sublation is a key concept both of this chapter and of the whole volume. The activity of Christ it seeks to describe is not unknown either to theology or to the church. The gains, however, that have been made in understanding Christ's relationship to the world, especially those captured by Vatican II, can be helped by this summary conception of sublation, I submit. Without it, too many in the postconciliar church have reverted to redemption as the only intention and activity of God in the world. Redemption undoubtedly is God's intention. Unfortunately, redemption usually connotes far less than God's full intention about this world.

Without supplying the term sublation, the council tried to widen the meaning of redemption. "Christ's redemptive work, while of itself directed toward the salvation of men, involves also the renewal of the whole temporal order."[44] While distinguishing "the spiritual and temporal orders" the council insisted that they "are so connected in the one plan of God that He Himself intends in Christ to appropriate the whole universe into a new creation, initially here on earth, fully on the last day."[45] The term I use to convey this appropriation of the whole universe is sublation. Redemption meaning "the salvation of men" is at the core of this appropriation, of course, but there is more to it than that. If this more is not taken into account, redemption can and often has been seen more like an act of excision, a process that has God cutting the spiritual core of people away from the world and from the wholes in which they become human beings. This way of seeing redemption reinforces a split consciousness since the world is then seen as ambiguous at best, dangerous to be in at least, and not part of what God esteems. The renewal of its social systems would then be the furthest thing from the mind of God. Since this is not what the church has taught, especially in this century and most particularly since the council, we must see the linkage between the well-being of the world and its systems and the redeeming activity of Christ in a closer relationship, in a mutuality in fact. Seeing part of Christ's activity in terms of sublation, I believe, could help to do this, since the term describes his activity in the temporal order.

The appropriate reaction to such a large order as the renewal of the temporal order, or the appropriation of the whole universe or the perfecting of the economy in its own "intrinsic strength and excellence," should be a feeling of helplessness. This helplessness can be alleviated somewhat if we remember that this is Christ's intention. But he needs the compliance of human beings. His followers are to play a key role in this. What is this role? They must learn to speak to money, to speak from faith to money. How can they go about this? The following chapters will be specific about what is entailed in the following of Christ with these intentions.

✤✤

CHAPTER III

Inclusion, the Second Function of Faith

If those who have incurred some form of the illness examined in the first chapter simply return to their culture and its economic system howsoever exorcised they might be, their healing will not last. Something more is necessary, namely, the sublation of the economic system. But that is a tall order. Notwithstanding the desirability of a change in the system, and the need to be ever-alert to assist in bringing this about, something closer at hand is necessary for individuals and groups. What this is brings us to the second function faith can play vis-à-vis our finances and in our role as actors in the American economy. My thesis in this chapter is that we will begin to move from a humanly healthy attitude toward money and possessions to a religiously more mature relationship to money and possessions by inclusion. We can enter the Lord's sublation of the economy by acts of inclusion.

Acts of inclusion are actions that make my financial interests or concerns cease to be solely mine because I include them in and surrender them to God. The act of inclusion is an exercise of faith in Christ that begins to deny a separateness to the realm of economic reality. Inclusion denies to the economic or financial structures represented by the yielded concern whatever sovereignty they might have been imagined to enjoy. The yielded interest or

concern can represent superficial or weighty things. The point is
that this aspect of the structure is now included within one's faith-
view, thus making it responsive to an order of values beyond itself.
The result of the act of inclusion of one's concern within the
mystery of Christ is that the concern can now be seen and handled
in a new way. It is not that the concern ceases but rather that one
is not alone in dealing with it. Since it has been made his concern
in addition to mine, it is from now on approached as our concern.
Faith has given Christ a stake in what had been handled as my
business. The frame of reference within which the object of interest or concern has been placed should help to keep it from being
addictive or threatening. It remains confined and relative, thus
not exceeding the boundaries of its finite reality because it has
been brought under God's gaze and care. This is only the beginning of a process but a significant beginning, since it can develop
into a habit of viewing the monetary, material, and economic conditions within which one lives in terms of faith. If the habit matures, activity in these areas can become an occasion for deepen-
ing union with God.

Acts of inclusion will be of different levels depending on the
depth of the faith of the believer. Taking our concerns to God can
be rather superficial. We can give our concerns over in a general
way at certain moments but then act the rest of the time as if we
had not. This might be called the "Morning Offering syndrome,"
because while, on the other hand, the relationship between the
concern and God is acknowledged, on the other hand, it bounces
back in my own court, soon after the acknowledgment. It is still
my problem and the only solution is for me to solve it alone. In
this case, faith only tangentially directs a person's behavior, his or
her heart, and his or her mind. It is not yet strong enough to give
the concerns a new orientation. There is, therefore, a vacillating
placing of one's concerns in the hands of the Lord and taking
them back. There is an act of inclusion here but the faith behind it
is weak. It could be strengthened if we knew more about inclusion.

The letter to the Romans has a description of what is entailed in
the act of inclusion. Paul begs the Roman Christians to "offer
your bodies as a living sacrifice, dedicated and acceptable to God,

that is the kind of worship for you, as sensible people. Do not model your behavior on the contemporary world, but let the renewing of your minds transform you, so that you may discern for yourselves what is the will of God—what is good and acceptable and mature." (Rom. 12:1–2) They are exhorted here to live a life of inclusion because they are "in Christ," a phrase that occurs 165 times in the Pauline corpus. They are to actively "offer" or include in the mystery of God their concerns or what they are about in the world. According to Ernst Kasemann, bodies here means "our being in relation to the world."[1] Therefore, all that our bodily existence touches in the world and the world that touches us is what there is to be offered. What I am alive to in created reality can become what is offered, by acts of inclusion of our concerns to God. The *creata* become the *oblata*. The ongoing decision to place at God's disposal whatever we are involved with in the world is done through the instrumentality of the life-giving Spirit. The Spirit makes these offerings "spiritual worship."[2] This Spirit which is poured out on Christians at baptism can transform the work of our hands. The transformation is not contingent on the stature of the matter we handle but on the inclusion and release of it into the mystery of Christ. By neglecting "to offer your bodies," that is, the things we touch, the concerns we have, these are not subsumed into Christ, at least not through human intentionality. The matter that interests us in this volume is anything we touch and that touches us, namely, bills, salaries, taxes, debts, securities, stocks, loans, and so forth. Nothing of the *creata* that can become the *oblata* is profane in God's eyes. Our financial situation is thus removed from its seeming profanity by becoming part of the "living sacrifice" which is "dedicated and acceptable to God." This way of seeing worship makes financial concerns appropriate matter for surrender and worship. Primarily through the exercise of his people's faith, the Lord "draws all things to himself." By inclusion of each of the parts, whole economic systems and financial structures are being "lifted up" to him who draws all to himself. (John 12:32)

The new meaning of worship in Christ was still evolving at the time Paul was writing, but coming into place by this time were the notions of the Spirit, the body of Christ, and the new age which was coming about in the midst of the world. These three themes are all locked together in Paul's few lines. For him, worship in the Spirit had to be worship from the Body and from bodies. This is the worship that is "acceptable to God." "God lays claim to our corporeality because he is no longer leaving the world to itself and our bodily obedience expresses the fact that, in and with us, he is recalling to his service the world of which we are a part."[3] By their offering of their concerns and what they are about, Christians "at all times and places stand 'before the face of Christ' and from this position make the everyday round of so-called secular life, transforming it into the arena of the unlimited and unceasing glorification of the divine will. At this point the doctrines of worship and ethics converge."[4] By their offerings they bring "the profane" into the eschatological age of which they have been given a share at their baptism.

By the ongoing offering of themselves and of all that their persons touched, and that touched their persons, the Roman Christians would be able to live in such a way that their lives would reflect the option they made: "Do not model your behavior on the contemporary world, but let the renewing of your minds transform you, so that you may discern for yourselves what is the will of God—what is good and acceptable and mature." (Rom. 12:2) Rather than subscribing to the version of values their age had dinned into them, these worshippers carried their renewed sense of themselves to their age. In our case this would mean we would not develop a sense of ourselves from efficiency, productivity, profit, economic growth—to mention some of the constants of our economic culture. We have been given a new measure by which to judge, Paul is saying. Insofar as we judge with this new criterion, the new Torah, which has been placed in our hearts (Jer. 31:33), we will be stronger than the determinations of our economic culture. When a single intentionality directs the flow of our lives, with the particulars we are immersed in offered, then we will have a facility in knowing what is "good and acceptable and mature" to God. By right judgments we live in the present age after the manner of the new age into which we are born through God's merciful love.

A distortion of faith in Christ, of course, would be the offering of ourselves to God with judgments that were wrong, either because they were unwittingly conformed to this age or because they were incorrect understandings of the faith. Our situation is similar to that which the Roman Christians faced. The majority of them had been pagan Gentiles who were drawn to a new age while living in the same world they had known before their lives had been touched by faith in Christ. For Paul, their former lives had meant vanities and pursuits that had stultified their minds. (Rom. 1:23) They had to sever their judgments from those who had "exchanged God's truth for a lie and have worshipped and served the creature instead of the Creator." (Rom. 1:25) God had taken them to Himself through His Son so that they then no longer belonged to that age, that world, or even to themselves. Therefore, anything that belonged to them had come from and belonged to the One to whom all things belonged. They were to put these and themselves at His disposal as Jesus had to his Father and his Father's will. Jesus who was the forerunner of their faith was also the forerunner in this continual inclusion of themselves and their concerns in God into whose service they had been called.

Being able to make right judgments, it would seem, required a gradual development of two different kinds of understanding: one, the understanding that came up from a heart rooted in a love of Christ which is sensitive to his presence and knowledgeable about his ways. The other was an understanding about the secular reality in question, in this case the economic reality in any of the subsets requisite and apposite for a given decision to be an informed decision and, hence, a good one. This is a tall order. Both of these understandings come slowly and even then are limited even in the most spiritually sensitive and secularly sophisticated. It can hardly be the perfection of these kinds of knowledge, therefore, that is necessary for the offering to be pleasing to God. God wouldn't have many occasions to be pleased if His pleasure were contingent on our reaching our perfection in both of these ways. It is, rather, by our attempts at knowing as much about the secular reality as is possible or necessary and in turn by acts of inclusion made with a mind being renewed by the power of the Spirit that we develop some facility in transforming secular undertakings and transactions into spiritual worship which is pleasing to God.

Given this Pauline insight into worship in and through the world, it is easy to see what would not be pleasing to God. These would be attitudes that harbored a false relationship to our corporeality, or which disesteemed our worldly concerns or interests, or disparaged our work in the world, or compartmentalized it, cordoning it off as not worth our best efforts or as unspiritual and of no importance to God. Also displeasing would be the attitude that used faith in God as an excuse for mediocrity or carelessness or ignorance about the secular reality in question. And, finally, what would displease would be such an immersion in the secular reality, such a preoccupation with it, that a surrender of it from the heart never takes place or its offering takes place with such a pallid degree of energy that it retains the form it has in the world. One is still conformed to this age in this instance and wholly of this age, a thing of time.

The notion of "the renewed mind" in these passages is "the power of critical judgment which can keep its distance."[5] The critical judgment is by no means limited to moral choices. The conversion process for the Christian is intellectual, moral, and religious, as we will see in the next chapter. The minds of Christians are to judge the world differently. They can take on the mind of the Lord into whose mystery their whole lives are inserted while they remain very much in the world. Like the master, they are not to despise the world but to love it. They are not to flee the world but from within it to serve God and the world while attempting to conform to the mind of Christ rather than to the world's "mind." One has to know its mind without conforming to its mind about itself through its ideologies. The Spirit is the gift that makes a sense of the mind of Christ possible. His Spirit is the gift that would breathe this mind into the minds and hearts of his followers of every generation.

The surrender of the concerns we are involved in is not the end of the matter but the beginning (or a continuation) of a different way of dealing with them. The act of inclusion is not an occasion for displacing responsibility for the concern. By our inclusions we assume no less responsibility than we had before except that coresponsibility is the way we now assume it. Christian faith does not relieve us of the concerns that torture the rest of humanity.

We are no less susceptible to its pain. But we can see purpose where another may see only meaninglessness. By retaining and handling the concerns we have in common with others, in a Christian manner, we can become instrumental to the Lord in his pursuit of his mission on earth.

Much has been written and taught in the churches about the criteria which a "transformed mind" will use to "discern for yourselves what is the will of God—what is good and acceptable and mature." (Rom. 12:2) These elaborations, however, are almost always concerned with ethical and moral criteria to be employed for infrequent, difficult choices facing the Christian. What is often overlooked by this concentration on ethical and moral dilemmas and criteria is the grubby, everyday stuff that keeps our noses to the grindstone in the myriad ways in which the economic systems impact our lives. These concerns tend to preoccupy us more than confuse us. Moral criteria are ordinarily less necessary than habits of mind and heart that will keep us aware of the person of Christ whom our faith makes real while attending to these everyday matters.

The most striking liturgical action of the Christian Church, the rite of baptism, is a dramatization of the act of inclusion and the life of inclusion. It seems to me to set the style for all subsequent offerings of our "bodies" and the inclusion of our concerns in the Christ mystery. The baptized release their whole persons, the stuff of their lives, the concerns of their hearts, into transforming waters of baptism. They take their autonomy and what they are immersed in into the water, thus drowning their preoccupation with it and denying it any pretense at autonomy, assertiveness, sovereignty. In like manner, we baptize our continuing material and financial concerns while we find them unceasing. Done from depth and by many, this posture can affect our immediate economic and financial structures.[6]

The central liturgical action of the Christian community is the Eucharist. A major feature of the Eucharistic liturgy is the offertory. The offertory brings together the acts of inclusion of the congregation and yields them in one action to the Father through the Son in the Holy Spirit. In the Roman Catholic Eucharistic liturgy, the priest's gesture of offering up the bread and wine sym-

bolizes the desire of each member of the congregation to be one
with Christ's offering of himself to the Father. They pray: "May
the Lord receive this sacrifice from your hands to the praise and
glory of his name for our good and the good of all the Church."

Raimundo Panikkar's liturgical vision of secularity helps put
Paul's vision in a modern perspective. This Indian theologian begins his volume *Worship and Secular Man* exuberantly: "Only
secularization can save worship from being meaningless."[7] His
optimism about secularization, or the world coming into its own,
is due to the fact that "it represents the regaining of the sacramental structure of reality."[8] At the same time, he observes, "only
worship can prevent secularization from becoming inhuman."[9]
Panikkar's understanding of worship and secularity assigns ultimate reality and created reality their respective worths and does
so in a way that integrates them at least conceptually. Economic
systems, and the concrete ways in which they impinge on our
everyday lives, fit into his scheme. Assigning sacredness to only
some moments, some objects, and some places is the tendency
worshippers are prone to. Dividing the sacred and the profane can
be found in virtually all moments of human history. But it was
not until human endeavor could uncover the inner structures of
our material, social, political, and economic worlds and discover
their "laws" that it could fully celebrate these. Worship without
secularization, like secularization without worship, leaves something to be desired.

This liturgical vision is rooted in Panikkar's Christology. He
sees in Christ a "theandric unity," the unity of the concrete and
the universal, the profane and the sacred, the immanent and transcendent. It is the constitution of the person of Christ that keeps
Christian worship from the two extremes of a world-escaping,
world-despising mysticism or an immanentism, a world-enclosed,
or world-exalting idolatry. The fact of Christ and the theandric
unity of his person, enables Christian worship to be integrated by
adding "the plus of matter when we are being too spiritual and the
plus of spirit when the intellect or the body take the upper
hand."[10]

By developing the habit of inclusion of the particulars of their
financial concerns in Christ, changes will begin to take place in

people, in their perception of their assets, and in their perception of Christ. What they treasure will be more focused. The worth they assign to things will have an order to it and a consistency. The psychology of the acts that assign the things of our lives their worth to us and the act of worship that acknowledges the object or source of worth par excellence is remarkably similar. The reason for this might be found in the etymology of the word worship. It is *weorp,* meaning worth.[11] Originally this referred only to material worth or value. It then widened to include the act of assigning to God ultimate worth, worth-ship; hence, worship. Inclusion is a habit of heart and mind that assigns each aspect of our lives its respective worth. Consequently, where business is transacted or commerce happens is not a place that has to be foreign to God or worship. Nor will they be if they involve the judgment of worth within a purview of worth that believes in the incomparable worth of God.

A scene in John's Gospel furnishes us with a happy confirmation of these Pauline themes. In it Jesus tells the Samaritan woman that "an hour is coming when you will worship the Father neither on this mountain nor in Jerusalem . . . authentic worshippers will worship the Father in Spirit and truth." (John 4:21–23) The whole world can become the site of authentic worship. The world of things can be given their due, can be assigned their relative worth, can be appreciated for what they are, and be so many occasions of worship. One would have to give each thing its due worth. But to do so, to live this way requires the Spirit of truth. Empowered by the Spirit, Christians singly and with their communities can offer authentic worship to God from hearts that include their financial and material involvements, interests, and concerns in Christ. By accepting their acts, God reaches after His creation through His people. By these acts Christians align themselves with God's intentions for His world as their faith clarifies these. They also frustrate the world's aspirations for autonomy as these make themselves known in its economies.

Inclusion as a Way of Life

By underscoring the act of inclusion we are not suggesting a piecemeal activity but an action that signals a whole way of thinking, valuing, and living. By this action one enters into a way of life in which confession of the worth of God will eventually be given primacy over all the other purposes of life. This is how humanity praises God. Acts of inclusion are a mode of ascent that reaches all the way to heaven. The lifestyle of inclusion or the "offering of our bodies" needs an example, an exemplar, a model. In Jesus we have such a one, of course. In this, as in other things, God has met our need. In the Gospels we see a human being living out a life of total inclusion. Jesus always dealt with his own and others' concerns in the same perspective and through the symbol of the reign of God. "In Jesus, the traditional expectation of God's kingdom is turned into one decisive perspective."[12]

The invitation Jesus extended to those the Father called to "the Way" (Acts 9:2) was an invitation to follow Jesus' way of handling his life with all the concerns he had in common with everyone else. How Jesus dealt with his own concerns became important information and guidance for the first Christians. The Gospels met this need. One of their clearest examples is the scene of the temptations. Famished, after forty days and nights, Jesus is described as dealing with his concerns from within his relationship to his Father. His concern for bread is undoubtedly imperious at this time, yet he refuses to deal with his need in isolation from his relationship with God. Another overwhelming concern at this moment would have been focused on the ministry God called him to begin. The second temptation, consequently, incites this profound concern of Jesus with the tempter's promise to put all the kingdoms of the world under his sway. Because of his love of God and his desire to put all in His hands, it was a consummation he would have yearned for. But Jesus insisted on relegating his concern to the primordial order he had learned in his thirty hidden years and in his (probably symbolic) forty-day desert experience. This was an order in which the worship of God took primacy and all else had to fit into this, even something that would seem to be as germane to his ministry, religious purposes, and commitment to God as the orientation to the homage of God of "all the kingdoms of the world." (Luke 4:5) His "You must do homage to the Lord your God, him alone you must serve" (Luke 4:8) describes his order of worth.

Finally there is the temptation to dream up the spectacular and test God with it. It was grosser than the other two in some ways and subtler in others. Its subtlety consists in its seeming inclusion. Throw yourself down from the parapet of the temple because Scripture promises "He has given his angels orders about you." (Luke 4:10) "Vanquished by Scripture or the Word of God in the first two temptations, the devil now quotes it to his own purpose: Surely if Jesus is God's Son then he stands under his benign protection."[13] The last temptation is an important one for clarifying the origin of the "inspiration" of what is to be included in order to avoid an abuse of the concept. In this instance, it does not come from need, faith, zeal, or love of God. It is an aping of trust. God is not being trusted but put on trial. Jesus is being invited by the tempter not to include but to observe whether God is trustworthy or His word true. In his sensitivity to the disorder of spirit such an action would entail, Jesus shows a knowledge of God, a knowledge rooted in his heart and a deeper grasp of the Word of God than merely quoting it which the devil showed himself able to do. Jesus said to the devil in reply, "Scripture says, 'Do not put the Lord your God to the test.' " (Luke 4:12)

Inclusion is too soft a concept if it simply means bringing to God any and all of our desires. It must be narrowed down to matters about which we find ourselves rightly concerned. In this restricted sense, the act of inclusion keeps us from reverting to the form of mammon illness referred to in the first chapter as "running," or being run by our desire to attain something appetizing greedily, compulsively, or addictively. The areas of concern that are appropriate matter for acts of inclusion are based on real needs, ours and others'—material, financial, spiritual, social, intellectual. What is, therefore, inappropriate matter for inclusion are wants and desires that are disordered.[14] Inclusion of these would serve only to camouflage the disorder.

Ignatius observes the ambiguity of spirit implied here in his meditation on the three types of persons. All have received a large

sum of money and all wish to rid themselves "of the burden arising from the attachment to the sum acquired" in order to find
peace in God and "save their souls."[15] The first type remains at
the level of wishing, velleity, inaction, never getting around to
doing anything specific, like making an act of inclusion. Those of
the second type "want to rid themselves of the attachment but in
such a way that they retain what they have acquired, so that God
is to come to what they desire." They are not prepared to give up
this sum of money in order to go to God. They might even, to use
our category here, have made repeated acts of inclusion but it is
conditioned inclusion, the condition being that they have their
way with the money and not in fact surrender it to God. The third
type of person manifests the desired responses to the situation,
one that involves an unconditional inclusion. This type will keep
the money only if it is "the service of God our Lord that prompts
their action."[16]

Jesus is not only a model includer of his own concerns, he is
also the model of a ministry done in the same manner. His ministerial actions appear to have taken place within this same way of
thinking, acting, and living. God received not only his concerns
but also those of others whom Jesus brought to Him. Each of
these latter is radically changed. Sometimes the change comes
about through a healing, sometimes it is contingent upon accepting his teaching, sometimes the concern is reworked,
refocused. But always the concerns are swept up into Jesus' powerful trust of his Father. They never remain as they were. An
example of his reworking the concerns brought to him can be
found in the Martha and Mary episode. Martha, who was busy
with all the details of hospitality, came to Jesus and said, "Lord,
do you not care that my sister is leaving me to do the serving all
by myself? Please tell her to help me. But the Lord answered.
'Martha, Martha,' he said, 'you worry and fret about so many
things, and yet few are needed, indeed only one. It is Mary who
has chosen the better part, and it is not to be taken from her.' "
(Luke 10:40–42) Martha is not prepared to release her concerns
here. She seeks Jesus' assistance in confirming her own agitation.
Jesus gives her a different perspective by which to judge her own
judgments about the things that concern her.

Sometimes he goes further and handles the concern by correcting the one petitioning him. "A man in the crowd said to him, 'Master, tell my brother to give me a share of our inheritance.' " (Luke 12:13) Jesus refused to meet this concern on its terms which did not involve surrendering it. The petitioner also sought to make Jesus play a role other than one that reflected his understanding of himself. "My friend, who appointed me your judge, or the arbitrator of your claims?" (Luke 12:14) Instead, Jesus deals with the concern by cutting into its underlying cause. This was not the need for justice, but apparently in this case greed was the stimulus motivating the request. Hence Jesus insists on the need to "watch and be on your guard against avarice of any kind." (Luke 12:15)

In general, those who brought their concerns to him were asking him to include them in his relationship with God and in the power of that relationship. Sometimes he did just that straightway. As a result the dead rose, the blind saw, the lame walked, and the poor learned about the wealth that was hidden from the eyes of the wealthy. The power that flowed from his personal and ministerial habits of inclusion were awesome to all who had eyes to see.

Inclusion and Christology

The Christology of the New Testament had its beginnings in the response of people to Jesus, Frans Jozef van Beeck notes.[17] Their response involved bringing to him what mattered to them and what they were concerned with. In this way Christology as action preceded what would become Christology as cognition.[18] The names Jesus is given in the New Testament and afterward derive from the transformation of people's concerns in his hands.[19] He shows himself capable of hearing, meeting, embracing, and with the resurrection, presiding over these. His titles have their origins in the concerns brought to him. When people's concern to know was met, he was teacher. When their concern to be safe from the raging sea was met, he was master or the one whom "even the wind and the sea obey." (Mark 4:41) When their concern was to find a way out of their religious and political maze, he was light and shepherd. (John 9:5; 10:11) When their need to be anointed in their hearts with God's own consoling presence and word was met by him, he became the one who had the words of eternal life. (John 6:68) In short, he begins to assume into himself all that mattered to them and transforms the assumed in the process. He leads into captivity the concerns that were holding them captive.

Their desire to surrender their concerns to Jesus began in the Godhead. "Everyone whom the Father gives me will come to me; . . . Now the will of him who sent me is that I should lose nothing of all that he has given to me, but that I should raise it up on the last day." (John 6:37–39) It was, furthermore, the action of the Spirit in Christians that enabled them to include their human concerns in what would be called the reign of Christ after the Resurrection. Subsequent generations were able to associate Christ with these same concerns by the initiative of the Father and the action of the Spirit. The titles of Jesus became carriers of common concerns. His titles helped to locate the meaning of their concerns in the Christ mystery.

Many of these concerns were in the area of material needs. For example, food, shelter, and drink were all brought into the naming process that linked their concerns with the discernment of who Jesus was. In the Gospel of John, we find the naming process has matured. It is also the Gospel in which Jesus is depicted as anticipating his disciples in this naming process. The Gospel of John can be seen first as a migration of Word to flesh and then as the return of the Word-suffused-flesh to the Father. This enfleshed word is laden with believers and their concerns. God sent His son into the world so that it might become worldly on His terms rather than on its own. A world that is worldly on God's terms is a world that becomes the Son's.

The world that Jesus enters is stuck in a materially fixated myopia, according to John. Throughout the Gospel, Jesus encounters a fixation that perceives on the material level but which he takes beyond itself to a level that does not disdain or circumvent materiality; rather it suffuses materiality with a whole new meaning.[20] The transposition is always from a vacuous materiality to a Christologized materiality. He becomes the Word that gives old matter a new form. Jesus' ministry is a ministry of transubstantiating all that he has been given from below and from above, so to speak, into the stuff of his own person. For John, that's a lot. "The Father loves the Son and has entrusted everything to his hands." (John 3:35) Jesus' followers can do the same as the Father with what they have—they can give everything over to him.

Again, the story of the Samaritan woman furnishes a ready example of the transposition from a mixed materiality to a Christologized materiality. Jesus, tired from his journey and seated there, said to her, "Give me something to drink." (John 4:7) In the rest of the narrative the skillful Evangelist transposes each of the woman's concerns for water, her people, worship, righteousness, the coming of the Messiah into matters Jesus wants her to associate with him. For example, he says to her, "If you only knew what God is offering and who it is that is saying to you, 'Give me something to drink,' you would have been the one to ask, and he would have given you living water." (John 4:10) Her thirst begins to assume greater depths until Jesus reveals his relationship to her many thirsts. ". . . the water that I shall give him [her] will become in him [her] a spring of water, welling up for eternal life." (John 4:14) A materially fixated optic is also evident in his disciples who upon returning "were surprised to find him speaking to a woman." (John 4:27) Confused and unwilling to ask him what he is doing, they urged food on him. "Rabbi, do have something to eat; but he said, 'I have food to eat that you do not know about.' " (John 4:32) Jesus locates his concern for food and for his ministry at its source as he had done in the temptation scene. "My food is to do the will of the one who sent me." (John 4:34)

Either the Johannine Jesus is monomaniacal or this Gospel communicates a fuller meaning of inclusion than do the other Gospels. The latter is the case. Jesus never described himself as acting on his own or for himself. His work, his will, his powers, his judgment, his way of life is described in terms of his Father. His life is so much a life of inclusion that he refuses to explain himself except in those terms: "In all truth I tell you, by himself the Son can do nothing." (John 5:19) "I have come in the name of my Father." (John 5:43) The Father is the law that governs his heart, his life, and his actions.

In the Gospel of John the theme of the reign of God virtually disappears.[21] In its place is not a lacuna but the figure of Jesus who even in his historical ministry John has "speaking from glory."[22] Thus, he does not exhort his hearers to focus on the reign of care their heavenly Father would exercise on their behalf to dispel their anxieties about tomorrow. Rather, the Johannine Jesus exclaims, "I am the bread of life." (John 6:35) Inclusion of their need for food and drink in him is the new way of seeing God and/or Jesus and dealing with their concerns. Christian faith functions differently than Judaism's did. "No one who comes to me will ever hunger, no one who believes in me will ever thirst." (John 6:35) Observing him is not belief. "You can see me and still you do not believe." (John 6:36) It is by coming to him with belief in him and our particular concern up front that Christian faith begins to function. Jesus assures his followers, "I will certainly not reject anyone who comes to me." (John 6:37)

Traditionally Chapter six of John has been associated with the Eucharist.[23] Given the thrust of the whole Gospel with its several levels of meaning, it can hardly refer only to this. It also refers to pedestrian, everyday moments with their worries. "So whoever eats me will also draw life from me." (John 6:57) This is a promise about all that is necessary for life.[24] The Johannine Jesus was not interested in satisfying only one sliver of their hungers. But he would be the bread for all their hungers. He would not disdain any of their hungers. As the centuries-old axiom stated it: "What is not assumed is not redeemed."[25] Jesus assumes into himself whatever is brought to him.

Several of the Johannine symbols convey this matter with a concreteness that a more conceptual form of communication fails to do. Thus, a concern surrendered is like "a wheat grain [that] falls into the earth and dies . . . it yields a rich harvest." (John 12:24) The concern that remains within the self doesn't change, "it remains only a single grain." (John 12:24) "Anyone who loves his life," or insists on autonomy or his own way, "loses it." (John 12:25) By contrast, "anyone who hates his life in this world" resists the agenda of the world, the world's way of self-providence and yields it up, "will keep it for eternal life." (John 12:25)

One of the clearest Johannine symbols for a life of inclusion is that of the vine and the branches. Jesus exhorts the eleven: "Remain in me, as I in you . . . I am the vine, you are the branches. Whoever remains in me, with me in him, bears fruit in plenty, for cut off from me you can do nothing." (John 15:4–5) Doing nothing apart from the vine means including in the vine all that concerns one's life. The consequences of a life of inclusion is that all things can come to be stamped by the character of the life that flows from vine to branches. The antithesis of inclusion, as we are developing this notion, is a secularistic individualism or autonomy. Habits of autonomy are ingrained in the American way of life.

Change for Christians is easier if they are able to trace the sought-for change to their image of Jesus. Specifically, here, if Jesus is seen as an includer in every particular of his life and ministry, then Christians will more easily change from acting autonomously, as the modern world teaches them, to acting inclusively. But if Christ is to be our forerunner in this inclusionist way of life, then the humanity of Jesus that is ordinarily presented in the churches has to be credible. It will not be credible if he is seen as a man who did not have to live his life as we are trying to explain it here because his inner core was divine.[26] From this divine center of control Jesus could proclaim a kingdom because he enjoyed an uninterrupted communion with God. This innermost center of his being transcends humanity.

In contrast to this kind of divinity-in-communion-with-divinity Christology, most recent Christologies understand the historical Jesus as having in the innermost core of his being a need to trust God and abandon himself to God from a center of freedom that could have chosen to be otherwise. He is not seen, therefore, as divinity-in-communion-with-divinity but humanity-in-touch-with-his-humanity which in turn is surrendered to God. But this surrender relationship is actualized and catalyzed by human needs and concerns, first his own and then those brought to him. In his innermost core Jesus is humanity asking divinity to be divinity to him, humanity letting God be God for him, humanity needing, inviting, trusting God to be God.[27]

Van Beeck is not alone in this emphasis. Jon Sobrino, Piet Schooenberg, John Robinson, and others suggest that Jesus' identity would be more truly perceived if he were understood in relational terms rather than in terms that try to define him in his own individuality. "Jesus' relationship to God must not be placed in a PERSONKERN. Instead, it must be seen as a qualifier, a modus of his entire person: his modus of being a person is one of absolute relatedness to the Father."[28]

Thus, twentieth-century understandings of Christology see Jesus' human consciousness developing humanly. In other words, his consciousness develops along with his habit of inclusion. As he brings his concerns to God he grows in so great a trust of God that he can name God "Father" because this is his experience of God. But this could only be the name he gave God if he needed and allowed him to be his Father by the care he found God took of him. If he didn't need God to be Father then he was only edifying his hearers. He would not then be the forerunner of our faith. (Heb. 6:20) "The mystery of Jesus is not a reality contained in an inner core of his person, but in his relationship to the Father, which makes the complete person of Jesus a mystery. In the lived life of Jesus, his abiding relationship of total abandon to the Father is what the tradition referred to as Jesus's consubstantiality with the Father."[29] What is at stake is an understanding of Jesus' humanity. Is he a man like us in all things, save sin, or is he not? (Heb. 4:15) "To put the human person of Jesus at one remove from the rest of humanity, for example by postulating a timeless, unchangeable inner entity in his humanity that would be unaffected by the human condition would amount to putting part of Jesus' person outside the common stock of matter and energy on which the stream of humanity moves forward."[30]

Before there was Jesus the teacher, there was Jesus the includer. Before there is confession of his messiahship, there were those who brought their concerns to him and he acted efficaciously on them. But he insisted that his efficacy stems from the relationship Jesus had with the One whose goodness he proclaims and whose power he counts on. It is into this relationship that he wishes to

attract his hearers. To enter into this relationship of trust he has
for his Father begins the reign of God in those who hear his word
and act on it.

Another reason this kind of perception of Jesus' identity has
not taken a deep hold in many Christians was the centuries-old
teaching that Jesus did not have faith. He didn't need it. One
needs faith because God is hidden from sight but for Jesus, God
was not hidden.[31] Thomas Aquinas's treatment is a classical example of this position. He observed: "The object of faith is divine
reality that is hidden from sight. Hence when divine reality is not
hidden from sight, there is no point in faith. From the first moment of his conception Christ had full vision of God in his essence
. . . Therefore he could not have had faith."[32] As modern theologians have been able to explain, this formulation owes more to
philosophy than it does to belief.[33] The Greek philosophy that
undergirds it, of course, also helped to formulate the incompara-
bly important Christological formulas of Nicea and Chalcedon.
These have not been surpassed but they have been nuanced by our
modern appreciation of truth as historical. Modern scriptural
scholarship has done much to break the thrall that metaphysical
categories have had for us especially in our perception of Jesus.[34]
It has enabled us to have access to the historical character of
Jesus' relationship with God, a relationship that did not grow
because of sight but because of trust and faith.

A final needed adjustment in Christology is noted by van
Beeck. It is needed because the titles of Jesus are all too often
dislodged from the human concerns from which they rose. They
begin to be frozen.[35] Christology functions, then, in a way that is
not patient of human concerns. It begins to be defensive and in-
hospitable to both its own inner development and to new human
concerns.[36] It begins to be a kind of Christolatry. Like the law in
ersatz Judaism, Christology grows independent of and above human concerns. It begins to be a body of doctrine that is to be
defended for the sake of itself and guarded against any further
development. "If we lose sight of the concerns' connection with
the culture we will then mistake Christological statements for
timeless, unhistorical truths thus ignoring the need for each generation as it is with its own dominant concerns, to surrender to

Christ."[37] For the presence of Christ to be vital in the world, Christians must be in touch with their culture and its concerns. In this way Christology grows. "Words will come to churches and to those Christians who are united to Christ and united with him in his love for the world. No new knowledge will come without participation in the experience."[38] In the final chapter we will see more about this way of developing Christology in relationship to the use of our material and financial resources. Suffice it to say here that Jesus himself exhorted his followers to a way of life that he himself lived. It was a way of living that was never without material needs and the necessity to procure them. He would have been tempted to anxiety all his life. He calls his followers to deal with it as he did.

Becoming a Priestly People

If the power of the historical Jesus was notable because of the way he included his own needs and all the needs that were brought to him, how much greater is the power of Jesus now that he has taken "his seat at the right hand of the majesty in heaven." (Heb. 1:3) The Epistle to the Hebrews is a trove filled with the significance of this new "position" of Jesus in his relationship to his Father. If the initial transformation of our concerns awaits our inclusion of them in Christ, how much more does their full transformation go beyond our own powers to rely on Jesus in his role as our merciful and faithful high priest. (Heb. 2:17) The Epistle to the Hebrews deepens our understanding of a spirituality of possessions and finances considerably.

The Christology of Hebrews is a High Priest Christology which is not tantamount to saying it is a high or descending-from-above Christology. Paradoxically, in the whole New Testament there is no Christology that is lower, or more of an up-from-our-humanity kind than this one is. Jesus is never more one of us than he is in this letter. For its author, Jesus was clothed in weakness; (Heb. 5:2) he had to offer prayers and supplications to be free from his anxiety; (Heb. 5:7) he learned obedience from the things he suffered; (Heb. 5:8) he was only gradually made perfect. (Heb. 5:9) The human Jesus, according to Hebrews, struggled with the human process of inclusion. The reasons for the struggle were several. The obvious one was the limitations endemic to being a human being and therefore, the virtual impossibility of a total, once and for all inclusion of oneself in God.

But a more pervasive reason for his struggle was that during his ministry, a judgment about the impracticality, even the imprudence, of what it was that he was witnessing to began to grow. He pointed to a way of life far too incalculable for many of his hearers to take a chance on. He was calling them to be like him who was like Abraham, whose faith "was reckoned to him as uprightness." (Rom. 4:3) Their way of being religious was more calculable, at least for many of them it was. If the law had many try to be righteous by reducing their relationship to God into acts of obedience to the law, then their religious lives were undergirded by an anthropology of achievement. They could perform themselves into righteousness. Jesus' religious life, on the other hand, was undergirded by an anthropology of entrustment. At its core was something God alone could do. This is the truth that inclusion liturgizes. One brings to God the kindling, like Abraham, showing thereby a willingness, to release even your most cherished Isaacs. In like manner we release our financial anxieties and interests.

Jesus performed many signs to encourage his hearers to heed his message about a caring, loving Father who saw all that they needed and who asked merely that they surrender themselves via the catalyst of their anxieties to Him. Some believed in his words and works; some even came to believe in him. He proclaimed a message so concrete that his hearers had to take a position for him or against him, for an inclusionary way of life or an achievement way of life. Jesus was the forerunner of the first way of being religious and of relating to the world and its transformation. Its warrant and foundation was in the Hebrew Scriptures. He showed the way for Israel to be renewed and true to what she had been called.

There are many modern equivalents in Christianity to unfaithful Israel's anthropology of religious achievement. These tend to be related not to law but to material possessions. Think of many of the good acts of modern Christianity, acts like thanksgiving before meals for what we have been given, or exercising stewardship over the things God has given us, or contributing to the support of the Church, or giving part of what we have to charity, or even in some few instances, tithing. While each of these acts is good all can also be performed while leaving one's own autonomy intact or one's security tightly wrapped around one's nest egg, thus confusing what are good religious practices with the essence of what is entailed in an inclusionary faith. What that essence is, is well attested to in the Epistle to the Hebrews. "Sacrifices and offerings, the cereal offerings, the burnt offerings and the sacrifices for sin, you [God] took no pleasure in." (These were offered according to the prescriptions of the law.) Then Jesus says, "I am coming to do your will." (Heb. 10:8–9)

We go back to Jesus to see the anthropology of entrustment take flesh. The ongoing, willing surrender of his heart and will to God was not an automatic nor a certain thing for him, according to Hebrews. It had to be learned. (Heb. 5:8) It was learned in part "through his sufferings." (Heb. 5:8) Paramount among the reasons for the suffering was the fact that his will and God's will were not the same. The deepest of reluctances came at the end of his ministry, as far as we know, when in such conflict and dread "his sweat fell to the ground like great drops of blood." (Luke 22:44) Notwithstanding, he did include his will in God's. Crying out to God, he was heard because of "his reverence." (Heb. 5:7) This word could be translated "anguish or fear of God or piety."[39] "If there is one point on which the Gospels, the Pauline Epistles, and Hebrews are in absolute agreement, it is on the voluntary nature of his death."[40] The struggle then was over whose will would win out. The deepest conflict Jesus ever faced was resolved in favor of inclusion of his own will in God because he had learned obedience in his whole life. Therefore, "Father, if you are willing, take this cup away from me. Nevertheless, let your will be done, not mine." (Luke 22:42) But even this heroic yielding required more prayer. "In his anguish he prayed even more earnestly." (Luke 22:43) His prayer was heard, his complete entrustment of himself to God was now possible. As a result, he could rise from prayer, (Luke 22:44) and proceed on with the execution of his Father's will even though the cost to him is his own life.

The Epistle to the Hebrews gives an insight into what constitutes perfection in this matter of inclusion. "He learnt obedience, Son though he was, through his sufferings; when he had been perfected, he became for all who obey him the source of eternal salvation." (Heb. 5:8–9) "When perfected" is what interests us here. The notion is not one of a moral perfection Jesus had to acquire but rather one that saw his life in terms of the stages he had to pass through in order to be perfected and thus become our Savior. For Jesus to become the priest, in fact the only priest of the New Covenant, the epistle lists the seven essential requirements: "He had to be appointed by God, identified with our humanity, sensitive to our need, victorious over sin, obedient to the divine purpose and willing to die to effect our deliverance."[41] His elevation to God's right hand is the final and definitive one.

These seven stages through which Jesus passes perfected him and makes it possible for our present inclusions to be received and raised to a wholly new stature or quality. That quality is "perfection," a favorite category of the author of the letter.[42] It contrasts, obviously, with the prior economy of salvation about which imperfect is predicated. In order to bring our acts of inclusion into this perfection, the writer has several enlightening recommendations. "We too, then, should throw off everything that weighs us down and the sin that clings so closely, and with perseverance keep running in the race which lies ahead of us." (Heb. 12:1) The race which lies ahead, however, we cannot persevere in if we are weighed down with things. The chief weight, however, is sin. The writer is probably not referring to sins in the plural and, therefore, exhorting us to be moral or ascetical. Sin is a way of life. The opposite of sin is also a way of life, a life of placing in the mystery of Christ our concerns to hold on to which would serve to hinder our ability to run in the race. One's concerns do not cease then but cease to be encumbering.

The epistle goes on to tell us how to run this race or to live this way of life. "Let us keep our eyes fixed on Jesus, who leads us in our faith and brings it to perfection." (Heb. 12:2) The letter would sometimes have the believer see him in his historical experiences and at others as seated at God's right hand. (Heb. 8:1) First of all, experiences in Jesus' life had to be kept in mind because the readers of the letter already had great trials.[43] The example of the historical Jesus was comforting to them in trials that included public insult, trial, prison. (Heb. 10:33) For many of them their adherence to Jesus in faith had already involved the confiscation of their goods. (Heb. 10:34) They were capable of resigning themselves to this insofar as they believed they had "something that was better and lasting" (Heb. 10:34) in him on whom they could fix their eyes. In this connection it is interesting to note how David Peterson takes issue with the R.S.V. translation "pioneer and perfecter of *our* faith" since the faith referred to here was first of all Jesus' own.[44] "Jesus is the one in whom faith has reached its perfection: he goes ahead of all others and enables them to follow his example."[45]

But it was not only on Jesus in his human experience, including his experience of the Cross, that they were to keep their eyes fixed, but also on him in his present risen status. Having finished the race, he is victorious and at rest, seated at the throne of God, having entered into the rest of God. This is more than simply a pedagogy operating here. It is also a soteriology. Because of his faith, he was perfected. But as perfected, he functions now as perfecter of those who follow him. Recall: "When he had been perfected, he became for all who obey him the source of eternal salvation." (Heb. 5:9) Our forerunner has not simply finished his own race, but "he has entered [inside the curtain] on our behalf." (Heb. 6:20) In his eschatological rest "his power to save those who come to God through him is absolute, since he lives for ever to intercede for them." (Heb. 7:25) We have a high priest who is ever in the Holy of Holies interceding for us. He makes possible our direct access to God. Behind this conception of intercession is "the presence of the glorified humanity of Christ with God, and the value of his act of salvation in confrontation and interaction with the divine power for the perfection of many in glory."[46] The rabbis had maintained that intercession was a ministry entrusted to the angels. To the author of Hebrews, Jesus' intercession is superior to theirs because he has experienced our humanity in his own. But more than that, his power to affect God because he is God's Son far exceeds that of the angels.[47]

Although we are not able to imitate his perfection, we are able to imitate his inclusionary way of life and by so doing he receives our *oblata* and perfects them as he does us who place them with him. The qualitative difference between the staples of Israel's spirituality and Jesus' role in our lives is spellbinding to the author of Hebrews.[48] The Covenant that God forged with us through Jesus was and is qualitatively different from that of the Old Covenant. So was and is the priesthood of Jesus in contrast to the former priesthood, so also the blood that spilled in sacrifice, the sacrifice itself, the promises, the hope. The author of Hebrews in contrasting all of these emphasizes that Jesus' "power knows no limits and his life knows no end. He is able to save his people fully and completely. Nothing is necessary to supplement their salvation."[49]

The contribution that the Letter to the Hebrews makes to the subject matter of this chapter can be even more appreciated when one knows something about the problem it was addressing. Its Jewish Christian readers had already undergone considerable suffering because of their faith and were expecting even more grief in the near future. The author was attempting to prepare them for this and also to counter their "spiritual lethargy which involved a loss of zeal, a lack of confidence and a faltering hope" by underscoring the perfection to which Christ attained because he was now in a position to perfect those who believed in him.[50] They had to unlearn their previous religious habits which had focused too much upon themselves and what they had done or failed to do. Instead the author presented them with a vision of Christ through whom a new way of living was possible both because of his death and because of his present risen state. His death was freely accepted, his self-donation total, his person without blemish. The effect of his death on believers was its power to "purify our consciences from dead works so that we can worship the living God." (Heb. 9:14) Dead works were those done without "the principle of life in them or that lead to death."[51] They had to repent of these dead, lifeless works. (Heb. 6:1) But they are also to cleanse their consciences of these works, that is to say, the attitudes they retained from their prior religious state about the place of their works. The failure to do so left them debilitated, joyless. It was urgent, therefore, that they cleanse their consciousness. This they could do by an awareness of the work already done on their behalf by Christ through the shedding of his blood and still being done now for them at the right hand of the Father.

It is the blood of Jesus that assures us of entrance into the sanctuary. (Heb. 10:19) Under the old dispensation with its annual, inefficacious Day of Atonement, "worshippers never experienced a definitive cleansing but continued to have a consciousness of sins."[52] Because of the blood shed by Jesus the great high priest who is over the house of God, "let us be sincere in heart and filled with faith, our hearts sprinkled and free from any trace of bad conscience, and our bodies washed with pure water." (Heb. 10:22) We draw near not empty-handed but believing, hoping, trusting, loving, and bringing to him the works we rouse one another to do. (Heb. 10:23–25)

Through Jesus and because of Jesus we are able to "offer God an unending sacrifice of praise, the fruit of the lips of those who acknowledge his name." (Heb. 13:15) This sacrifice of praise includes cultic moments, obviously, but it is also a continual offering of praise by the yielding of any and all things that occupy our lives.[53] The way that Hebrews advocates this continual sacrifice of praise be made is one in which believers keep their eyes fixed on Jesus, his life, death, resurrection, and intercessory role at the Father's right hand.

The First Epistle of Peter was written in similar social conditions and at approximately the same time.[54] The context was one of persecution of the Christian communities probably during the reign of Emperor Domitian (A.D. 81–96). Both letters evidence a post-apostolic situation, in which the "cover" of Judaism no longer protected the new Christian faith because the split with the synagogue had been fairly well established by this time.

The Christian communities also had a more stable way of life by this time, one that was centered on worship. The First Epistle of Peter adds a note missing up till this point in the New Testament writings, namely, the priestly character of this new people of God. Jesus' followers had become like him while at the same time he never ceased to be one of them. They are told to "Set yourselves close to him so that you, too, may be living stones making a spiritual house as a holy priesthood to offer the spiritual sacrifices made acceptable to God through Jesus Christ." (1 Pet. 2:4–5) The whole of this people was priestly, as Jesus was now seen to be. Their activity was priestly, as Jesus' was and is. Their offering of their sacrifices was received with delight by God because they were offered in the Spirit and through Jesus. Their discontinuity from civil society and its ways as well as their unacceptability to that society is seen in very positive terms. "You are a chosen race, a kingdom of priests, a holy nation, a people to be a personal possession to sing the praises of God who called you out of the darkness into his wonderful light." (1 Pet. 2:9)

Both letters contribute to the development of our theme in this chapter since they describe who it is who receives our offerings now and what they become as a result of the one who receives them. Roman Catholic doctrine picks up and unifies these emphases. So, "the baptized, by regeneration and the anointing of the Holy Spirit, are consecrated into a spiritual house and a holy priesthood."[55] Baptism confers on them a capacity for "participation in the one priesthood of Christ."[56] The priestly character of their lives is exercised "by the witness of a holy life," by joining in the offering of the Divine Victim to God and the offering of themselves along with it; "by receiving the sacraments, by prayers, thanksgiving, self-denial, and active charity."[57] But in addition, "All their [the baptized] works, prayer, apostolic endeavors, their ordinary married and family life, their daily labor, their mental and physical relaxation, if carried out in the Spirit, and even the hardships of life, if patiently borne—all of these become spiritual sacrifices acceptable to God through Jesus Christ."[58] What both letters lack and the Second Vatican Council begins to develop is a theology of secularity or of "earthly realities," one that gives a positive understanding and evaluation of human endeavor and human institutions in the light in faith.[59] If this is not developed to add to the biblical categories already examined, a world fleeing or world disparaging attitude can easily accompany this "priestly" understanding of the meaning of inclusion. We will develop more on this in Chapter V.

With this understanding of the priestly Christ, however, we can relativize the importance of our financial and material needs. A growing anxiety because we are without hope or recourse or alone in handling them is unwarranted now. Surrendered, these concerns are "stripped of their inherent power and disarmed."[60] As a result, "they can stop asserting themselves with force since they have found their justification in Jesus Christ. They now become capable of being given up, shared or taken away."[61] In this connection, the image of Jesus sitting at the Father's right hand is noteworthy. In the Epistle to the Hebrews, Jesus' sitting is in sharp contrast to the standing of the High Priest in the Holy of Holies. A seated Christ celebrates the liturgy of the eternal Sabbath rest.[62] Israel did not know rest because of her unbelief. "It was their refusal to believe which prevented them from entering" into the rest of God. (Heb. 3:19) "Hearing the message did them no good because they did not share the faith of those who did listen. We, however, who have faith, are entering a place of rest." (Heb. 4:2–3) "There must still be, therefore, a seventh-day rest reserved for God's people, since to enter the place of rest is to rest after your work, as God did after his. Let us, then, press forward to enter this place of rest, or some of you might copy this example of refusal to believe and be lost." (Heb. 4:9–11) What the author is saying is that to act in faith and to surrender oneself and one's concerns to God will leave one's concern and oneself at peace with and in the rest of the Lord who like the Creator in Genesis is sabbathing eternally. (Gen. 2:2) The effect of Jesus' total sacrifice of himself to his Father's will out of love was that Jesus has entered the rest of God. The effect on those who include themselves and their concerns in Jesus and receive this word about him and his sacrifice with faith is that they will participate in this same rest of God now.

This examination of the transformation of concerns in Jesus' hands has informed us about several things: the power of faith when it is freed to function; the special relationship Jesus had and has to human concerns; the priestly character of Jesus; the extension of Jesus' priesthood to us and the manner of its exercise in us who believe.

Clarifying Inclusion

There are a number of objections that could be advanced against the emphasis of this chapter. By dealing with them we hope to deepen and clarify what has been said so far. First of all, the emphasis on inclusion could be heard as an invitation to stick one's head in the sand by refusing to deal with the very complex relationship each person, family, and institution necessarily has with the economy. Further, it could be said that the religious handling of this complexity and the amount of religious language that is brought to bear to promote this thesis only obscure the more necessary worldly tasks of understanding the economy in its particulars. Lest there be such a misreading, let me clarify my position further. First of all, what is being recommended is *NOT* a word change but an action, a different way of life, a change in the horizon we take to our participation in the economic culture. Inclusion is being advocated on the basis of a theological and religious understanding of the character of possessions and capital, the nature of Christ and his saving act and the specific meaning of faith in him vis-à-vis possessions and capital. What is being called for is a new way of going about actions already being done such as buying, investing, selling, consuming, and so forth. The recommended change was described in terms of its religious intentionality because integration requires a point beyond economic transactions. Certainly it shouldn't require any proof to see that much of the economic and financial interactions that take place in our present culture are undertaken in a way that is without perspective, compulsive, opportunistic, and self-interested. If de Tocqueville was correct in his observations, this pattern of self-interest was alive and well from the earliest years of our country.[63]

Self-interest is a very slippery notion. It tends to be caricatured by moralizers and extolled by economists.[64] It was baptized by the father of modern economics, Adam Smith, in 1776 in his *Wealth of Nations*. He assured his readers that the pursuit of self-interest has a beneficial effect on the whole of society. Individuals acting from self-interest and spurred on by a profit motive will produce a society that will be orderly, efficient, and productive because in effect an invisible hand will regulate it. This societal mechanism is

the result of each pursuing his or her self-interest.[65] To enter into
the literature and the many interpretations of Smith, self-interest
and the regulatory ingenuity of this invisible hand would take us
far afield.

Two things will have to suffice here. One is to note that self-
interest is ordinarily used as a category in economics and in economics it is a respectable notion that is not dependent on Adam
Smith. The second comment wishes to continue the negative observations already noted above by de Tocqueville about self-interest as he saw it being pursued in American society. He recorded
the ready justification Americans had for their self-interest. He
concurred with the idea that it had some good consequences. "It
disciplines large numbers of people in habits of regularity, temper-
ance, moderation, foresight, and self-command."[66] But unsurpris-
ingly it also engenders a peculiar form of American individualism
and self-immersion. De Tocqueville describes this individualism as
a feeling, which disposes each member of the community "to
sever himself from the mass of his fellows and to draw apart from
his family and his friends."[67] The result of this is that each person,
"leaves society at large to itself."[68] Unlike selfishness, the individualism that de Tocqueville observed "proceeds from erroneous
judgment more than from depraved feelings; it originates as much
in deficiencies of mind as in perversity of heart. Individualism at
first only saps the virtues of public life; but in the long run it
attacks and destroys all others and is at length absorbed in down-
right selfishness."[69] What he is describing here, I believe, are the
personal and social effects of a life of non-inclusion of one's material and financial interests in a site beyond oneself. What I am
promoting is not only for the good of those who practice this way
of life but for the society in which they do so.

A third objection that could be raised against this brief for
inclusion is that it is too privatistic and overly attentive to the
spirituality of individuals. One must be concerned with systems,
the objection runs, and with changing the injustices of the economic system. There are several levels to this objection. First of
all, there is the key issue about systems or the injustices of the
system, and what to do about these. It is important to note that
the included matter need not only be personal, in fact, is not likely

to be merely personal. Each includer is a member of the human community, a member of a civic community, and usually a member of a religious congregation. Our economic and financial actions, therefore, already take place on many levels of communality. They are caught up therefore in different kinds of "liturgies." One would have to formally deny our participation in the social reality of each of these levels in order for those discrete acts to be privatistic acts.

But a point that is foundational to all of these is the character of Christian prayer of which inclusion is only a part. In the Roman Catholic view of it, at least, all personal prayer is in a direct relationship to the liturgical prayer of the church. The prayer of the People of God whose vocation it is to participate in the Priesthood of Christ is always done "through him and with him and in him," as the Canons of the Eucharistic liturgies of the Roman rite always conclude. Inclusionary acts are acts looked at from the side of the individual. But they can, in turn, be seen from the eyes of the Son who knows his sheep and hears their voice. In turn they can be seen from the eyes of God who receives these from the Son. He sees many members of His own Son's body generating this liturgy of need that arises from all over the world.

Of course we have to take responsibility for justice, big justice, out-there money, but we must do so according to who we are. A Christian anthropology gives an account of itself to the systems by dealing with them from within its own horizon of truth. This truth is that we are dependent on a Creator and a Redeemer. The dependency is acknowledged by every act of inclusion. As members of this priestly people we also know and celebrate the truth of material, created and socially constructed reality, namely, that it, like us, is dependent. The opposite would be a life of self-assertion, the exclusion of ourselves and created reality and socially constructed reality from its source and finality.

The objection about privatism also ignores the degree of transformation anything can undergo which by virtue of faith we formally make a part of the Christ-reality. The included does not remain as it was. We do not remain as we were. And he to whom the included is taken does not remain as he was before it was brought to him. If faith is weak, however, then it retards the process of transformation. When faith is weak it expects everything to remain pretty much the same after such acts have been made. Then faith is tantamount to a superficial "offer it up" attitude. If faith is strong, nothing remains as it was before faith was exercised. For example, death becomes life or life becomes gift. So also wealth becomes gift. It ceases to be life. It can aid life or diminish it. All of these changes occur when Christ actively functions as Lord over that which has been placed in his care and made part of his reign.

To see the option facing the Christian as either going the route of social change or going the route of personal faith is wrongheaded. Inclusion is not a displacement of responsibility for the world. Rather, it is a judgment about an ever-present way of going about being responsible in it and for the social systems that make up our social existence. It believes that faith's power is the main ingredient needed to arrive at some degree of social order. That faith can be in error, of course, by being too private, a me-and-Jesus kind of faith, just as it can be too insistent on a social change that does not involve personal conversion.

For Lonergan, social disorder has its roots in the human reluctance to transcend oneself and one's own interests. Nothing substantial happens in a society that desires or seeks social change if its citizens insist on a formula for change that ignores personal self-transcendence, he would contend. "The problem of warring egoisms keeps recurring as long as inattentiveness, obtuseness, unreasonableness, irresponsibility, keep producing and augmenting the objective social surd or the unintelligible and irrational situation."[70] Instead, for him, the very possibility of social transformation pivots on the three modes of personal conversion. "What alone goes to the root of the problem is the new person, converted at once intellectually, morally and religiously."[71] This, of course, does not mean that conversion must be achieved before there are any programs, strategies, or tactics for social change. Rather, these latter will only be effective if the conversion process is going on concomitantly with efforts to affect the order of society.

The more important objection is not to the purported privatism of inclusion but to its seeming elitism. It would appear, in other words, to be something only the Christians and elite ones at that, do or can do. This objection forces us to realize that inclusion as conscious acts is only one part of a much deeper and more cosmic liturgy of groaning. "We are well aware that the whole creation, until this time, has been groaning in labor pains." (Rom. 8:22) The movement of all created reality is one of inclusion though only that part of creation that is human can locate its groaning and posit it in God. And only some small portion of this population, those who "have the Spirit" would be able to say that they "are groaning inside ourselves, waiting with eagerness for our bodies to be set free." (Rom. 8:23) Christian inclusion, in other words, is only the tip of the iceberg.

By the same token it is not automatic that all human beings are part of this liturgy of groaning simply because they are created. There are non-groaners. They are those who are rich, full, laugh now, are spoken well of. (Luke 6:24–26) They have their consolation now. Satiety removes them from the liturgy of groaning that is the soil from which Christian inclusion springs. We become includers because we are among those who groan. One will not begin or persevere in this if need is not one's middle name. To be human is to be needy and, therefore, a groaner. But this endemic condition can be superseded at least for awhile by those who "laugh now," or are "rich" or "full." These are the actual elite. Their social and material condition has placed them outside of the truth of their humanity and its basic posture of needing to be completed.

A theological objection that could be posed against the thesis of this chapter is that it is concentrating on a "work" and, therefore, it errs because we are not justified by works but by faith. Theology has, of course, developed beyond this either/or dichotomy. By refusing the dichotomy, faith or works, the objection loses its force. We are justified by faith, we are righteous in the eyes of God by faith. But that faith is not only gift, it is gift acted on, gift opened and used. Inclusion is faith acted on. Inclusion is an entrusting of ourselves to God via our concerns. Faith acted on makes us whole.

The final objection is that faith categories are being read into economic and financial structures and, in effect, denying their reality and autonomy. If this is what we have been doing we are guilty of integralism and are rightly castigated for so doing. Integralism is "a tendency to apply standards drawn from the faith to all the activities of the Church and its members in the world."[72] The world is to take shape, in other words, under the direct or indirect authority and action of the Church. It is an effort to explain or master reality exclusively in the light of faith.[73] It is at the same time a denigrating of reality, and disdaining of the knowledge needed to understand it.

Integralism had been developing since the Middle Ages in some parts of the Church.[74] In its earlier stages it was eager to get the emerging political powers to obey the Pope and the Church by applying Church directives to the affairs of the state. The term itself, however, did not appear until the twentieth century when modernism's excesses sharpened the reactionary response from which it takes its name. The twentieth-century form of integralism was most destructive to the Church. Unfortunately, at this time its proponents also had positions of influence in the Vatican. Pope Pius X's Encyclical *"Pascendi dominici gregis"* in 1907 is the best indication of the depths of this influence. This document did much to freeze Catholic theology before Vatican II. It propounded a notion of "the faith," which was a system of thought interlaced with philosophy undergirded by Aristotle and Thomas, plus a body of dogmas that could not evolve and were to be preserved as a whole since it was as a whole that they communicated revelation.[75]

In the light of this, one can appreciate what the Second Vatican Council did to encourage history, historical consciousness, the evolution of dogma, the role of science, the importance of the social sciences, and so forth. The Church eschewed the validity of integralism by its affirmation of "the proper autonomy of the secular" at the council.[76] It affirmed that all created reality and its societal constructions should enjoy their own autonomy. "By the autonomy of earthly affairs we mean that created things and societies enjoy their own laws and values which must be gradually deciphered, put to use and regulated by men."[77] The council gives its reason for its affirmation: "For by the very circumstances of their having been created, all things are endowed with their own stability, truth, goodness, proper laws, and order. Man must respect these as he isolates them by the appropriate methods of the individual sciences or arts."[78] By a respect for inquiry that accords a proper independence to temporal affairs, human beings can become "the artisans and authors of the culture of their community."[79]

While the council was concerned to legitimate modernity (for those who needed it to be legitimated) it also insisted that "in the socio-economic realm, the dignity and vocation of the human person must be honored and advanced along with the welfare of society as a whole. For man is the source, the center and the purpose of all socio-economic life."[80] The council's concern was not that there is an economic dimension to our lives that has its own laws. The concern was that the laws by which our economy runs usually run us rather than us it. What is missing is a capacity for human valuing which modifies and shapes the economic system rather than the economic system determining human values. Human beings were not made for the economic system, the economic system was made for human beings.

As long as our purchase and use, production and consumption of material goods take place in ways that express our human values, all is well and good. But an autonomy of the secular reality, in this case the economic system, that is not kept relative to human purposes becomes autocratic. When the laws of economic life, such as the need for growth, efficiency, and profit ride roughshod over people then we have gone beyond a proper autonomy of the secular. The proper synthesis will not be arrived at, of course, by opting out of the system or into it, or by being anarchic or sectarian or totally conforming to it. It does involve relating to the system in a way that makes it responsive to one's values. Vatican II stressed the autonomy of the secular because it was concerned that the *creata* not lose their proper place by a secularization process that went too far in one direction. At the same time it was concerned with a secularization process that went too far in the other direction. Proper autonomy is a perception that frees up a process whereby political and economic systems and technologies operate under the dominion of human purposes for personal and common good. While this appreciation of the autonomy of the created order is called for, it is clear that systems can develop into being our sovereigns. That which is the work of God's hands, and by extension our own, can begin to tie our hands. Can and all too often does. So there is a fine line between what we have constructed expressing who we are and our becoming the pawns of that which we have constructed. One ingredient we propose to assist the complex process of balancing these seemingly irreconcilable opposites is the act of inclusion.

The thrust of the previous chapter should be helpful in keeping inclusion from becoming integralist. In the concept of sublation developed there, there is the resolution of opposites into a unity. Recall that the resulting unity or synthesis doesn't destroy what it supersedes but completes it and raises it to a fuller and richer context.[81] Recall also the role of theory in the process of sublation. Vatican II helped develop theory not about the economy but about how Christians can interact with the economic order without it being denigrated by them. Even when it functions poorly and unjustly, Christian faith "can resolve through grace and forgiveness those anomalies of egoism, prejudice and non-reflexivity which cannot be fully abolished" by an economic theory that overlooks the importance even to the economy of the ongoing conversion of citizens.[82] Lonergan's own theory complements and deepens Vatican II's theory because it is built from the structures for authentic knowing and acting within subjects who while they can critique and act in society on the basis of theory have a theory "contingent on a prior change within the theorist, and enlightenment resembling the experience of the man dragged from Plato's cave into the full light of the sun."[83] Inclusion is a habit Christians can develop that would have them always bring into the sun and under the Son their economic and financial concerns. In this manner, at the originating points of social and economic life a process of sublation goes on in which economic reality can be given its due while the Lord of peoples and systems is acknowledged.

❖❖❖

CHAPTER IV

Obedient Hearing—The Third Function of Faith

It is not enough to have included the financial matters and concerns in the mystery of Jesus. This is not the end of the affair, but the beginning of a whole new stance toward that which has been included and to the Lord whose concern it now also is. What is now a mutual concern is capable of becoming like a sacrament, an outward sign through which we grow in union with God and God comes to us. Faith functions not only in the direction of inclusion described in the previous chapter, it also functions in the direction of obedience, the subject matter for this chapter. After the concern has been included in the priestly mediatorship of Jesus this further function of faith begins. If faith is freely operating in people they will move from inclusion to obedience. Once I make my business his business, he becomes its chief executive officer and I look to him for how we will go about conducting what is now our business.

The most profound frame of reference for understanding these connections, at least for the Judeo-Christian, is the notion of covenant. This basic paradigm communicates an understanding of who we are to God, who God would be to us, and how to go about the ever-changing task of meeting our needs and making ends meet. Historically, covenant was the most radical change in the relations between God and human beings. It invited and still invites a most drastic reformulation in how we are to imagine and approach God. God's choice was to show His passionate love of His people by lavishing Himself on them precisely through the created realities we are examining in this volume. Covenant promised them there would be nothing He would not do for them, that there was no particular they would lack if they yielded to His decision to covenant Himself to them. Covenant means embrace, His embrace of them as beloved.[1] He would hold Israel as His own and care for her as His Beloved if she would yield to this startling initiative.

The evidence that Israel accepted Yahweh's covenant invitation would be by what she did with her needs. If she routed them through Him that would be the sign of her acceptance. If she sought to meet them autonomously that would be the sign she didn't want the embrace or she did not trust that she would be taken care of. For the embrace to be congenial, both parties had to be "in sync." Yet this was not an embrace of equals but of creatures by their Creator, of the limited by the Infinite, the endemically needy by the Source of all Goodness and Power. He asked the embraced to look for and obey His promptings as also His ways and His commands; to trust where He was taking them; and the way He would care for them. "Trust My care of you" this theme says. "Obey My statutes and you will have life."

Covenant was and still is a two-way risk. God risks having what is, in effect, an act of remarkable vulnerability rejected. And Israel risks the future of the business, so to speak, to new management. Since it had precedents, it wasn't a total risk He was asking. Their obedience would gain assurance by recalling the past experience of His special care of them. At Shechem, for example, when under the leadership of Joshua, Israel was asked to commit herself, Yahweh reminded all the tribes of Israel what He had already done for them. "I have given you a country for which you have not toiled, towns you have not built, although you live in them, vineyards and olive groves you have not planted, although you eat their fruit." (Josh. 24:13) Since He had done this and more for them, Yahweh calls His people to trust and obey Him "truly and sincerely." (Josh. 24:14) The people exclaim, "Yahweh our God is the one whom we shall serve; his voice we shall obey" and "banish the foreign gods which [we] have with [us] and give [our] allegiance to Yahweh, God of Israel!" (Josh. 24:23–24) After the historical moment of the disclosure of Yahweh's desire to be with the believing community in a covenantal manner, Israel could not revert to a pre-covenant relationship. To serve Yahweh then would mean to serve a covenanting God. Any other posture would mean to serve the one true God strangely or truly strange gods.

The Book of Deuteronomy is the primary locus par excellence of the covenant theme. It emphasizes the concreteness of the ways Yahweh would care for His people. It enjoins constant "follow[ing] his ways and fear[ing] him . . . [lest you] become proud of heart . . . Beware of thinking to yourself, 'My own strength and the might of my own hand have given me the power to act like this.' Remember Yahweh your God; he was the one who gave you the strength to act effectively like this, thus keeping then, as today, the covenant which he swore to your ancestors. Be sure: if you forget Yahweh your God . . . you will perish . . . for not having listened to the voice of Yahweh your God." (Deut. 8:6–20)

God made covenant with His people first through Moses on Sinai. "I carried you away on eagle's wings and brought you to me. So now, if you are really prepared to obey me and keep my covenant, you, out of all peoples, shall be my personal possession, for the whole world is mine. For me you shall be a kingdom of priests, a holy nation." (Ex. 19:4–6)

Although it involved every material item needed by Israel, the covenant was to be a commitment made by hearts. For His part it was a disclosure that they were His treasure, containing a plea that He would be theirs. "If serving Yahweh seems a bad thing to you, today you must make up your minds whom you do mean to serve." (Josh. 24:15) It was a promise of His largesse for their obedience of the heart. Neither Yahweh's largesse toward them nor Israel's obedience to Him was to be interior merely or immaterial but concrete and horizontal. The evidence of this obedience to the covenant would be in part at least Israel's care for the weaker members of the community. The poor, the widowed, the stranger, the weak, are an intrinsic element in Israel's response to covenant. If she really believed that what she had was from Yahweh, she would be ready to release her hold on it if the needs of others required since the land and all that came from it was His. (Lev. 25:23) Covenant drew the economics of Israel into its sweep. In the Book of Deuteronomy, for example, there is the ordinance of the release of all debts every seventh year and the freeing of those enslaved by them. (Deut. 15:1ff.; 12ff.) There is also the year of jubilee ordinance whereby every fiftieth year all land that had been sold in that period was to be returned to its initial owners. To observe redistribution statutes such as these would be the proof of her fidelity and her trust in Yahweh. Israel's cleaving to God, therefore, was to have considerable empirical evidence to make obvious to the other nations the wholehearted-ness of the covenantal relationship between God and a people.

Israel was more unfaithful to the covenant than faithful to it. Think of her desire to have a king like the other nations, her indifference to the past, her neglect of the Jubilee and Sabbath years, the split of the kingdom between North and South, the overestimation of their cultic practices, the multiplication of laws, norm obedience to the neglect of the heart component—all of these developments in the history of her infidelity kept her from enjoying the care and consolation Yahweh had intended her to know when He covenanted Himself to her.

While the covenant, it could be said in general, created a cul-ture that gave Israel her identity, pride, and esprit de corps, at the same time, her response was generally so meager that much of the nation was blind to what was being asked of her. Hence she was continually on the lookout for and responsive to other forms of power while serving Him with her lips. She continually took prov-idence into her own hands only to find again and again she did not have the wherewithal for self-provision. She was repeatedly called to purity of heart by the prophets. But they were treated cruelly by Israel because she could always preen herself with the evi-dences of fidelity to which her practices testified. She had learned how to be religious while withholding her heart. She could always point to the ongoing sacrifices in the temple, her direct lineage from Abraham, her knowledge of the law, the practices of religious austerity in her midst, her religious superiority to other nations, to name a few evidences. Her Maker, however, would not be fooled and would settle for nothing less than betrothal. "I shall betroth you to myself for ever, I shall betroth you in uprightness and justice, and faithful love and tenderness. Yes, I shall betroth you to myself in loyalty and in the knowledge of Yahweh." (Hos. 2:21–22) The covenant passion of Yahweh refused to be satisfied with the games Israel had learned to play, her ways of make-as-though-she believed, loved, trusted.

As if the daring "idea" of covenant weren't enough, Yahweh had one more surprise. Since His vulnerable proposal of marriage was being met by a spouse with a heart of a whore, He could either withdraw and leave her to her lovers or He could supply her with what she was too profligate and phony to develop from within herself. His new idea: I will give her a new heart. Wooing hadn't worked. A transplant alone would save the marriage initiated by God and resisted by Israel. A New Covenant is promised, one which goes even further than the already extravagant forms in the earlier stages of the revelation.[2] This new covenant is described as gifting Israel with a new heart and a new spirit. "I shall give you a new heart, and put a new spirit in you; I shall remove the heart of stone from your bodies and give you a heart of flesh instead. I shall put my spirit in you, and make you keep my laws, and respect and practice my judgments." (Ezek. 36:26–27) In order to do this Yahweh will have to "pour clean water over you and you will be cleansed; I shall cleanse you of all your filth and of all your foul idols." (Ezek. 36:25) He will do this in the sight of the nations so that "the nations will know that I am Yahweh . . . when in you I display my holiness before their eyes." (Ezek. 36:23)

The passion and purpose that was evident in the former remains in the new covenant. The new Israel is to match the steadfast covenanting ardor of God. Israel's love of God is to be very concrete, an obedience of the heart. She will remain faithful to what she hears in her (new) heart, because she has a heart that now knows Yahweh and His law. (Jer. 31:33–34) That law does not abrogate the old law. At the same time, however, it appears in

a wholly different light because its form is Jesus. It is reducible to
one commandment: love.

Recall that we are interested here in the third function of Christian faith in relationship to our finances and possessions. That
function is obedience. What has been included must now be subject to a will other than my own. Self-provision was the posture of
spirit that Yahweh sought to eradicate when He covenanted Himself to Israel. Self-provision is still the posture of spirit God intends to eradicate by the New Covenant. Christians are to see the
things they need and the way they procure them in the light of
covenant, using the old as framework and the new as a source of
power, new order, and commitment.

The obedience of Jesus is the reason we even have a New Covenant. The obedience of Jesus was all the more remarkable because
it was learned, as we have seen already. How the New Covenant
came about remains astonishing even after all these years. One of
us, Jesus, said the unreserved human yes that God had wanted to
hear from our side all along and didn't hear. The New Covenant
begins with the yes of Jesus. But by the will of God this yes can be
entered, so to speak, by us. He can supply our yes to the longed-
for embrace by God of us and us of God. This covenant becomes
the Father loving us who belong to His Son and our response to
the Father through and with and in His Son. The first conse-
quence of our being so intimately conjoined to the yes of the Son
is that our sinfulness, the past acts that cumulatively said no,
become nonexistent to God, choosing as He does to hear only the
yes we say to and with and through His Son. We will never even
guess how unworthy we were (and are) for the embrace of God so
great is His mercy toward us. Nor will we guess how efficacious
the action wherein Jesus said yes to God.

Obedience to Shema

The foundation of obedience in Israel was Shema. New Covenant obedience is still rooted in Shema. Its formula was "Listen,
Israel: Yahweh our God is the one, the only Yahweh. You must

love Yahweh your God with all your heart, with all your soul, with all your strength. Let the words I enjoin on you today stay in your heart." (Deut. 6:4–7) Deuteronomy insisted that the people of Israel "tell [these words] to your children, and keep on telling them, when you are sitting at home, when you are out and about, when you are lying down and when you are standing up; you must fasten them on your hand as a sign and on your forehead as a headband; you must write them on the doorposts of your house and on your gates." (Deut. 6:7–9) Devout Judaism recited these words every morning and evening. Their recital was a form of consecration. In the late postexilic period each phrase was taken apart.[3] We will do this here to bring Christian obedience back to its roots.

"Listen, Israel." Obedience begins by hearing. It presumes the ability to listen and the desire to hear. The words are addressed to the innermost part of listeners, their hearts. Obedience is hearing with the heart. What Israel hears is that "Yahweh our God is the one, the only Yahweh." (Deut. 6:4) Yahweh is her God and Yahweh is to be the object of her attention, affection, allegiance, and worship. The Hebrew of the very first line of the Shema is peculiar. "Yahweh, our God, Yahweh one" is the literal meaning.[4] It has been surmised that this emphasis comes from the fact that the many shrines in ancient Israel at which the earliest Israelites worshipped had left the people insufficiently focused on the fact that there was only one God, Yahweh, who was the object of worship at each of these. No other loyalty was to usurp the primacy and claim over them that Yahweh is demanding here.[5] The oneness of Yahweh, furthermore, calls to and invites Israel to be single in her heart toward Yahweh.

The Shema continues, "You must love Yahweh your God with all your heart." (Deut. 6:5) Israel's wholehearted response to Yahweh's very particular and concrete care of her had much evidence for her to reflect on: a land flowing with milk and honey, large cities she had not built, "houses full of good things you have not provided, with wells you have not dug, with vineyards and olive trees you have not planted." (Deut. 6:10–11) Israel's response was to be with her whole heart. For Israel, heart would have meant "one's innermost being, the center of one's thoughts, will, feelings, instincts."[6]

Hearing with hearts and loving from hearts that perceived Yahweh's love, precipitated and anticipated monotheism long before it is defined.[7] The theodicy undergirding Shema is done long before monotheism is named. The problem Israel had been faced with we could call a pantheon consciousness. The polytheism of the cultures from which Israel came and within which she lived and by which she was continually affected made it necessary for her to be constantly alert to "not follow other gods, gods of the peoples round you, for Yahweh your God among you is a jealous God." (Deut. 6:14–15) These gods were not to be accorded any homage nor were they to usurp any of the loyalty Yahweh insisted upon having undividedly. In effect, Israel is warned: Divided allegiance will win for you separation from the land and national death. (Deut. 4:25–27) Attention to any of the many gods in the pantheon divided each believer. It led to a diffusion of allegiance and idolatry.

"You must love Yahweh your God . . . with all your soul." (Deut. 6:5) This is drastic, meaning "even if God requires that you face death for his sake you are not to renounce the good and proper allegiance God demands in order to escape it."[8] Because God is who He is and we are who we are, not even our lives should be held in reserve from Him but placed at His disposition. His loving kindness is a greater good than life. (Ps. 63:4)

Even more germane for our theme: "You shall love the Lord your God . . . with all your strength." This was explained as meaning with all your mammon by the scribes and rabbis. "Mammon here covers wealth and the power and status which accompany wealth."[9] In other words, loving God from one's innermost being entails not only a love which places oneself at His disposal, but also includes loving God with all one has in the area of material resources. They are placed at His disposal. This lifts mammon from either neutrality or a position of ambivalence to something of positive value for expressing where one's heart is. To love God with all one's heart, therefore, will be shown by willingness not only to forgo life, one's most intimate possession if God should ask it, but also to reduce to an instrumental role all that one has.

Possessions, material resources, assets, capital are to be instrumentalized, kept in a position of subordination. They are to serve as means to the ends to which an obediential love draws us. If mammon is loved in or for itself, it loses its instrumental quality and becomes an end from which every disorder ensues. Since this easily happened, mammon had a seamy reputation by the time the term gets to the New Testament.[10] It becomes a symbol of the sickness referred to in the first chapter.

The New Obedience

Hearing with one's heart and responding with a love that places one's life and possessions in God's hands is the way Jesus and in turn the early Church are depicted in the New Testament. In the parable of the sower, for example, we can see the structure of Shema operating in Matthew's Jesus. We can also see in this parable what Jesus teaches about obedience and how he personally obeys. (Matt. 13:4–23) The sower sows his seed, some of which falls on the footpath where it is snatched up by the birds. (Matt. 13:4) The parable's explanation of this is that the word Jesus spoke was not understood and that it was snatched away by the evil one. (Matt. 13:19) The word never gets to the soil of the heart. The hearers' hearts hardened against hearing or receiving it. The response of many to Jesus reveals a division in the population and a split consciousness as the spiritual condition of many Israelites. Within Israel there is both the true Israel which hears Yahweh with her heart and the rest who intercept the word in the outskirts of the heart, warding off its penetration.

The rest of the parable only adds to our reasons for interpreting the parable of the sower within the Shema's frame of reference. The second type hear the word in the soil of their hearts. It penetrates but the soil is rocky and shallow. (Matt. 13:5–6) Initial enthusiasm soon gives way to disappointment when heavy weather in the form of "some trial . . . or some persecution on account of the word." (Matt. 13:21) Only the superficial reaches of the hearers' hearts were affected by the word, whereas obedience to Yahweh required reserving no part of the heart for the word's growth. Jesus' God would not settle for a little of Israel's loyalty and allegiance. (Deut. 6:15) Although there was faith in this second response, the word that was heard begins to meet with ambiguity and a reserve about how costly its entry would prove to be.

Even more pertinent to our interests is the third type's response. "Others fell among thorns, and the thorns grew up and choked them." (Matt. 13:7) This type "hears the word, but the worry of the world and the lure of riches choke the word and so it produces nothing." (Matt. 13:22) Although possessions, monies, and assets might appear to be religiously innocuous, their seeming neutrality is deceptive. Their use as means to express one's heart takes constant vigilance. Possessions not firmly located as means begin to emit their own commands. Once one listens to them, they easily become ends in themselves or valued outside of the intentionality of love of God, making obediential faith problematic. Things loved for themselves at first appear religiously innocuous but what eventually happens is that their very limitations make more of the same desirable or more from them is sought. The parable isn't as concerned with the quantity of the person's goods as with the anxiety which attends their acquisition or possession.

Some seed, finally, falls on good soil and yields somewhere between thirty- and a hundredfold because it has been taken into the heart without obstruction and acted on. (Matt. 13:8–22) It's only in hearts that the word can grow. Some speculate that the difference in this growth is that the thirtyfold yield grows in the hearts of those who are not asked to renounce their possessions and that the sixtyfold yield comes from those who give up their possessions and that the hundredfold yield is realized in those whose very lives are the price they are asked to pay for their obediential faith.[11]

The new holiness that is to surpass that of scribes and Pharisees will come from the heart and be received in the heart. It will place "love of neighbor as yourself" within the formula of Shema; this second commandment is "like the first," Jesus says, insisting that these together are the foundation on which the law and the prophets rest. (Matt. 22:38–40) This is notable! The reduction of all material resources to the level of instrumentality is now coupled with the elevation of others (persons-neighbors-enemy) into the same sphere of love the Shema had reserved for God alone. The one heart which is called to love wholeheartedly is now to include neighbors, even enemy neighbors, in its ambit. The inspiration of this activity is not to be contingent on the goodness or lovability of the neighbor (Matt. 5:45–47) but is to rest on the character of God as it has manifested itself in unconditional love. Our behavior toward one another is to be in the manner of God's behavior toward us. Since God's love is not meted out in proportion to or in view of our goodness neither is ours to be toward others, foreigners, neighbors. "In a word, you must be made perfect as your heavenly Father is perfect." (Matt. 5:48) Perfect here implies "complete, undamaged, undivided, and unimpeachable in the attitude of one's heart."[12]

The one who is most like God, of course, in his attunement with the holiness called for by Shema is Jesus. He responded to Yahweh with all his heart, soul, and strength. His love developed into a humanly perfect love because he learned to hear Him who alone was good, perfect, merciful, just. His love was not small-minded or self-concerned. (Matt. 23:23) Where the religious professionals of his day stressed ritual purity, his concern was for neighbor. (Matt. 9:9–13) His Sabbath cures are only one example of this. (Matt. 12:1–8)

Jesus developed a listening capacity both by being apart from people and by being with people, especially with hurting people and needy people. They were like the frequencies on which God would speak to Jesus' heart. His listening evoked a response from his heart, a response of love both for those he heard and of the One he heard speaking to him from within people. This love was of a piece.[13] His obedience to his Father showed itself by his willingness to "deny his very self" for the sake of those who approached him, losing in the bargain at times his solitude or rest, and eventually his reputation or acceptability to many. His ministry was Shema lived out loud. The Cross was Shema lived so totally that the last possession he had to give, his life, was freely put at the disposal of those who took it and of Him who received it.

When people follow Jesus' way of living the spirituality of Shema, their lives will be lives of love shown in deeds. Others will be the beneficiaries of a love which is wholehearted and single-minded. They will be the beneficiaries because the believer's "soul" is available to them in small ways or big. The most frequent way for expressing this love will involve their strength, their mammon, the material resources that believers have at their disposal and have learned to use to express their love of God. This mammon, however, must be sternly situated in the role of means, to express our loves, values, and purposes. This was the special "English" Jesus put on Shema.

He called his followers to follow in his way of obedience. "If anyone wants to be a follower of mine, let him renounce himself and take up his cross and follow me." (Matt. 16:24) It is largely from this world of mammon that the wherewithal comes by which obedience to the Shema can be expressed and made deeds of love.

Obediential hearing cannot be reduced to a system. Trying to do so is alien to its basic character, which is love. What does love call for? is the ever-unfolding question it is always answering. Sometimes love calls for giving, at others for receiving; sometimes for waiting, at others for acting. In any case, the hearing does not take place in a vacuum but within an affectivity which has its own history. That history is both recent and remote, personal and corporate. Part of this data operating in a person's affectivity is the matter that has already been included, which is described in the previous chapter. About this first and foremost, the obediential hearer is prepared to take orders, hear a word, be given a sense. In addition, the grid of one's affectivity is being constantly bombarded by a topsy-turvy, ever-changing series of circumstances and events, foreseen and unforeseen. As it was with Jesus, so it is with his followers, the word that is spoken to hearts will sometimes come through these events and circumstances and thus require a special attentiveness to them. It is equally possible that the word God would speak will come through more clearly if one is apart from others and at a distance from immersion in events. Whether a situation is the carrier of signs or distractions, the first calling for attention, the second for withdrawal, cannot be known abstractly, or before the fact. In the course of time by trial and error, hopefully, the art of knowing how to do both develops. One can be given some guidance by those who have a developed discernment as well as from traditions of discernment.

The relevant proximate data for obedience is anything connected with the included concern. The relevant remote data is that which has been mediated through the community of faith. This community has communicated doctrine, norms, customs, practices—in general its understandings via all of these. A Christian does not generate the content of faith out of thin air. The relationship between this communicated content and obedience as we are conceiving it here is not simple. It would be simple if one's understanding of Christian obedience was one of learning norms and living in accordance with them. In the matter we are dealing with here, for example, this would mean that all one would have to do is learn and conform to the norm that people in need are to be loved with the mammon one has at hand. But obedience to this norm, if that's all there is to it, would lead rapidly to being broke or guilty—broke if the norm is obeyed, guilty if it isn't.

It is important to understand, therefore, the distinction between norm obedience and obediential hearing. While obediential hearing needs and cherishes authentic norms that have arisen from Christian tradition, it does not simply learn them and obey them since they are only one part of the process it uses. Furthermore, when one faces a situation of clear right or wrong then conscience recalls the norm and the course of action is indicated. In this case, the norm obeyed pretty much exhausts the problem of obedience. But norm obedience tends to be inadequate and infrequently the issue with respect to the matter we are scrutinizing in this volume. Obedience to God speaking to the heart in and through the living, topsy-turvy circumstances, events, and people who are part of or intrude on our days and consciences is a more difficult obedience. It presumes a relationship of discipleship. Norm obedience, on the other hand, is clearer, more measurable, simpler. You don't have to develop an inner ear. Obediential hearing goes beyond norms not against them. It cannot ultimately be argued to. This is not to say it isn't reasonable but that its reasons come from the heart. Love, in the final analysis, is its only explanation, a love that is indivisibly from God and for God, for people and from them.

A good illustration of norm obedience is the story of the rich young man. "I have kept all these since my earliest days." (Mark 10:20) The limitations were evident when he could not respond to Jesus' invitation to follow him. A norm obedience was operative but his heart was not free. It was weighed down with the mammon Jesus invited him to sell and give to the poor. Jesus advances no argument why he should do this nor does he give any reason why he made himself vulnerable by inviting the "very rich man" into his own life. Jesus' heart is a stark contrast; it is free and open to a future, one that would have had this man in his company. Mark notes Jesus' motivation, "Jesus looked steadily at him and he was filled with love for him." (Mark 10:21) Jesus obeyed his heart and the word that emerged from it in the encounter. That word was love.

Not all norms are of the stature of the commandments the very rich man claims to have kept. The believing community communicates norms mixed with customs as well as customs that grow apart from norms. One example from the Gospels should serve to remind us how tricky the subject of obedience can be because in this instance Jesus' particular complaint was: "In this way you have made God's word ineffective by means of your tradition." (Matt. 15:6) In this context Jesus realized that the word that had to be obeyed would come through needy mothers and fathers to their independent children. They could have honored their parents by concrete support with the resources they had at their disposal. (Matt. 15:1-5) Instead, their "devout" children chose to dedicate their mammon to God, thus making it inaccessible and unavailable to their parents to whom concrete expressions of care and honor were due. Obedience to a norm selectively chosen and intentionally abstracted enables them to justify withholding themselves and retaining their mammon. Quoting Isaiah, Jesus skewers their behavior. "This people honors me only with lip service, while their hearts are far from me. Their reverence of me is worthless; the lessons they teach are nothing but human commandments." (Matt. 15:8-9)

This is a good illustration of how good norms, holy principles, sacred traditions, and religious customs can become like mammon which keep those employing them from seeing what goes on in their hearts or discerning what love calls for. Because of their close, confused association with God, these norms become a surrogate for God, receiving the homage and obedience due to God alone. Norms can function like golden calves, substituting for knowing and loving God. This need not be the case. Properly taught and used, norms help believers to have their consciences informed, their hearts schooled in the meaning of the Gospel. The norms are part of a process of formation in Christ.

Still the question must be answered more specifically. How do we learn to obey in the manner described here as obediential hearing? So far we have examined covenant, Shema, and Jesus. But more is needed to better understand how the heart hears God. I will examine in detail mentors who have something important to contribute to this answer.

Schooling the Affections

The first of these mentors is Ignatius Loyola and his Spiritual Exercises. These are still being "done" even though it is four centuries since they were in a sense received by Ignatius during several periods of intense enlightenment beginning at the cave in Manresa.[14] The dynamics he proposes in the Exercises are particularly relevant to growing in obedience of the heart. While the efficacy of this instrument presumes that one formally undertakes to do them over a protracted period of time, usually thirty days, some knowledge of the process they propose can also be helpful to those who do not have the freedom to "come aside" for that period of time. More and more people are making the Exercises in the present day.

There is an implicit theology of providence behind the Exercises. It is far from a deist theology of providence because Ignatius believes, as the retreatant must, that God's relationship to each human being is such that He has a particular "will" for them and that this will can be known in the heart in its particularity. This "will" can be heard in those who are disposed to see this kind of providence operating between God and ourselves, who want to

know what God would have them to do or be, and who are willing
to undergo the discipline of love needed to hear God. In general,
this discipline presumes a willingness to put oneself in a space
where the ordinary round of responsibilities, relationships, and
the general din of life are far from one, insofar as that is possible.
This is done by any religious person, of course, anytime he or she
undertakes a session of personal prayer. The only difference here
is that the apartness lasts for the entire period of the retreat.

Two other things should be noted about these Exercises. The
first is that much of what goes on in the drama of the heart during
the time they are done is a war over attachments and detach-
ments, over possessions, money or the lack of same, over gain and
loss. The second has to do with attractions or repugnances, with
the affections and disaffections. Seeing these more clearly, dealing
with them more directly than we tend to do in our everyday lives
and interpreting their significance for hearing one's particular
"call" are the most delicate part of the retreat and one of the
reasons why a director is necessary. The Exercises have been
called a school of the affections because of the help they afford in
discerning one's affectivities which are usually more pronounced
at this time.

More important than all of the above is the experience these
Exercises unleash, according to the testimony of Ignatius and
many of those who have made these since then. This experience is
of the person of Jesus Christ who can become so much a part of
one's heart through the petitioned graces of the Exercises that in a
sense one's life is no longer one's own, by choice.[15] He is so much
a part of one's heart that he becomes the norm by which choices
to do this or that, be this or that, have this or that are made in
light of him. He is the new, interpersonal "attachment" which I
now follow. Maybe not wholly new, but newly appropriated,
grasped, savored, loved.

This doesn't happen miraculously or in an instant, although
such an experience could happen, of course, since nothing is impossible with God. It ordinarily happens over time as one learns
to hear one's heart from within one's affectivities and hear the
bridegroom of one's heart in the midst of these. There are two
main forms of prayer recommended by Ignatius. One is medita-

tion which is an exercise in reflecting on and considering the proposed matter. This gets one's heart straight through the use of one's head, so to speak. The other is contemplation. This helps to get one's heart straight through one's imagination. The person enters into the scene where Jesus is, there to see him and others, listen to his words and others', and observe how he goes about the enterprise of living, loving, serving God. Ignatius clearly anticipates and is something of a precursor of our modern perception that text and personal consciousness interact.

One of the more interesting effects of these Exercises is the uniqueness of the responses they evoke. Perhaps it would be more accurate to say that the sought-for, prescribed graces which are firmly specific and even somewhat predictable in their formulation are received in markedly unique and unpredictable ways. The rationale behind this is that God has a different will for each retreatant which is heard with varying levels of openness in consciousnesses that are sui generis. In addition to this, it should be noted that the Exercises do not intend to predetermine the response, nor do they intend to teach or to win those making them to one state of life.

In what follows, I will describe very succinctly the direction of the considerations or meditations Ignatius prescribes to give the reader a sense of the matter prayed over when they are made. The first considerations tend to be teleological. What have I been made by God to be and do in the course of my life? And how are other things meant to be related to this finis? The first consideration: a person is created to praise, reverence, and serve God and by doing so attain salvation. The second consideration: things are to be used to the extent that they help us attain to this, our purpose for being. They are to be disregarded or discarded to the extent they prevent this finality from being realized. The third consideration: we must seek to come to a disengagement of our affections from things not aligned to this purpose so that in all earthly matters, such as having much or little, "riches or poverty," we can come to desire and choose only those things that help us "to attain the end for which we are created."[16] In just a few lines the Exercises give retreatants much to ponder. Not just the mind, but the whole person must be exercised in a process involving feelings, personal

history, conviction, and desire which will take a long or short time
to sort out depending on one's ability to center oneself and look at
things in these starkly simple terms.

It is not only the fact that different calls are issued that makes
retreatants' responses vary. It is also their conditioning, attachments, and personal history of fidelity or infidelity to God's grace
that affect them. This leads Ignatius to propose a second series of
considerations to address the heart and its attachments. These
"First Week" considerations seek to have the person come to an
abhorrence of sin, a sense of compunction for sins committed, and
a sense of astonishment that God has treated me so compassion-
ately and in a way that is contrary to what I have deserved for the
degree of disorder I have come to with my life and use of resources. To be prepared for a new way of living the former way
must be left, abhorred, and renounced. These considerations are
undertaken in an attitude of great neediness because God must
supply in one's own spirit what it is not able to confer upon itself.

What is hoped for from these initial considerations is freedom.
What is inimical to attaining this freedom is "any inordinate incli-
nation or attachment." If one finds oneself so attached, "it will be
most useful to work as forcefully as possible to attain the contrary
of that to which the present attachment tends."[17] Ignatius gives
the example of some office or "benefice" one either has or is seeking to acquire. If the person is inclined to seek or keep this and to
do so, not for the honor and glory of God our Lord nor for "the
salvation of souls," but for personal convenience and temporal
gain, there must be a change in the direction of his or her affections. By earnest prayer and other exercises one must ask the
contrary of God our Lord. That is to say one should desire to
have no such office or benefice, or anything else, unless God, re-
storing order to the wishes of the heart, changes the desire, so that
now the reason for desiring or holding such office or benefice is
solely the service, honor, and glory of God. This is not a world-
despising attitude Ignatius is harboring here but an order-seeking
one. God can restore this order if the person sincerely seeks this.
Ignatius encourages a person undertaking these Exercises to do so
wholeheartedly, with courage and generosity, so that God "might

make use of one's person and all that one possesses in accordance with His most holy will."[18]

The next series of considerations seek out God's particular will by evoking and focusing the affectivity of the seeker. They are calculated to attract one to a deeper attention to and identification with the person of Jesus. The paradigm here is one of companionship with him. Howsoever the call is particularized, all who would follow him are informed by Christ that "whoever wishes to come with me must labor with me so that following me in suffering, he/she may also follow me in glory."[19] From here on, if people find a desire to say yes to Christ's call, Ignatius brings their hearts to school by many exercises that have as their purpose a greater love for the person of Jesus whom they more and more desire to follow. This is done usually by the prayer of contemplation by which the person is shown how to enter into the word that describes Jesus' actions, word, and personality.

By entering into the word about Jesus and opening up one's affections to be seized by him, one can come in time to hear and follow his invitation to the particular way he wishes to have the person serve him. In the very first exercise of this "Second Week" of the Exercises the issue of possessions and comfort are brought to the fore. One's relationship to them is symptomatic of the lengths one is willing to go in answering this call. "Those who wish to distinguish themselves . . . will work against their own sensuality and carnal and worldly love" by indicating their willingness to bear "poverty both physical and spiritual" if God chooses to call them to this.[20]

As the personality of Christ reveals more and more of itself to the retreatant through the contemplations, Ignatius recommends two axial meditations which are also particularly germane to our volume.[21] In one of these, he depicts Christ and his tactics in terms that sharply contrast with the tactics of his archenemy, "Lucifer." Lucifer's tactics have possessions as their basic lure. These subtly bring a person into bondage first by tying one to the possessions themselves and then by the distance they create between Christ's way and the person's desires for these attachments. Having succumbed to the seduction of things that will seem innocent or neutral enough in themselves but in turn begin to draw

one to a particular way of living usually connected with attaining
some honor or attention, people find themselves caught in a chain
that pulls them to aspire to being "themselves," and to security
and independence. Lucifer's message has many minions who communicate it even though they do not know they are doing this.
Nor do they ordinarily know whence the message originates or
the effect it has in them or will have on its subscribers. Ignatius
contrasts this strategy of "the mortal enemy of our human nature" with that of Christ who wants his followers to be prepared
to undergo the absence of things, or "actual poverty," if they are
called to it and to dishonor, which is the second kind of deprivation they must be prepared for. It is not that poverty or dishonor
as such is of value, of course, but the detachment of one's heart
from desires to have both Christ and good things or Christ and
honor or God-and-mammon is of incomparable value. They do
not give Christ a free reign with which he can work by trying to
have it both ways—being religious and having their security and
their reputation elsewhere.

When we find ourselves unfree and attached to something, Ignatius advises, "It will be of great help in overcoming our inordinate attachment to beg in the colloquies [one-to-one discourses
usually with our Heavenly Father, Jesus, or Mother of God] that
our Lord chose to have us serve Him in actual poverty [even
though our flesh opposes it] and that we desire it, beg for it and
plead for it, provided that it be only for the service and praise of
his Divine Goodness."[22] The repugnance, brought to prayer, can
be subdued through prayer. Ignatius' own experience as well as
his pastoral experience was that God brought this change about in
hearts that at least desired to have such desires. He was adamant
about the need to be free from the things that attach themselves to
hearts without being integrated into one's sense of God, His purpose in making us and His call to us to be followers of His Son.
He insists that one must not shape or drag the end for which one
was created into consideration after one has chosen something for
itself, something that ought to be a means to achieving our end.
"Many, for example, first choose marriage which is a means and
secondarily to serve God in the married state, which service to
God is the end. Likewise there are others who first desire to have

benefices and afterward to serve God in them. These individuals do not go straight to God but want God to come straight to their inordinate attachments. Acting thus, they make a means of the end and an end of the means so that what they ought to seek first they seek last."[23]

A second meditation to be made in this "Second Week" of the Exercises imagines these different responses to a hypothetical event. The event: a large sum of money has been acquired by three different "classes of men."[24] For none of them was it acquired "purely or for the love of God." All subsequently wish to be at peace about the money and free of any "serious impediment arising from their attachment to the acquired money." The first type's reaction is one of inaction. These people would like to be at peace and detached "but up to the hour of death they do not take the means." The second type desire the same thing, "to free themselves of the attachment but in such a way as to retain what they acquired. They thus want God to come to what they desire."[25] Both of these classes in fact want to have it both ways.

The third type's reaction is the most noteworthy.

> They wish to free themselves of the attachment, but in such a way that their inclination will be neither to retain the thing acquired nor not to retain it, desiring to act only as God our Lord shall inspire them and as it shall seem better to them for the service and praise of His Divine Majesty. Meanwhile they wish to consider that they have in their hearts broken all the attachments, striving not to desire that thing nor anything else, unless it be only the service of God our Lord that prompts their action. Thus, the desire of being able to serve God our Lord better will move them either to accept things or to give them up.[26]

This is a good description of the kind of indifference that makes us available to hear God. God has heard their prayers and made them free to be moved by the Spirit of God.

In the next two weeks the affections are seduced even further by love of Jesus. The third and fourth weeks of the Exercises are devoted almost entirely to two experiences of Jesus—that of his

passion and death and that of his resurrection. Again identification with him, love of him, is what is primarily sought. The contemplations are highly interpersonalized. The grace of the "Third
Week" seeks an inner sense of sorrow, affliction, and confusion
because the Lord is going to his passion on account of *my* sins.[27]
He is also seen to be suffering *for me* and my salvation. Instead of
privatism there is the personal realization of God's personal love
and care both of the person and of all peoples. In the "Fourth
Week," great joy and the consolation of the Spirit is sought in the
fact of the Resurrection event. The victory of the one who invites
followers into companionship with him is celebrated. The followers of Jesus anticipate their own eschatological future as they
rejoice at the triumph of Jesus who goes before them as forerunner and the first of many brothers and sisters.

The aim of this whole Ignatian process is to change the character of the heart by a disengagement of one's heart from lesser
attachments in order to become more and more attached to
Christ. These lesser attachments can be to people, "Anyone who
comes to me without hating father, mother, wife, children, brothers, sisters, yes and his own life too, cannot be my disciple. No one
who does not carry his cross and come after me can be my disciple." (Luke 14:26) Or their attachment can be to things: "So in
the same way, none of you can be my disciple without giving up
all that he owns." (Luke 14:33) Detachment and hearing the particularization of one's call follow as surely as dawn follows night.
When hearts are attached to the One and detached from things,
then Christian life is a matter of using possessions to express discipleship. They make it possible for the disciple to express his or her
freely chosen, wholeheartedly embraced, interpersonal finality. By
their use one executes the responsibilities that accrue to one by
reason of his or her particular way of being his disciple.

The final exercise of the four weeks is a résumé of the whole
process. It is also a form of prayer that can consolidate "the
graces" received in the retreat. Its two pre-notes about the character of love are deceptively simple. First of all: "love ought to be
manifested by deeds rather than by words."[28] The discipleship
that is being specified and intensified is not intellectual or interior.
It is not thought but done. It will be etched in relationships, en-

tered and left, possessions received or renounced, acquired or foregone, used or donated, enhanced or discarded, increased or depleted. The second pre-note is in continuity with the first: "love consists in a mutual interchange by the two parties . . . the lover gives to and shares with the beloved all that he has and can attain."[29] The petition made by the retreatant is for a deep knowledge of the many blessings received, in order to be filled with gratitude for them and in all things love and serve the Divine Majesty. The petition is more likely to be answered if the petitioner is disciplined enough to "reflect on how God dwells in creatures . . . how He dwells in me giving me life, senses, intelligence; and makes a temple of me . . . Consider all blessings and gifts as descending from above as rays of light descend from above."[30] Ignatius anticipates that a dynamic relationship will build between Christ and the follower who has come to see his love and be gripped by his attractiveness. It will grow in proportion to the perception that God in Christ particularizes his love for him or her all the day long. If this perception develops, then life becomes a response to love by love, a mutual interchange. What he has he shares with me. What I have I share with him, for example, "honors, riches and all things."[31] At his disposal is "all that I have and possess. Thou has given all to me, to thee O Lord I return it; dispose of it according to Thy Will. Give me only Thy love and Thy grace for this is enough for me."[32] This final exercise opens up the possibility that one could develop a continual perception of God acting out of love for me through particulars with my own actions being done as a response to God's love. When this is coupled by a sense of a particular call heard and assented to, then one's possessions, finances, and economic concerns will be caught up in an all-consuming love.

There is a final aspect of the Spiritual Exercises that needs to be explained so that their value for what we are treating in this volume can be more fully appreciated and utilized. How does one know to what God is calling one? A particular call or a particular way of being a disciple that cannot be deduced from general Christian principles or from the Gospels must have some way of being known or "objectively" verified. At the same time, this call will not be known ahead of time by anyone else, like the director, since it is being issued uniquely to me.

Ignatius gives guidelines for this delicate and complex expectation in his Rules for the Discernment of Spirits.[33] The discernment of and decision about a particular way of being a disciple of Christ, called "the election," is not expected to take place before the person is in the "Second Week" of the Exercises, namely, when Christ's own person strongly attracts the retreatant. By this time the end for which a person was created and the personalizing of that end by Christ, plus many considerations about God's goodness and love and mercy, as well as a deep abhorrence for what could deflect one from that end—all of these considerations would have begun to impact the affectivities of the retreatant. At the same time, they would have grown more sensitive to the experience of consolation which is a sensed presence of God or of desolation which is a sensed absence of God. How to read and deal with these two different moods or conditions of spirit is covered in the Rules for the Discernment of Spirits.

In the course of these experiences of the different spirits that afflict the retreatant, one who has entered upon the Exercises to make a choice about a state of life or about a specific way of living their faith will begin to weigh that particular matter and to surface attractions and repugnances. The object of the Election will always have the character of being a means to praise, reverence, and serve God and follow His Son. The important ingredient for weighing this particular means and for discerning whether it is a call is this matter of consolation and desolation. In this connection Karl Rahner notes, "The object of the Election is always a means to God, not God himself. Consequently that object is finite and different from the term of the fundamental and divinely effected consolation which represents the first of all principles of the Election. This consolation never, therefore, has as its direct and genuine object the means, which is the concern of the Election. Second, the starting point and ultimate criterion of the consolations themselves and of the Election built on them can only be this really fundamental and certainly divinely effected consolation."[34] Since these two things—the object of the Election and the experiences of consolation or desolation—are so intimately intercon-

nected, Ignatius proposes that their connection provides a way of
testing whether the proposed course of action is in fact the way
God is particularizing His call to the retreatant. Consequently,
"by frequently confronting the object of Election with the fundamental consolation, the experimental test is made whether the two
phenomena are in harmony, mutually cohere, and whether the
will to the object of Election under scrutiny leaves intact that pure
openness to God in the supernatural experience of transcendence
and even supports and augments it or weakens and obscures it;
whether a synthesis of these two attitudes, pure receptivity to God
(as concretely achieved, not as theoretical principle and proposition) and the will to this limited finite object of decision produces
'peace,' 'tranquillity,' 'quiet,' so that true gladness and spiritual
joy ensue, that is, the joy of pure, free, undistorted transcendence;
or whether instead of smoothness, gentleness and sweetness,
sharpness, tumult and disturbance arise."[35]

If there is a harmony between the proposed choice and the
experience of consolation or between the proposed choice and an
experience of transcendence, this would augur well for the means
being apropos and what God wants. Without such, this would
augur poorly for the nexus being apropos and what God wants.

This supernatural concrete logic, as Rahner calls this process,
"of discovering the will of God through the experimental test of
consolation," can and should become a habit so that lesser
choices, less than direction-setting decisions would be made in the
same manner.[36] The Exercises and the choice of a way of life done
in this mode of discernment set one's feet on a course that can also
clarify lesser decisions and how to go about them. The ongoing
decisions to do this or that with one's finances and one's resources
in view of the major choice of a way of life made in the Exercises
follow upon this choice, perfect this mode of discernment, and
deepen the unitary consciousness with which these were made.
These are highly idealized aspirations, of course, but these means
are being used and found helpful by more and more people. The
purpose for spelling out the process here is not to promote the
Spiritual Exercises but to describe a process that is traditional and
used in many analogous ways by many Christians who have never

heard of the Exercises and who are not likely to have the chance to formally make them.

Ignatius' contribution needs a complementary scheme that can give an account of some of the developments that have taken place since the sixteenth century, one in particular that can take into account the growth of secularity, pluralism, and the social sciences. Modern consciousness deals with many more factors than Ignatius could have known. The explosion of the social sciences and the knowledge and theories that derive from them must be exploited if we are to do our humanity justice in the name of faith.[37]

Obeying Reality, Oneself, and God

Lonergan's insight into the process of self-transcendence takes into account the complexities that modern consciousness deals with. His conversion methodology shows how listening with the heart also requires a keen use of intellect and considerable capacity for sorting out the activities of consciousness. The religious obedience of modern Christians is not as simple as that of first- or sixteenth-century Christians.

The Lonergan framework of obedience, as I believe it can be called, involves different foci, one concentrated on conversion, the other on the sources of meaning. The first of these, conversion, has three levels. The first level is intellectual and involves knowledge. To the extent it is possible, one must know enough about the financial matter being weighed to make a good judgment. For example, in the area of social security, medicare, insurance, interest rates, annuities, or something as specific as the trade-in value of a car, and so on, ignorance is overcome by knowledge. One must move beyond the "seems-to-be" toward the "is," thereby transcending one's ignorance of the matter.[38] Knowing is a form of obedience. Remaining uninformed when one knows how to become informed is a form of disobedience to reality.

Appropriate financial choices or a good use of material resources must be preceded by the hard work of acquiring knowledge. One must leave subjectivity and bias in order to understand whatever technical and objective data are needed to give the inquirer sufficient mastery of the matter to make a good decision. Lonergan calls this intellectual self-transcendence. In this process he would include being open to understanding whatever theory or theories help to explain and interpret the matter when these are pertinent. To be willfully underinformed about available information puts too much stock in one's intuitive capacities. To do this in the name of God or religion is not far from fanaticism, fundamentalism, or integralism in some form. Listening with one's heart is not an invitation to shut down one's mind or to avoid the intellectual effort needed to make critical judgments.

To some extent a degree of ignorance in financial matters and economic affairs is, of course, universal, but I am referring here to intentional ignorance. If the character of the obedience we are examining in this chapter has religion as its only referent, it will be deeply flawed since it will then deprecate the secularity of Christianity, not to mention history and the knowledge and information accessible to us in modern life. A Christian vision of obedience has to include listening to nature, the matter being weighed, and the bodies of knowledge that are pertinent to understand it. Accepting, appreciating, and seeking to know all we can about nature, society, social systems, economic structures, and the data needed for a particular decision is not the same as conforming to them. Indifference to being informed by available information needed to understand the piece of reality germane to one's choices and responsibilities consigns one to the world of the immediate. Religious people are frequently susceptible to this as they are to alienation. One who is alienated refuses to accept the reality of the world one lives in, by a deliberate blocking of the data it could continually furnish in order to remain in a predetermined sphere which is reality as I choose to interpret it.

A second kind of obedience or self-transcendence is of a moral character. When one's choices concerning finances or possessions are so riveted to the immediate object that appetite is more operative than freedom, or desire for satisfaction than intentionality, then moral self-transcendence is needed. Moral self-transcendence gets beyond the present want, desire, comfort, or satisfaction. To be worthy of our humanity the choices that relate us to others, the world, nature, systems should represent more than the satisfaction of immediate desires. "Moral conversion changes the criterion of one's decisions and choices from satisfactions to values."[39] When one has already glimpsed and chosen a particular value yet acts on the basis of its opposite, moved by mere satisfaction, one is not being authentic, consistent, or true to oneself. When particular choices about possessions, assets, and so forth are disconnected from one's values and purposes, one is being disobedient to oneself. A wedge is driven between one's authentic, valuing self and one's compulsive appetites.

Moral conversion and intellectual conversion cannot be separated. Ideally growth in knowledge should accompany growth in value perception and vice versa. The task of scrutinizing one's responses to values and one's implicit scales of preference is never complete. One has to listen to criticism "to uncover and see one's individual, group and general bias. One has to keep developing one's knowledge of the human reality and potentiality as they are in the existing situation."[40]

Our obedience is only as good as its rootage in solid judgments of fact and value. Absent either or both and our obedience will not be worthy of the name Christian since it is not even worthy of the name human. Such judgments of fact and value, in turn, rest largely on beliefs. These beliefs in turn are affected by our judgments of value, according to Lonergan.[41] He distinguishes beliefs from faith and notes that "judgments of value relevant for religious belief come from faith, the eye of religious love, an eye that can discern God's self-disclosures."[42]

Besides the need to be obedient to the world of fact and value there is a third kind of obedience, which requires the transcendence of self-immersion. When self-immersed people pursue self-interests these will be privatized or deprived, because these people will not act with a sense of the larger whole, of which a person is a part. This is not, of course, the same as saying that personal concerns, needs, and interests are illegitimate. It is, however, saying that our personal concerns, needs, and interests are legitimate if they are pursued with an awareness of our solidarity with the social wholes of which we are a part. Hence our choices are to be made with formal attention to those affected by them, taking into account first of all our responsibility for those with whom our lives and resources are directly linked. Ideally this awareness will flower into a religious self-transcendence which Lonergan describes as "being grasped by ultimate concern" or an "otherworldly falling in love."[43] This conversion is religious when and insofar as the person is transformed into "a subject in love, a subject held, grasped, possessed, owned through a total and so an other-worldly love. Then there is a new basis for all valuing and doing good."[44] These forms of self-transcendence, especially this last one, come slowly. These three forms of self-transcendence all interconnect as one attempts to be authentic.

Lonergan's understanding of human consciousness can be abstract and intimidating. His categories are important, however, and not altogether foreign to anyone. In more common parlance, our need for, pursuit of, and use of financial and material resources can be obedient or disobedient. We can be disobedient to God, ourselves, or the matter being chosen by choices that self-immersed, want-blinded, or willfully ignorant. We will be obedient if we are attentive to the matter at hand, as well as our selves as valuing subjects and God as the value par excellence in our lives. The contemporary term that best describes disobedience in these matters is "consumerism."

American consumerism is a favorite subject for moralizing. Resisting the temptation to join the lamentation, we would be well advised to root consumerism in the social meaning of acts of consumption and the social context of these acts. The anthropologist Mary Douglas sees the consumption decisions of a population as the vital source of and index to a people's culture at any given moment.[45] Goods that are the materials of our culture, "in their assemblage present a set of meanings, more or less coherent, more or less intentional."[46] She develops a communications approach to consumption that sees goods and their use as "a live information system."[47] "Moralists who indignantly condemn overconsumption will eventually have to answer for whom they do not invite to their table [and] . . . for where their old friends are today. Goods are neutral, their uses are social; they can be used as fences or bridges."[48]

By the same token, every culture is not healthy simply because it is a culture. Nor is every pattern of consumption a socially responsible one in which citizens are acting freely and obeying their own humanity seen in terms of its capacity for self-transcendence. The move beyond consumption to overconsumption, beyond consuming to consumerism, has been profitably examined by means of social analysis by Christopher Lasch. He situates his analysis of personal consumerism in the social context of mass production and mass consumption.[49] The economics of the social context thrive if there is within the citizenry a propensity for immediate gratification, one that resists postponing the use of its resources. There is also increasing dependency on social systems and their technologies which induce passivity and discourage initiative and self-reliance.[50]

Lasch records the psychological impact on individuals of these technological and economic elements. "A culture organized around mass consumption encourages narcissism (a disposition to see the world as a mirror, as a projection of one's own fears and desires) . . . which makes people weak and dependent. It undermines their confidence in their capacity to understand and shape their world."[51] This mass culture which began in the United States in the 1920s began to discourage people from providing for their own needs and socialized them into being consumers of goods and services increasingly mass-produced and impersonally delivered. With more and more dependency "on these intricate, supremely sophisticated life-support systems" infantile feelings of helplessness begin to develop which "re-create oral patterns rooted in an even earlier stage of emotional development, when the infant was dependent on the breast. The consumer experiences his surroundings as a kind of extension of the breast, alternately gratifying and frustrating."[52]

A deep disobedience to oneself develops in people who allow their perceptions of themselves to be altered by the strong impress made on them by commodity production. It is not the omnipresence of things that are the problem as much as the fantasies about oneself that these things invite. It is a common occurrence that people begin to "see themselves with the eyes of strangers and shape themselves as another commodity offered up for consumption on the open market."[53]

Social and cultural analyses such as these can leave one informed but helpless since there isn't much one can do about the fact of mass production and its twin, mass culture, except stand over against it. But it is precisely the value of Lonergan's insights that they can furnish a grid of consciousness that enables one to stand over against the culture long enough to operate more freely and self-awarely within it. Consciousness analyses complement social analyses.

Recall the need described by Lonergan for us to be able to move between the several realms within which human consciousness is capable of operating. These are common sense, theory, interiority and, finally, "the realm of transcendence in which the person is related to divinity."[54] In more primitive times people's consciousness was undifferentiated so that the first and the fourth realms were operative while the second and third realms were virtually nonexistent.[55]

The first realm for producing meaning, common sense, is attentive to the immediate, the concrete, the particular. The ever-present procedure by which we achieve common sense is "a self-correcting process of learning. Experience gives rise to inquiry and insight. Insight gives rise to speech and action. Speech and action sooner or later reveal their defects to give rise to further inquiry and fuller insight."[56] When these insights are shared by a group, the group has a communality, a way of understanding itself and discoursing within itself. For a differentiation of consciousness to take place, common sense has to suspend and relinquish its pretensions at omnicompetence. Although it cannot be disparaged or disregarded without endangering the other realms of meaning and human knowing, its limitations must be appreciated.[57] In the matter of finances and material resources, we cannot afford to lose our common sense. But, by the same token, it cannot be taken to be the only realm from which meaning derives.

Enter theory. Theory, too, is a mode of knowing, a way of attaining meaning. It, too, has its own cognitive procedures. By our use of common sense we look at the object that is occupying our attention in its relationship to us. By theory we look at the same object to understand what it is apart from us, what it is in itself. The spontaneous element diminishes as consciousness seeks to be more objective. The object is weighed "with some approximation to the logical ideal of clarity, coherence and rigor," and with particular attention to the language, which is technical and objective, that conveys this.[58] In the realm of theory "things are conceived and known not in their relations to our sensory apparatus or to our needs and desires but in the relations constituted by their uniform interactions with one another."[59] By theory Lonergan means any form of systematized meaning. Questions are raised by common sense that it can't answer. Theory is born out of a systematic exigence. More was needed historically than was known through common sense. More is needed personally than common sense can supply. In the complex modern world of finances and consumption, common sense alone will not suffice.

If theory is born out of a systematic exigence, interiority develops from a critical exigence.[60] Interiority, a third realm from which meaning arises, is like the other two, a mode of knowing with its own peculiar procedures. A person cannot simply shuffle back and forth between theory and common sense. One must bring these two realms into a working relationship with one another by making them one's own in a third realm, interiority. This realm involves a self-appropriation that sifts common sense and theory. It will use and acknowledge both while critically grounding each. This font of meaning which Lonergan calls interiority constitutes a quantum leap in the capacity of consciousness to see itself operating. One can reflect on oneself intending the various object of consciousness and on the norms being employed by the choice of the objects of consciousness. One has become capable of a self-critical reflexivity. "Differentiated consciousness appears when the critical exigence turns attention upon interiority, when self-appropriation is achieved, when the subject relates his different procedures to the several realms, relates the several realms to one another, and consciously shifts from one realm to another by consciously changing his procedures."[61]

Lonergan is, in part, describing human consciousness in its historical development. He is also exhorting or promoting a heightened use of consciousness by that which grounds it, interiority.

Otherwise, "our attention is apt to be focused on the object while our conscious operating remains peripheral."[62] The move to interiority is a step beyond being simple intenders and choosers of objects to an enlargement of one's interest so that what comes to the center of consciousness is the intending subject.[63] The capability that is developed here is that of "(1) experiencing one's experiencing, understanding, judging, and deciding; (2) understanding the unity and relations of one's experienced experiencing, understanding, judging, and deciding; (3) affirming the reality of one's experienced and understood experiencing, understanding, judging, and deciding; (4) and deciding to operate in accord with the norm immanent in the spontaneous relatedness of one's experienced, understood, affirmed experiencing, understanding, judging, and deciding."[64] This might sound terribly complex but it is the move from simple intending to a more self-aware intending. The essential ingredient is freedom, a consciousness moving freely over the data and freely choosing its choices, judging its judgments, and so forth.

Finally, there is the fourth realm of meaning. Like the third realm which is a must, this fourth realm is also a must, or a transcendent exigence, as Lonergan calls it. Because of it, each of the other three realms of meaning are experienced as limited. "There is to human inquiry an unrestricted demand for intelligibility. There is to human judgment a demand for the unconditioned. There is to human deliberation a criterion that criticizes every finite good. So it is that we can reach basic fulfillment, peace, joy only by moving beyond the realms of common sense, theory and interiority into the realm in which God is known and loved."[65]

This realm of transcendence does not develop after the first three are in place. It was there from the beginning. "As the question of God is implicit in all our questioning, so being in love with God is the basic fulfillment of our conscious intentionality."[66] "Before it enters the world mediated by meaning, religion is the prior word God speaks to us by flooding our hearts with His love."[67] The fourth realm is the least susceptible of consciousness in an explicit or fulsome way. "Ordinarily the experience of the mystery of love and awe is not objectified. It remains within subjectivity as vector, an undertow, a fateful call to a dreaded holiness."[68]

Our capacity for self-transcendence "becomes an actuality when one falls in love. Then one's being becomes being-in-love."[69] Being intelligent is a function of being in love, not the other way around. "Being in love with God is the basic fulfillment of our conscious intentionality."[70] Our deliberations and choices in the matter of what to own, and disown, how to use what we own, how best to make use of our financial resources, these are all matters that rightfully move toward ways of loving God. A growing awareness of the opportunities implicit in our choices will make us materialistic in the right sense of the term. An immaterial Christianity is a Christianity that will never know its role in the real world of money and possessions. A Christianity that is ever materializing the love that is being poured into our hearts (Rom. 5:5) is at the same time a faith that is maturing and a mission that is engaged in the world.

We should be able to see now the importance to our study of both of Lonergan's grids. The one sees obedience in terms of self-transcendence. The other is a chart of the four realms within the structures of consciousness for deriving meaning. Even though, for Lonergan, the core meaning of being human is love, this is not an invitation to live unreflectively nor unintelligently. Quite the opposite! We owe it to our humanity to listen with our hearts but to exercise our critical capacities in so doing. A love that can keep reason in its employ is what Lonergan's schemes see as ideal, both humanly and in the Christian reading of what it is we are called to become.

I believe Lonergan's four realms of meaning serve to clarify the business of obedience of the heart with respect to the use of money, possessions, and goods. One has to know about the matter to be purchased or sold or used or invested and so forth. The reality in question has to be obeyed. But to the extent that common sense is operative and theory is necessary, reality is being obeyed. But these must, in turn, be grounded in the reflective self. Interiority is an ability to obey oneself. Interiority is self-possession without being isolated from the communities within which the self lives or the culture within which the self consumes and produces, buys and sells, and so on. But interiority, in turn, chooses to value itself in the other. A process of choosing that went straight from common sense meaning to transcendence without passing through the mediations of theory and interiority would be humanly and religiously defective. The realm of theory, as also the realm of common sense, must in turn be grounded in interiority. The subject must appropriate itself in the light of these. But interiority is drawn beyond itself into love. In all our choosing, we are propelled by an "eros towards divinity."[71]

Our choices and behavior as consumers are, of course, much more spontaneous than the Lonergan grids seem to suggest. Their purpose is not to load us up with a complex apparatus for our everyday consumer behavior or act as a philosophy of life. They describe the routes hearts, minds, and wills take when they are functioning freely and fully. Their formal use would be infrequent. When there is an opportunity to get back from our day-to-day consuming patterns to examine whether we are using all the possible routes of a healthy, whole life they are invaluable.

CHAPTER V

✦✦

Extending the Tent Poles

Several objections easily arise as a result of the last chapter that can serve to introduce this one. The first. As a matter of practical fact, isn't this theme of obediential hearing a bit beside the point in the everyday matters of paying bills, keeping solvent, making a living, and so forth? Are not most matters involving finances and possessions decided for us by the system we find ourselves in rather than by us? It is true, our choices will be limited by our resources and opportunities as well as the responsibilities we have. Every choice we make about financial material matters is made from within definite constraints imposed on us. Our decisions are made on the basis of a series of givens that seem largely intractable. I can't determine the interest rate, for example, nor the sales tax nor the price of flour. Nor can I manipulate the mortgage. Our freedom and our faith are not expected to operate where there are no constraints but where there are many. Our freedom and our faith operate within history, within a culture, within particulars. Our faith becomes functional first of all by the reading it gives to these constraints and opportunities. The response faith makes to the givens can range anywhere from action or the refusal of action, submission, or renunciation. The fact that one acts from within constraints does not mean one has acted unfreely. Our acts are unfree only if they are conformist or compulsive in relationship to these constraints and opportunities and ultimately to the system from which these come.

Another objection would be about the "subjectivity" of the proposed obediential hearing. It is posed by those who see Christian obedience as objective matter whose contents can be found in the Ten Commandments, the Church's moral tradition, and the discipline with which the Church surrounded the various states of life. Of course Christian obedience is an objective matter, but it is not wholly so. These accessible articulations of the objective side of Christian obedience are undoubtedly part of the contents of obedience. They require no comment since they are more or less in place for knowledgeable and sincere Christians, the variations coming largely from the particular Christian tradition the believer has espoused. But if this is all there were to Christian obedience then the uniqueness of people and their relationship to God, the particularities of their circumstances, and of their call, the peculiar challenge of their moment of history and their relationship to their contemporaries would all be taken to be of no moment. Any Christian anthropology worthy of the name would not be that succinct about obedience.[1]

In this chapter I wish to extend the tent poles of Christian obedience in three directions. The purpose of the extension is not to widen or enlarge the matter about which obedience is required but to lodge the obedience of modern Christians more firmly in the freedom of the subject, the character of membership in Christ and the concrete situation of deprivation that so many suffer today. Each of these directions is warranted for two reasons. First, contemporary Christians are increasingly obeying or responding to the call of Christ in the manner we will describe. And, second, all of these three extensions of obedience find their warrant in the tradition of the Church and in the praxis of the saints who have faithfully followed Christ.

These three can be briefly described and distinguished from one another. In terms of direction, the aspiration of the first extension is toward singleness of heart. The aspiration of the second is toward social wholeness. It is generated by the social character of human life, the social purpose of the goods and resources of the earth, and the communal nature of the body of Christ. The aspiration of the third is toward solidarity with the poor. As can be seen already, these are not separable but have different optics and, as we will see, different emphases. Each, furthermore, admits of degrees. Each measures growth in obedience in a different way. Of the three, the first is the most familiar to Christians. The second and third modes are understood less well, at least by Christians in this country. The third has come into its own only in the last few decades but is seldom seen as a mode of obedience. All three, furthermore, as I will explain later on, have different measures of disobedience or different enemies to the practice of their peculiar mode. The enemy to the first is rote behavior referred to in the previous chapter. Also inimical to it is addictive behavior in general and consumerism in particular. The enemy of the second is individualism in general and looking-out-for-number-one in particular. The enemy of the third is a faith insufficiently distinguished from the culture or an enculturated faith.

The First Extension: Equipoise

The first of these might be characterized as the habit of making choices in equipoise. By equipoise I mean that people (and by extension the group) have sufficient self-presence that their material and financial resources are kept in a position of means while their hearts sort out the good to be chosen, the value to be expressed, or the purpose to be pursued. Synonyms for this are singleness of heart or indifference, that is, notwithstanding one's feelings one chooses to do this or forgo that, and so forth. Equipoise is a poise of spirit that can weigh conflicting pulls and not act compulsively or addictively so that one's choices or use of things express one's deeper self, one's interiority. What is traditional in this understanding of obedience for Christians is that they pursue their purposes through their use of things, having appropriated in some way the key teleological principles of the purpose of their lives and the purpose of the things they have or could have.[2] These (usually inchoate) principles come from a combination of personal experience and the received wisdom of forebears and mentors in the faith.

An extension of this traditional understanding of obedience would place it within the framework of a call ethic.[3] The Spiritual Exercises could be characterized in these terms. Indifference or equipoise is the precondition for hearing the call and living it out. Recall the three types of men who were faced with the acquisition of a large sum of money. The third group show the equipoise kind of obedience we are describing here. They also show that they are prepared to use things in light of the particular way they are called to serve God.

This kind of obedience is no small attainment. It is a feat of grace and nature to develop the degree of union, love, self-knowledge, and self-control that is ever prepared to employ material means to pursue faith-glimpsed ends or to embody one's values with one's resources or to act on the basis of an interiority that is alive to God and others. This consistency of heart and mind matures only slowly over time and presumably will grow along with a developing sense of God and discernment of the state and manner of life God would have one pursue. Equipoise is Lonergan's interiority in action.

Just as one grows in this singleness of heart by degrees, so one falls short of it by degrees. Failure to aspire to single-mindedness is the ordinary state of affairs in our American culture that does not encourage a way of life that grasps a means-to-an-end relationship to material goods. We are invited to a level of consumption we don't need by the ethos of our culture of conspicuous consumption.[4] A harmony between one's inner sense of oneself and what one has by way of external possessions is difficult to maintain when the direction of our culture's pull is always toward *more* while less and simplicity of life is the pull of the Gospel.

The classical story of someone who was disobedient to this mode of obedience was the man with the superabundance of grain. (Luke 12:16–21) Here was an accumulation that had lost touch with the ends for which the rich man was made and the purposes of his possessions. The grain dictated to him his sense of himself, his lifestyle and, his vision of the future—rather than he determining it.

The presuppositions behind this aspect of modern Christian obedience are several. First of all that we are free to make choices. Illusion or addiction or compulsion or moral weakness are the usual fonts of unfreedom. Second, that while knowledge of the traditional moral norms of the Christian tradition is good and even necessary to make moral choices, the application of these norms to our existential situation, and specifically to the allocation of our material and financial resources, will not necessarily lead to a clear moral imperative.[5] A morally clear course of action will not ordinarily be deducible from the moral norms the Church has articulated over the centuries about the disposition of goods.[6] Third, that God has a particular will about such matters and, if it is sought, it can be known.[7] Equipoise will enable the individual (or the discerning group) to hear a particularization of God's will for him, her, them.[8]

The particularization of God's will is binding on those who come to understand the call that is being issued to them even though its "binding force, which regards the individual reality as such, cannot be expressed in a general proposition."[9] What is operating in this case is the conscience of the individual, not in the sense that it is applying a universally moral norm to one's own situation but in the sense that it has grasped "what has not yet been made absolutely clear by the situation and the universal norms" but which nonetheless "must be done by me individually."[10]

For our material and financial wherewithal to be transubstantiated, equipoise is necessary. Certainly when the choice will substantially affect one's material and financial condition the consumer needs to come to a point of "equilibrium (about it), without leaning to either side, that I might be ready to follow whatever I come to perceive is more for the glory and praise of God and the salvation of my soul."[11] Certainly God could bring the person who was willing to this equilibrium and, having done so, God could move the will and bring to mind what ought to be done with the matter in question if the person begged God to so dispose him or her.

It is necessary to extend the tent poles of our contemporary obedience beyond where they are too often lodged. Equipoise as the precondition of a mature obedience goes far beyond the superficial sense of simply avoiding what offends God. "We treat sin too exclusively as the mere offense against divine universal norms . . . [and neglect to see that sin] is also and just as much an offense against an utterly individual imperative of the individual will of God . . . [and] the failure of a personal-individual love of God."[12] Equipoise is concerned to discover this utterly individual imperative and obey it.

There is a further way of examining equipoise, one that I will only allude to here, namely, that being the appropriation of freedom. What grows by equipoise is the capacity of people to determine their lives. What shrinks is the amount of determination exercised on their lives by forces outside of them. Extending the tent poles of obedience, therefore, in this direction enhances the possibility of a commitment of oneself in freedom and love, the stuff of which eternity is made. (See my volume on commitment, *Should Anyone Say Forever?* published by the Loyola Press, 1985.)

Brethrenomics

The second direction in which modern obedience must be extended has also been introduced in the previous chapters. Any number of formulations are possible but the main ingredient of each of them is the use of material and financial resources with a sensitivity to others as one of the constant criteria. This sensitivity grows with the increase in knowledge of the needs of others. It is alert, first of all, to those to whom we are already linked by natural bonds such as spouses, parents, children, kin, or by commitment such as friends and associates. There are degrees of this kind of obedience, with the more perfect extending in the direction of a sensitivity toward the needs of those with whom one is not ordinarily or naturally associated.

The concreteness of this second mode of obedience has never been better depicted than by the several parables already touched upon. Negatively there is the rich man who dressed well and feasted daily and who chose not to hear the the ill and hungry Lazarus at his gate. (Luke 16:19–31) More positively there is the wily manager who, after his hand was forced, had to learn this kind of obedience. The commendation he receives is a good formulation of what I mean by brethrenomics. "Use the elusive mammon you have at present to make friends so that when it gives out you will be welcomed into dwellings that will last." (Luke 16:9)

The optic of the first mode of obedience was more personal and individual than this one. This second mode is a necessary complement to the first because Christian obedience has to be both individual and communal. While the mode of obedience called equipoise is more likely to be discerned from interior impulses, this one is more likely to be occasioned on the streets.

The "brethren" must become a norm for the disposition of one's resources. This mode of obedience is an attitude of mind that consistently includes others in its purview and is prepared to act on the basis of one's relatedness to others or one's perceived responsibility for them or their evident needs. While brethrenomics is a sexist term it captures the spirit and scope of this kind of obedience insofar as money or goods are essential to it.[13] It also suggests the way in which Christianity could affect the economy.

Brethrenomics is not new. One of the earliest evidences of this form of obedience is the practice of almsgiving as Israel practiced this and the early Church followed suit. The needs of others were a norm for giving. Almsgiving has its etymological root in the Greek word *eleemosuna,* meaning compassion.[14] One gave alms to a needy person because one's "fellow-feeling" was evoked. In time, the compassion that evoked the act became the name of the act itself. So compassion manifested itself in almsgiving. Firmly instituted in Judaism, its rationale was that the compassion of God was to be made manifest especially to widows, orphans, and the needy by the regular giving of alms by devout Jews. Jesus' critical attitude about it relates not to the practice itself, but to the use to which it was twisted by those who wished to be seen as holy. Instead of displays of almsgiving which were "parade[d] . . . to attract attention" (Matt. 6:2), Jesus recommended that the practice be done in such a way that God who sees the heart can reward it because its compassion reflects His own.

Almsgiving is an important theme in Luke and the Acts. Like

Matthew, Luke saw how almsgiving was an occasion for hypocrisy. But he also emphasized that it would have the marvelous effect of wiping the heart clean if it were done out of compassion. (Luke 11:41) The occasion for Jesus' teaching on the subject is a dinner given for him by one of the Pharisees. He is surprised at Jesus' indelicacy in not having "first washed before the meal." (Luke 11:38) Jesus reacts by describing a religious attitude that fixates on this and other external practices as being tantamount to cleaning "the outside of cup and plate" while the heart from which the observance springs can be "filled with extortion and wickedness." (Luke 11:39) Jesus recommends instead that you "give alms from what you have and, look, everything will be clean for you." (Luke 11:41)

This connection between almsgiving and redemption was not novel. Judaism had earlier begun to develop a "doctrine of redemptive almsgiving."[15] In Proverbs 19:17, for example, we read: "Whoever is kind to the poor is lending to Yahweh who will repay him the kindness done." The Gospels imply such a doctrine, for example, in Luke 18:22, because what is given to the poor is described as becoming treasure in heaven. The Fathers of the Church deepen this connection. Irenaeus argues that almsgiving erases past avarice.[16] Origen argues that there are a number of actions that remit sins, the first of which is baptism, the second martyrdom, and the third almsgiving.[17]

This feature of the religious effect that the giving of alms has on the giver is a major reason why money doesn't get a wholly negative report in either Judaism or Christianity.[18] Money and wealth, furthermore, are given a conditional acceptance by the Church because their communally enlightened use was one of the easiest ways Christians had of acting concretely in view of the communality they were brought into by being baptized into Christ. In addition, as the Christian communities became institutionalized, they needed funds to build and maintain their institutions.

Paul developed what we might call a theology of the collection which was a combination of almsgiving institutionalized, Christology materialized, and ecclesiology concretized.[19] The rationale he gives to the collection builds on but goes beyond Judaism because the responsibility is that of a member for other members of the same Body and that of one part of the Body of Christ for another part. This Body of Christ motif gives Christian obedience a bottom line.

For Paul the Body motif meant that there had to be a sharing of one's resources and a meeting of the concrete material needs of those who were baptized into Christ. This was more than a local sharing and caring. Through collections taken from one part of the Body of Christ, another part of the Body was to be supplied. To be particular, from communities in Macedonia and Corinth, the Jerusalem community was sustained. The Jerusalem Church had experienced much hardship as a result of its severe marginalization and persecution from the dominant culture.[20] Paul believed that the bond between members of this new "Body" was so intimate that one member could not suffer or rejoice without the effects being felt by the whole Body. Or better, "should not" since the many members are one. (1 Cor. 12:12–13)

Two Corinthians, Chapters 8 and 9, describe Paul's efforts to motivate Corinthian Christians to have the same impulses of the Spirit that had the first community share all things in common. (Acts 4:32) He describes the generosity of the Christian communities in Macedonia to the Corinthian Christians so that they might be moved to imitate their generosity in giving to the Jerusalem community. These Macedonian Christians, though themselves quite poor, upon hearing of the needs of the Jerusalem Christians produced monies and goods "beyond their resources." (2 Cor. 8:3) Even more remarkably they saw this sharing as a favor to themselves, or so Paul claimed. "They had kept imploring us most insistently for the privilege of a share in the fellowship of service to God's holy people." (2 Cor. 8:4)

Paul's nuances in the following verses speak volumes. He is not giving them an order, he says, but is holding up two pictures for their contemplation. The one is of Macedonian Christians: test "the genuineness of your love against the concern" they have shown. (2 Cor. 8:8) The other: recall "the generosity which our Lord Jesus Christ had, that, although he was rich, he became poor for your sake, so that you should become rich through his poverty." (2 Cor. 8:9) Paul, therefore, called upon each member and household to give "so far as your resources permit." (2 Cor.

8:11) Not beyond your means, however, because "it is not that you ought to relieve other people's needs and leave yourselves in hardship." (2 Cor. 8:13) Paul hopes this will be done graciously "not an imposition" or grudgingly. (2 Cor. 9:5; 9:8)

He even foresees a time when the surplus of another part of the Body will supply the Corinthian Christians' needs just as "your surplus at present may fill their deficit." (2 Cor. 8:14) He articulates a principle: "There should be a fair balance," (2 Cor. 8:13) because through baptism they have all been brought out of isolation from one another and made one in one Spirit. He likens this sharing with other members of the Body of one's material resources to a sowing which if done generously results not in having less but having more because of the origin of the resources themselves. "The one who so freely provides seed for the sower and food to eat will provide you with ample store of seed for sowing and make the harvest of your uprightness a bigger one." (2 Cor. 9:10) The God Paul is familiar with in Christ is not outdone by generosity. By contributing from their means God can bring them beyond sufficiency to an increase of favors. "God is perfectly able to enrich you with every grace, so that you always have enough for every conceivable need, and your resources overflow in all kinds of good works." (2 Cor. 9:8)

The enemy of this mode of obedience is a culture that teaches all of us to look out for ourselves and "our own," to take care of ourselves, to value ourselves in isolation from one another, and to define our individuality in terms of our economic and financial conditions instead of others, their needs, and our faith. Our economic culture foments competition and self-interest. Competition and self-interest are not in themselves inimical to human needs or to faith. They are hallowed ways of generating and regulating an economy. They can and usually do, however, go beyond their economic functions and affect the area of personal values and interpersonal relations. When this occurs, a faith that proclaims a solidarity with neighbor or a member relationship to others in the Body of Christ is up against a consciousness already predisposed to the opposite. This opposite is a competitiveness toward one another and looking out for one's own interests despite of or with a disregard for others.

The Option for the Poor

This is a third way Christians' obedience is developing. It is more difficult to pinpoint because of the considerable variation there is both in the understanding of its key category, the poor, and because the Church's pastoral relationship to the poor is uneven at present. This mode of obedience is only now maturing. Nevertheless, in some ways this mode of obedience is ancient, antedating even Christianity. The Torah, for example, prescribed a regular system of relief for the poor, financing it by a mandatory payment of poor tithes every third year. (Deut. 14:28–29) Concern for the poor, the widow, and the orphan were a constant theme of the prophets.

What is most difficult to locate in the argument is not that the poor should receive something whether these be tithes or alms or "charity." Rather, who the poor are, what their relationship is to God, and God's attitude toward them—these are the issues that specify this mode of obedience and, at the same time, give it its still developing character. Those who live this mode of obedience voluntarily often claim that the poor are in a privileged relationship to God. The argument is that those who would follow Christ should be in solidarity with these poor because of who the poor are in God's eyes. The so-called preferential option for the poor, therefore, can be seen in terms of obedience to Christ who has already opted to identify himself with them.

In this claim there is something very old and something new. Old because the *anawim* of Israel were considered to be the object of predilection by God.[21] Old also because Christ identified the hungry, the naked, the friendless, "the least of these" with himself. (Matt. 25:45) But there is something new here, too, because many of the present-day followers of Christ are seeing social and ecclesial implications in this mode of obedience not previously perceived. While this mode of obedience, like the other two, admits of degrees, one moves within it in a definite direction, from concern for the poor to identification with the poor to depriving oneself for the sake of the poor and finally to a sharing in their conditions. As one's life begins to be related more and more to the poor, the implications in the initial attraction to this way of living usually become clearer. Not the least of these is that, according to the testimony of those who have gone in this direction, one will come to see that the attraction is to Christ himself.[22]

To be for the poor is not unusual. In fact, it is the usual sentiment. (It would be hard to see how we could be counted Judeo-Christian if we were not.) But the ranks get thinner and this wide road narrows. Being one of the poor voluntarily is the final stage of the journey or the steepest, narrowest part of this road and the most complete form of obedience possible in this mode. Of those who persevere along the road, some will be called, to put it in Ignatius' terms, to "actual poverty." This condition differs from being for the poor because they voluntarily forgo their more comfortable circumstances out of a sense of being called to be poor. They do so not because they have reasoned to it or talked themselves into it or deduced their decision from some scheme for radical social change but out of conviction, attraction, a sense of the rightness of this for them. Equipoise vis-à-vis possessions made it possible to hear the call and obey it. They voluntarily place themselves in circumstances that are deprived at least by comparison to the ones they were in, and could have remained in, circumstances that are now the same as those of the poor with whom they seek to be in association. The relationship of their choice to God might not always be clear, at least at first, as I have already noted.

Because of changes that take place in the perceptions and social location of those who have chosen to throw in their lot with this lower "class," the voluntarily poor can become the catalysts and bridges for the rest of those who have some attraction to this mode of obedience but who have yet to concretize their own choices. The voluntarily poor begin to see society through the lenses of the poor.[23] Not only see, of course, but feel and experience the same neglect, discomfort, indifference, fear, powerlessness, corruption, and so forth. This is not their only experience. There are also joys, camaraderie, sharing, and community. People who are voluntarily on the side of the disadvantaged of society after having been on the side of the advantaged often find themselves "spiritually" better off than they were before. At least they measure "better off" in terms other than the way they had previously. As aspirations appropriated from the dominant culture recede, new aspirations succeed them. The Gospels are discovered to have a dimensionality they weren't seen to have before. They begin to generate new energy for the reign of God, for justice, and community. Life together is likely to become more important if, for no other reason, there isn't as much to occupy or distract those who have little (as long as their condition is not abject or desperate). Furthermore, growth as economically construed and subtly coerced can be discriminatingly judged. Having chosen to be free of the dominant culture's economic dictates, one can embrace alternative ways of being a consumer, citizen, friend, colleague. What would previously have been seen as basically a decent economic order, give or take a little, because one was a beneficiary of it, will now be recognized for its insensitivity, its greed, its anticommunity dynamics, its option for capital over the laborer, its all-consuming interest in people insofar as they are consumers, and so on.

Leaving the economic class within which one lives to live in a different relationship to the economic culture, the followers of Christ in this mode of obedience will be forced to take their cues about particulars from the poor with whom they feel called to be in association. The change involves a different social location not simply an interior movement. Furthermore, it begins to affect a change in where one lives, with whom one lives, and how one lives. The new social location places one (or the family or group) in circumstances less commodious. Because they do not reinforce the economic system's "growth ethic," its induced covetousness, in small ways the voluntarily poor are a counterweight to the system in its present functioning which has made a preferential option for upward mobility, a higher class, more capital, an increase in security, and comfort—an option made even by the majority of laborers.

I have focused this mode of obedience largely on the poor understood in an economic sense. As Monika Hellwig has observed, however, "the poor" are more appropriately considered as an "ideal type."[24] If this is done then material deprivation which is the focus of much Latin American theology which has spearheaded this mode of obedience would be merely the prototype of

many different kinds of deprivation. "The poor," then, would include those who are physically handicapped or politically or culturally deprived by margination, contempt, or oppression. "The
central factor at issue appears to be powerlessness and suffering."[25]

By identifying with those who suffer deprivation in these several ways and by sharing their plight in practical ways, one comes
to enjoy "the hermeneutic privilege of the poor." The privilege
this ideal type of "the poor" enjoys is hearing the Gospel, not
because they are virtuous, but being in a situation of bad news
they are continually ready to hear the good news about a savior.
There is a very good chance that they will be open to give welcome to the great hope to which they are called, if it is preached
to them. Their vulnerability makes it likely that many of the following assertions will be true of them, according to Hellwig:

The poor have no exaggerated sense of their own importance.

The poor have a sense of their interdependence on one another.

The poor expect much from cooperation, little from competition.

The poor rest their security more on people than on things.

The poor have no exaggerated need of privacy.

The poor can distinguish between luxuries and necessities.

The poor can wait because they have acquired a kind of dogged
patience.

The poor know they are in urgent need of redemption.

When the poor have the Gospel preached to them, it sounds
like good news and not like a threat or a scolding.

The promise of future salvation is truly present joy and therefore present incipient salvation for the poor.

The poor can respond to the call of the Gospel with a certain
abandonment and uncomplicated totality because they have so
little to lose and are ready for anything.[26]

It should be obvious that the three extensions of obedience we
have outlined here are very much interrelated. In fact, one without the other two would be very likely to go awry. Equipoise
alone could become scrupulous or privatized. Brethrenomics
could become imprudent if it were untempered by equipoise. And

the option for the poor could become alienated or ideological without the modifying influences of the other two directions.

But this third mode, the preferential option for the poor, is the one that needs most discernment at present. To exercise this option is not ordinarily understood to mean choosing to be among the poor or to be poor. Should it be? Is the step that goes beyond being for the poor to choosing to be of the poor a particular call within the Body of Christ? Or is it only seen to be such at present because we are only now being brought to see the character of the call of all Christians? Is there something intrinsic between being faithful to following Christ or hearing the Gospel more clearly and being among the poor? Are those who are choosing to be poor now forerunners of where the whole people of God will be called? I am not sure of the answer to these questions. I am sure, however, of the importance of our asking them and our becoming more enlightened about them. Some of this light should come from the magisterium of the Church. We will examine the discernment it is giving to this impetus.

The Official Church as Leader and Follower

Thus far I have looked at this third extension of obedience both as a call and in terms of the rationale it has developed from the experience of those who live it out. Before proceeding further it is important to examine the official Church's perceptions on this subject. I am particularly indebted in the following pages for the research of Donal Dorr in his *Option for the Poor,* published by Orbis, 1983.

Rerum Novarum (1891) was the first of a host of encyclicals and official teachings by the Church in modern times that touched on the subject of economic disparity and injustice. Pope Leo XIII put the Church on the side of the poor and the working class in this encyclical. It contains the seeds of the subsequent option for the poor as I have described. While Leo XIII favored the poor and called for society to change for their sake, nevertheless, his notion of society saw these changes coming about from the top down, initiated by those who were the beneficiaries of the system as it existed. If the proposed changes threatened to destabilize society, then the injustices were to be tolerated. As Dorr notes, Leo's spirituality "actively discouraged the poor from confronting the wealthy to claim their rights; it promised reward in heaven to those who were victims of injustice on earth."[27] Forty years later, however, Pius XI's *Quadragesimo Anno* called the Church to assume a major role in the needed sociopolitical changes. It held out an alternative model of society. Unfortunately, that alternative was quite ambiguous. It was also too influenced by the Italian political efforts of the day which were attempting to implement a corporatist form of social order.[28] These first two social encyclicals were issued at a time "when the Vatican was very unsympathetic to left-wing economics and politics."[29] In fact, in the whole seventy-year period that began with Leo XIII and ended with Pius XII, the Church theoretically offered a third way between capitalism and socialism but practically speaking it was much more explicit about its opposition to socialism than it was to capitalism. A chastening attitude toward capitalism tended to legitimate it in contrast to its hostile attitude toward socialism.

By 1961 and John XXIII's *Mater et Magistra,* a much clearer direction began to be taken by the Church with respect to the poor. This new direction put distance between the Church and the forces of society that were resistent to structural change. This beloved Pope's favor "of what amounts to a welfare model of society," disconnected the Church's social teaching from those who had used Catholic social teaching to give free enterprise or private property a carte blanche or pride of place.[30] Paul VI, two years after the Vatican Council ended, continued this new direction in his *Populorum Progressio,* which in effect, called for "the replacement of the present structures of international capitalism" not through violence or confrontation but "by negotiation and consensus."[31]

The Latin American bishops in 1968 at Medellin took a further step by their commitment "to renounce the patronage and privileges which the state can offer," thus enabling the Church to speak and act prophetically over against "those who hold power."[32] The Medellin document commits the bishops and the

Latin American Church to give "effective preference to the poorest and most needy sections of society."[33] Even more radical than this was their view of the key agency in bringing about social change. This would be the poor themselves. Medellin validated the already widely used processes of conscientization whereby the poor become insightful about the causes of their oppression and seek to organize themselves to overcome these.

Pope Paul VI issued two documents subsequent to Medellin which continue the development of the Church's perception of and relation to the poor. The first, *Octogesima Adveniens* (1971) explicitly derogates the perspective of the advantaged liberals who see the world's poor as not yet developed peoples "but with a little help from us" they can become so in time.[34] It is sensitive to the political factors that keep the economically poor, poor and the need for political action to remove them. *Evangelii Nuntiandi* (1975) is concerned to give a more comprehensive view of the social mission of the Church than one that is merely attempting to affect a change of social structures. It calls for "conversion of the minds and hearts of those who live under these systems as well as those who have control of them."[35] How this is done? The Good News effectively proclaimed changes "the standards by which people make judgments, their prevailing values, their interests and thought patterns, the things that move them to action . . . it is capable of reaching into and out from the core and the roots of life . . . it can penetrate all cultures while being neither subordinate to any of them nor the monopoly of any."[36] The significance of this document is its refusal to dichotomize structural and attitudinal change. It takes our personal ways of thinking, valuing, and feeling as structures "that are within the person without being private" and that need to be evangelized and reformed.[37] (This is similar to the perspective of Lonergan as we saw in the previous chapter.) Conversely, the Pope notes, "even the best of structures and the most widely planned systems soon become dehumanized if the inhuman tendencies of people's hearts are not healed."[38] This is true of those who are wealthy, those who are poor, and those who are middle-class.

Finally there is the pontificate of John Paul II. Within a few months after his election to the Chair of Peter he journeyed to

Puebla, Mexico, in January 1979, to play a difficult role in the Conference of the Latin American Church. What made the conference tense was the opposition which had gathered momentum since Medellin (1968) and sought to halt the direction taken by that conference. The conflict that interests us most is over the "preferential option for the poor." Medellin had been criticized in the intervening years by conservatives for its implicit abandonment of the universal mission of the Church. It was also contended that an option for the poor was really an option for a class-struggle conception of social change which was Marxist in inspiration. The document that was hammered out by the bishops, however, not only reaffirmed their previous stand, it went even further. It "affirmed the need for conversion on the part of the whole Church to a preferential option for the poor, an option aimed at their integral liberation . . . This option, [is] demanded by the scandalous reality of economic imbalances in Latin America . . . We will make every effort to understand and denounce the mechanisms that generate this poverty . . . the witness of a poor Church can evangelize the rich whose hearts are attached to wealth, thus converting and freeing them from this bondage and their own egotism."[39]

At Puebla, John Paul relied heavily on Paul VI's *Evangelii Nuntiandi* and its liberation-cum-conversion conceptions. He rejected an image of Jesus as a political activist who was involved in a class struggle as some liberation theology had suggested. In backing the Latin bishops, however, in their reiterated preferential option for the poor he did not use the same phrase. His subsequent speeches give a further indication of his mind. To poor Mexican Indians he proclaimed the need for "bold changes which are deeply innovating" such as "a social mortgage on all private property" so that "if the Common Good requires it there should be no hesitation even at expropriation, carried out in due form."[40] In another address he told his audience of poor people, "I feel solidarity with you because, being poor . . . you are God's favorites."[41]

Back at the Vatican he issued several encyclicals that are less related to the Latin context but they are not for that reason any less confrontative. In one of these, *Redemptor Hominis,* he contemplates the existing international economic order through the parable of the rich man and Lazarus. The institutions on which this seeming "order" rests, control trade, finance, and production. This order is incapable of bringing about social justice or acting ethically. Even those people who benefit most from this disorder are increasingly feeling its limitations, for example, by the sense of enslavement to the very products it produces. Structural economic changes are necessary. These presume moral commitment and conversion. At the same time these structural changes will make this kind of conversion more likely. Hence, there is a mutuality between conversion and structural change. Solidarity of peoples with peoples is a central conception of John Paul's. It was the rich man's refusal of solidarity with Lazarus that landed him in Hades.[42]

The Pope returned to Latin America eighteen months after Puebla, this time to Brazil. His talks there show how his own consciousness was developing in this matter. While the Church does not seek to exacerbate any of the divisions of society or condone violence in bringing about social change and does not identify with the interests of only one part of society, nonetheless the Church wishes to be the Church of the poor, the Pope insisted. When he explains what he means by being poor, it turns out to be more of an evangelical than an economic quality. The poor for John Paul II are those who are merciful and generous and aware that they have received everything they have, such as it is, from God. The poor, furthermore, are those who are open to God and to their neighbors. He associates this openness with the first beatitude—Blessed are the poor in spirit—and proceeds to explain that this beatitude has something different to say to each of the three economic tiers of Brazilian society:

"To those who live in want, it says that they must maintain their human dignity and their openness to others.

To those who are somewhat better off it says: 'do not close yourself off inside yourself. Think of those who are more poor . . . share with them . . . in a systematic way . . .'

To those who are very wealthy, the Church of the poor says: 'Do you not feel remorse of conscience because of your riches and abundance? . . . If you have alot . . . you must give alot . . .

in such a way that it will tend to bring about equality between people, rather than putting a yawning gap between them."[43]

A change took place in the Pope's emphases during his trip in Brazil. In one of the first speeches he seemed to regard change in the structures of society as primarily the responsibility of the wealthy and/or the decision-making elite of society. The poor, on the other hand, he attempted to console.[44] Whether he was advised after this by some of the Brazilian Church's leadership or whether he himself sensed the need, a few days later he told the shanty dwellers at Favela dos Alagados that they must shape their own destiny. "You are the prime authors of your human advancement and the rest of us must offer you unselfish cooperation in order that you may free yourselves from everything that enslaves you . . ."[45]

Since Brazil, John Paul II has, if anything, become more insistent on these themes. One of his most trenchant critiques of the present economic order was delivered during his September 1984 visit to Canada. What was new in this was his use again of the Dives/Lazarus parable to warn "the rich and becoming always richer north that the poor and becoming always poorer south will judge it."[46] The poor, as also the poor nations, "will judge those people who take these goods away from them, amassing to themselves the imperialistic monopoly of economic and political supremacy at the expense of others."[47] Again the aspiration is for solidarity achieved not via class conflict. The vision he has is for a world where "freedom is not an empty word and where the poor man Lazarus can sit down at the same table with the rich man."[48]

The Poor and a Discriminating Faith

The main impediment to the growth of this third mode of obedience is a faith that is *en*culturated. All faith is *in*culturated because it doesn't exist apart from people and people always exist in cultures. Their faith, therefore, comes through some culture and is usually an ingredient of the dominant culture in which believers live. But an enculturated faith is so interwoven with a culture it is not clear to the faithful what the faith is apart from the culture or where the culture stops and the faith starts.[49]

The possible combinations between faith and culture are complex and many. I will cite the three most evident. First, faith can disdain the larger culture within which it finds itself. By doing so it is not thereby cultureless but will try to ignore this larger culture by having its members hew to judgments and a normativity developed elsewhere.[50] These norms and judgments would come, in fact, from an outside culture. Much of Christian missionary history has operated in this manner. Second, faith can attempt to relate to culture as Vatican II prescribed, namely, in a way that is discerning, perfecting, and strengthening of the larger culture. The Good News of Christ "makes fruitful the spiritual qualities and gifts of every people of every age."[51] This is the ideal relationship between faith and culture, one that avoids the two extremes of separation and of identification. And third, faith can accommodate to the culture, subordinate itself to the mores of the culture, and become indistinguishable from many of the mores of the culture in which it is situated. In this state of affairs, faith has been enculturated.[52] The salt has lost its flavor. (Matt. 5:13) When this is the local Church's condition, personal and communal obedience will be problematic because what is heard will be interpreted by a faith that is insufficiently differentiated from the culture. This is all the more destructive when the inauthenticity of the faith is unsuspected or is even defended if it is called into question.

Faith is easily enculturated where there is a naïveté or ignorance in the Church's membership about the ordinary impact on citizens of the economic institutions of the culture in which they live. The economic institutions of a given society enable members of a culture to buy, sell, own, and finance their lives, and so forth. A culture's structures not only organize the life of the culture, they also convey values. To miss their value communication is the surest way of enculturating faith.

The dynamic features of our American economy are profits, the profit motive, the interests, self-interest, competition, economic efficiency—to mention a few of the hallowed devices and formulas by which our economic system functions.[53] That portion of the population and of the Church whose interiority and sense of transcendence are virtually inoperative are certain to reinforce the values that these dynamisms convey. The problem is not with the dynamisms themselves but with their becoming a source of values, a font for defining the worth of our humanity and its agenda. A failure to proceed in the several ways toward self-transcendence mapped out in the previous chapter is a guarantee that people will live uncritically and indiscriminately within our culture. Economically fueled interests engineer citizens into responding to devices, formulas, and stimuli rather than to values. They are induced into confusing wants and needs. Even without intending it, they reinforce, even promote, a mass consumption culture that acts as if we were made for the economy and by the economy. Consumption and life's meaning are confusedly joined together. The result is an economic interpretation of the purpose of human life, not theoretically, of course, but operationally and functionally. A culture whose majority chooses from within an ethos of economism, as John Paul II calls it, heightens the difficulty but adds to the necessity for people of faith to develop a discriminating faith.

A discriminating faith must accept the fact that we live within a context of modernity.[54] Modernity is undoubtedly the phenomenon that has most influenced the cultures of the last four centuries and, hence, the faith through the influenced cultures. Modernity has four structural traits that characterize it. The first of these is technology. The degree of social and environmental change still taking place in modern societies through technology is simply incalculable. We have mentioned mass production; from it there is the telephone, television, the automobile, the airplane, the computer, to name only a few. The technetronic revolution which conflates technology and electronics is overtaking us at present and promises to be even more revolutionary. We are in only its initial stages. The more these technological and technetronic changes revamp our social environment and our ways of doing things, the more they impact our consciousness.[55] The second characteristic of modernity is a pluralism in personal and group identities. This has a positive side to it when contrasted to bygone days when personal values and group identity tended to be much more defined and confined. Interiority and self-appropriation are one of the sources of pluralism. The negative part of this is the confusion, identity-diffusion, and anomie of so many modern people. The third characteristic of modernity is secularization, in particular "the attempt to give rational explanations to natural phenomena as well as the predominance of immanence over transcendence."[56] It has frequently been fashionable for those who become enchanted with this aspect of modernity to have little use for a religious explanation of phenomena since there is evidently such value in a more immanent and scientifically verifiable explanation of phenomena. Secularization, as we have noted, has ambiguous results.

The fourth trait of modernity is the development of economics and economic rationality.[57] The unending efforts to systematically comprehend and effect the world through economics is one of the most humbling glories of moderns. Humbling because economic phenomena are so complex. Economic rationality is a glorious pursuit, as long as it is also modest and accurate about its own scope. It isn't if it purports to give an account of the purpose of human life. It isn't if it denies the evidence from the other three realms of meaning. Theory unchecked by common sense, transcendence, and interiority leads to economism. We are all familiar with Captain Ahab in *Moby Dick* whose means were all rational but whose ends were insane. "To do more efficiently that which should not be done in the first place is no cause for rejoicing."[58]

An enculturated faith is ideological, one that owes its perceptions as much to the economic dynamics of the larger culture within which its adherents live as it does to the actual content of faith, objectively considered in its sources. If this modifying influence were seen for what it was there would be no problem, since authentic faith could outweigh the values and perceptions imparted to it by the culture's economic interests. But since the modification of faith by the economy is not seen, an ideological faith develops. It begins to take its cues from a culture it should be able to critique and confront.

Several things go into making an ideology, one is a consciousness that cannot reflect on itself. Such a consciousness can only focus on objects rather than itself intending those objects. The other is the impact of social location on consciousness.

An ideology is a worldview that is bought into rather than

reasoned out. It is a consciousness and, at the same time, an absence of consciousness. The former because it has definite interests. The latter because it is unaware of the refractions its interests bring to perception. This unawareness becomes obdurate when religion confirms its way of operating. It is also unaware of any disservice it performs or the negative impact it has on others by the pursuit of these interests. It is also a false consciousness because as a lens through which reality is being read it is uncritical of itself because it is unaware of (or unwilling to be made aware of) the extent to which interests have ground the lens.

Every social location mediates interests and interests mediate an ideology.[59] A change in social location, therefore, is the surest way to come to see the refractions that a given group (or individual) has developed and, therefore, conveys however unconsciously. If social location tends to mediate an ideology, then the social location of those who are most marginal to society are also, all things being equal, the least motivated to pursue or maintain the interests of the majority's ideology. They are, therefore, more likely to uncover the ideological rendering that faith has undergone in a given society.

What follows from all of this is that one of the most important subgroups in the Church for assisting it to discern the difference between an enculturated or ideological faith and a discriminating faith is the poor, whether they are voluntarily or involuntarily poor. The reason for this statement is not theological, for example, that the poor are those for whom the Gospel is intended or the poor are those whom God hears. It is sociological. The poor will have benefited least from society's arrangements. Therefore, we can presume that they will be the least likely to see these arrangements as sacrosanct. They should be keenly aware of its rationalizations, its compromises, its indifference. They should be more sensitive to the accommodation of the faith community to the culture than those who are more comfortable in the culture. Therefore, the poor should be in a privileged position to help the Church purify itself and move away from an enculturated faith.

Proof of this contention seems unnecessary since the development of the Church's relationship with the poor as has been articulated especially in the last century is due largely to those who

were poor and tried to be faithful or those who were faithful and
concerned themselves with the poor. These have been certainly
the teachers of the Church. The hierarchy of the Church, the
Popes and the magisterium, in turn have been the teachers of the
rest of the Church.

Three Witnesses

The truth of the above assertions about the role of the poor in
purifying our faith *discrimen* comes through praxis. We will in
this section, therefore, examine three people who together with
the poor with whom they have associated have affected the
Church considerably. They have also exemplified the third mode
of obedience by their own lives since they have elected to be
among the poor.

The first of these is Gustavo Gutierrez, a Peruvian mestizo who
had the opportunity of receiving a first-class theological education
in Europe before he returned to Rimac, a slum of Lima, to minister to its poor. He found that most of his European theology was
irrelevant for the poor to whom he ministered. By contrast, he
found that they were capable of trenchant reflection on their faith.
The theology he had been taught which had been articulated by
those who were in a socially privileged position in society had
little appeal to those who were "the underdogs of history."[60] Consequently he proceeded, like Abraham, to leave the security of his
learned categories to become more of a hearer and learner of
Christian faith as it came to be articulated by the underdogs.
Gutierrez furnished them with a process of reflection which was
not wholly originally his but one that specified features of the
conscientization process whose main proponent was the Brazilian
educator, Paolo Freire.

There are two moments that complement each other in the
Gutierrez/Freire process. The first is action undertaken by the
poor because of their situation. It is a commitment, a struggle
against their wretchedness. The second is a critical reflection on
their actions in the light of the Word of God. Both of these actions

are attempts to attain to a degree of human dignity in a society that denies their personhood or treats them as nonpersons. The reflection process takes place within communities of like-minded and similarly situated peoples, those who are politically and economically on the outskirts of their societies.

In the course of their action/reflection process a number of previously held perceptions fall away, and new ones take their places. First of all the complex fecundity of the Scriptures begin to reveal a pattern. God's action from the beginning seems to be consistent in bringing those who are oppressed into freedom through trust in Him. Second, the image of Jesus begins to change; he looks more and more like a new Moses who was himself in a mortal conflict with the authorities and powers that sought alternately to ignore, corrupt, and destroy him. Considerable social energy develops out of this combination of a God who is concerned with their situation plus a Christ whose plight was redolent of theirs. Thus they develop a warrant for remaking their own history with the help of God and Christ. Third, the locus for expressing their faith is their own political and economic circumstances. This faith does not have as its bottom line merely interior changes. Spiritual growth is not only measured by union with God or greater trust in Him. As these develop the poor must also attempt to change their social conditions. They aspire to nothing short of the transformation of society.[61]

Gutierrez observed that while the poor's (and his) previous notions of faith had allowed society to remain as it was, their new process was socially and politically sub-versive. They had accepted others' theologies, social analyses, or reading of their history with an interpretation that came from the top down; hence it was socially and politically super-versive. Super-versives were those who made and reinforced the status quo. In contrast, "we shall not have a great leap forward into a whole new theological perspective until the marginalized and exploited have begun to become the artisans of their own liberation—until their voice makes itself heard directly."[62] This is subversive activity both societally and theologically.

Not satisfied that this approach is valid only for poor people, Gutierrez is convinced that Peru's poor as also other poor are the bellwether of a new moment and stance for the whole people of God. "The great wrong is to become—or, perhaps to continue to be—a super-versive, a bulwark and support of the prevailing domination, someone whose orientation to history begins with the great ones of this world. But a subversive history is the locus of a new faith experience, a new spirituality and a new proclamation of the Gospel."[63]

The final and most difficult change of perception is an ecclesiological one. Gutierrez sees the Church as it is presently constituted being called away from its immersion in the dominant cultures of the first world of the northern hemisphere. He articulates "an ecclesiology whose point of departure is Christ calling out to us from the midst of the oppressed."[64] These are the ones whom the rest of the Body of Christ must hear. "The Lord speaks to us from among those on the bottom, on the underside of history."[65] The Church which hears the Lord speaking to it from these peoples is called "to descend into the hell of this world, into communion with the misery, injustice, struggles and hopes of the wretched of the earth—for of such is the kingdom of heaven."[66] He calls this a process of being reborn, except in this moment in history we are to be reborn "from below" which means, in effect, to die to every shred of complicity with oppression.[67] Gutierrez sums up the effect the poor have had on him when he observes, "One gradually comes to see that what is ultimately important is not that the Church be poor but that the poor of this world be the people of God."[68] He will not be content till the Church en masse goes back to the very beginning when the poor had the Gospel preached to them, when being poor was the condition that made it possible to accept the Gospel.

The Puebla Conference is a good example of the influence of this line of reflection based on experience. It begins to ground the teaching of the Church in Latin America. Puebla noted that "the witness of a poor Church can evangelize the rich whose hearts are attached to wealth, thus converting and freeing them from this bondage and their own egotism."[69]

At the same time, a wider discernment process is going on. For example, the Sacred Congregation for the Doctrine of the Faith in September of 1984 and Pope John Paul II in October of 1984 voiced fears that some of the sentiments of liberation theologians had become too radical.[70] The Vatican's concern was with the tendency to make an ideology out of the option for the poor, so that in the name of faith, a discrimen would be articulated which was itself beyond critique based on its experience, while it was capable of critiquing the rest of the Church.[71] Their fears are not without some basis if the experience of the poor and their struggle are taken as the only criteria for judging authentic faith. If "theological criteria for truth are subordinated to the imperatives of the class struggle,"[72] then the questions of theologians and the magisterium can be dismissed as coming from the oppressor class whose theology or argumentation is taken to be merely a reflection of hidden class interests.[73] Unhappily the option for the poor is then reduced to an option for class conflict in this turn of events.

This reduction would be avoided if one were to extend obedience in the other two directions examined in this chapter, namely, to brethrenomics and equipoise. Notwithstanding the danger of such reductionism, the light that comes to the whole Church from processes and directions forged by a Gutierrez et al. is highly beneficial in enabling not only Latin American Catholicism but the rest of the Church to come to see how much of modern economic culture has adversely affected her collective discrimen. The wattage from this light will increase in proportion to the fidelity of people and groups to an obediential hearing of God through the poor. It will decrease insofar as the poor and their facilitators among the theologians try to reduce obedience to merely a political option.

More modeling of this third mode of obedience is necessary to prove that being poor places one in a privileged position with God. If that evidence were to come from our own culture and from those who obeyed this way without ideology, it would be even more credible. There are such models. The one who immediately comes to mind who has embodied this kind of obedience is Dorothy Day. She came to the point in her life when she was sure that "poverty is my vocation, to live as simply and poorly as I can, and never to cease talking and writing of poverty and destitution."[74] She arrived at this only slowly, by very small steps. "What we avert our eyes from today can be borne tomorrow when we have learned a little more about love. Nurses know this, and so do mothers."[75] Since she found the destitution of the poor repugnant, she only gradually came to accept her vocation to be one with the poor. Even so, toward the end of her life she observed of herself and those who had joined her that "we are always foreigners to the poor. So we have to make up for it by renouncing all compensations."[76]

The noted historian of American Catholicism, Dr. David O'Brien, has referred to Dorothy Day as "the most significant, interesting and influential person in the history of American Catholicism."[77] Monsignor George Higgins is no less enthusiastic, describing her as "a true sign of how God is speaking to us today."[78] More by her life than by her words, but ultimately by both, she led many to be effectively concerned about the poor and to go beyond organizing for them by putting their own people and resources at their disposal. "One must live with them, share with them, their suffering too. Give up one's privacy, and mental and spiritual comforts as well as physical."[79] This was a radical call, one she could issue only because she herself responded to it for fifty years of her life as the founder and inspiration of the Catholic Worker Movement, a movement that is still vigorous today with approximately eighty houses of hospitality in the United States, each of them attempting to embody her ideals.[80]

Three catalytic events seem singularly important for understanding how Dorothy Day came to see her Christian vocation specified by the ideal of voluntary poverty. The first was her socialist past, the second the hunger march of 1932, and the third was the entrance into her life of an eccentric Frenchman.

The first of these, more a period than an event, extended from 1916–28. At the age of nineteen with only two years of college completed she began her lifelong avocation as a writer. She began as a reporter for a socialist paper and then became a journalist for two other radical papers. Her two passions in this socialist period of her life were the poor and women's suffrage.[81]

The second of these catalytic events was the hunger march held on December 8, 1932, in Washington, D.C. She had become a Roman Catholic in 1928, but she had been unable to integrate her previous passion for the poor with her newly embraced faith. This hunger march which had thousands of poor and unemployed converge on the seat of government painfully reminded her of this and fired her with the desire to get these two parts of herself together. She later described the event.

> As I stood on the curb and watched them, joy and pride in the courage of this band of men and women mounting in my heart, and with it a bitterness too that since I was now a Catholic, with fundamental philosophical differences, I could not be out there with them. I could write, I could protest, to arouse the conscience, but where was the Catholic leadership in the gathering of bands of men and women together, for the actual works of mercy that the comrades had always made part of their technique in reaching the workers?[82]

She was sure the distances between her faith and these comrades must be bridgeable. What she was not sure about was what to do to bring these two parts of herself together—not only of herself, of course, but of the Church and society itself.

> When the demonstration was over and I had finished writing my story, I went to the national shrine at the Catholic University on the feast of the Immaculate Conception. There I offered up a special prayer, a prayer which came with tears and with anguish, that some way would open up for me to use what talents I possessed for my fellow workers, for the poor.[83]

Her prayer was answered within one day. The answer brings us to the third catalyst, Peter Maurin (1877–1949). He had wandered around for years putting his ideas into practice personally while developing even more radical ideas from his radical practice. His ideas were either derived from or corroborated by the two social encyclicals, 1891 *Rerum Novarum* and 1931 *Quadragesimo Anno.* He profoundly personalized the abstract panorama they presented and reduced them to concrete programs. Try as he might he could get no one in the religious community or from the members of the hierarchy he approached to accept his version of the kind of relationship Catholic Christianity should take toward the poor. As a result he began to preach or, as he would prefer to describe his role, "agitate" before the unemployed and the radicals at Union Square and Columbus Circle in New York City. He had realized for a long time that he needed someone to help him bring his vision to realization. He found that companion in Dorothy Day, who was twenty years his junior. He was waiting for her when she returned from the hunger march in Washington. Every day for the next four months he would knock on her apartment door at three in the afternoon and talk to her till as late as eleven at night "until, exhausted from it all, she would turn him out."[84] He was the unexpected answer to her prayers as she was to his. He had a plan and a call. She had call and a need. Together they would change the lives of many both materially and religiously. American Catholicism still has a lot to learn from these two figures about its relationship to the American economic system.

The first lesson, it seems to me, on the relationship between a Christian's faith and the economic system is that one must jump in with actions as they did in order for the logic of the faith to shed its light in this area. One sees only as far as one does. Take the few economic processes Maurin had some discretion over as an example of this. He noticed the impoverished kind of relationships there were at a luncheonette situated under a railroad viaduct where he frequently ate his meals in his vagabond days.[85] It was a place to which neighborhood down-and-outers would repair to warm themselves over a cup of coffee. He decided he would nail a little box on the wall of the luncheonette. Over the box he wrote, "If you have money to give, put it in, and if you need money, take it out. Nobody will know." His experiment worked at least for a while until one day twenty-five dollars disappeared. Several anxious weeks went by before it reappeared with a grateful note attached saying that it had been urgently needed for bus fare. Maurin rejoiced that his trust in people had been thereby vindicated.[86]

His insight grew apace of his actions. Soon after meeting Dorothy he developed a scheme comprised of three programs which, as he saw it, had to be launched on a large scale in order for the Church to be faithful to her mission to society and bring about a new social order. These programs were first of all sessions of value clarification, second, hospitality houses, and third, "agronomic universities."[87] All of these needed to be created from scratch. The rationale behind each of these appeared over time in their new newspaper, the *Catholic Worker*. It is still being published since its first issue appeared May 1, 1933.

The first of the proposed programs, called roundtables, began in June of 1933. They were convoked to discuss and clarify social issues. Maurin was eager to have all segments of society represented at these, especially scholars and laborers. The former could help "the untrained minds of the laborers from becoming superficial" and the latter could help the scholars' "trained minds from becoming academic."[88] With a deep Catholic instinct for reconciling classes he distrusted ideas or actions that would exacerbate the divisions or fragmentations already in society, whereas he trusted whatever gave promise of adding to whatever solidarity society could achieve.

The second part of his social vision, hospices, began the same year. He thought of these as serving both the poor who needed food and lodging and those who served them who needed to be with the poor since they were other Christs in Peter Maurin's and Dorothy Day's eyes.[89] In the third issue of the *Catholic Worker* (which Maurin wanted to be called *Catholic Radical* "because he was more interested in deep-seated social transformation than in addressing only one group of people such as the laboring class"[90]) he published an open letter to the Catholic hierarchy of the United States which suggested that houses of hospitality be established in every parish and with this as a stimulus, that rooms for hospitality be made available in every home. Urging a personalization of hospitality, he felt that Christianity had been derelict by allowing hospitality to be institutionalized or municipalized. He lamented its many forms that came from taxes rather than from hearts. He also saw these houses of hospitality as places where bishops and people could meet, where religious instruction, vocational training, and the education of the clergy could be imparted.[91]

At the center of his thought about social transformation was voluntary poverty. His ideal in this was St. Francis of Assisi. He grew to cherish several books as well as five papal writings on the subject of St. Francis of Assisi that were issued from 1882 through 1926 by three popes. He used the personal religious emphases he found in these sources to complement the institutional and analytical emphases of the Social Encyclicals to keep whole what would otherwise have never come together. What kept these two worlds together for Maurin and, as he hoped, many others was voluntary poverty. It was an ideal he only gradually discovered. By 1934 he had given up everything he could call his own. Voluntary poverty was an ideal he saw individuals and communities called to.[92]

His pithy verse about this reads:

> St. Francis thought
> that to choose to be poor
> is just as good
> as if one should marry
> the most beautiful girl in the world.
> We seem to think
> that poor people
> are social nuisances
> and not the Ambassadors of God.
> We seem to think
> that Lady Poverty
> is an ugly girl
> and not the beautiful girl
> that St. Francis of Assisi
> says she is.
> And because we think so,
> we refuse to feed the poor
> with our superfluous goods—
> What we give to the poor
> for Christ's sake
> is what we carry with us
> when we die.
> Pagan Greeks used to say
> that the poor
> "are the ambassadors
> of the gods."

> To become poor
> is to become
> an Ambassador of God.

His written words are so quaint it is easy to miss the depth of the reflection behind them. The form they took is due in part to his desire to make them understandable to unlettered derelicts who had been the only ones who listened to him before he met Dorothy. They are deceptively simple, however, the way Gospel is simple. His reflections, furthermore, were continually being fed by what he read. He read hundreds of books by the most sophisticated authors of his day, on matters of philosophy, economics, history, and social commentary which he synopsized and critiqued for his friend Dorothy and the workers with whom he lived.

He called their program a communitarian revolution. He distrusted social change that did not evoke personal responses to people. His starting point is the diametrical opposite of class conflict.

> The Communitarian revolution
> is basically
> a personal revolution.
> It starts with I,
> not with They.
> One I plus one I
> makes two I's
> and two I's make We.
> We is a community,
> While "they" is a crowd."[93]

Accepting the dictates of their economic culture kept Americans from undergoing this kind of conversion and resisting the needed communitarian revolution, as Maurin saw it. At the heart of the culture was the growth ethic, the endless attempt to be better off.

> The world would be better off
> if people tried to become better.
> And people would become better

if they stopped trying to become better off.
For when everybody tries to become
better off,
nobody is better off.
But when everybody tries to become better,
everybody is better off.
Everybody would be rich
If nobody tried to become richer.
And nobody would be poor
if everybody tried to be the poorest.
And everybody would be what they ought
to be
if everybody tried to be
what he wants the other fellow to be.[94]

He refused to accept the choices modern societies were given as
simply between capitalism and communism. Taking a bit from
each of these he promoted a third possibility.

Christianity has
a capitalism of its own
and a communism of its own.
Modern capitalism
is based on property without responsibility,
while Christian capitalism
is based on property with responsibility.
Modern Communism
is based on poverty through force
while Christian communism
is based on poverty through choice.
For a Christian,
voluntary poverty is the ideal
as exemplified by St. Francis of Assisi,
while private property
is not an absolute right, but a gift
which as such can not be wasted,
but must be administered
for the benefit of God's children.[95]

"Lady Poverty," which was embraced out of love for God who called individuals and communities to it, furnished society with examples of the shape of its own eschatological future when community would win out over the desire for personal security in the form of possessions and the pursuit of self-interest. Maurin anticipated twentieth-century theologies both the political and liberation varieties by his insistence on praxis and on the role of personal faith in the transformation of society. Probably more important, however, is his insight into the mediating role of voluntary poverty in integrating personal conversion and structural change.

Dorothy spent the rest of her life, after meeting Peter Maurin, both practicing and reflecting on this Lady she had definitively embraced through the ministry of this man. She does not romanticize poverty and is careful to distinguish between inflicted poverty, which she calls destitution, and voluntary poverty, the mystery of which was not simple to her. She condemned the first kind of poverty and advocated the second. She gradually lost her life fighting the first kind of poverty. She gained the attention of the world and, we can safely presume, a high degree of holiness by embracing the second kind of poverty. She mused how most religious communities that had begun in poverty paradoxically soon began to "thrive" after their initial simplicity, thus making it difficult to continue in poverty.[96] Precarity or precariousness was an essential element for retaining the ideal, she noted, but constantly having to await the "miracle of increase" by living in that way never became easy for her or her compatriots.[97] Neither her own nor Maurin's poverty was "an end in itself. It was a means to an end, a way of sharing with others."[98] She and Maurin fully shared in the vulnerability of the poor by becoming one with their lot. The effect of this shared vulnerability was community. Their poverty was a way of expressing their love; it was a way of being with Christ both by feeding the hungry and by having their own hunger fed through them and one another.

She had both a problem with the Catholic church and at the same time a profound love of the Church. Part of her dissatisfaction was due to the attitude of too many of the clergy toward the poor.

> The scandal of business-like priests, of collective wealth, the lack of a sense of responsibility for the poor, the worker, the Negro, the Mexican, the Filipino, and even the oppression of these, and the consenting to the oppression of them by our industrialist capitalist order—these made me feel often that priests were more like Cain than Abel. "Am I my brother's keeper," they seemed to say in respect to the social order. There was plenty of charity, but too little justice.[99]

She hoped that the training of future priests would involve their exposure to poverty so that they might "be haunted by the sufferings of the world."[100] To be prophetic in their ministry they will have to be seen to be "standing in poverty near God and proclaiming God's judgment on human indifference. To convert the poor you must be like them; to convert the rich you must be unlike them."[101]

She expressed this mystery of voluntary poverty in the starkest of terms in her *On Pilgrimage: The Sixties:*

> The mystery of the poor is this, that they are Jesus, and what you do for them you do for him. This is the only way we have of knowing and believing in our love. The mystery of poverty is that by sharing in it, making ourselves poorer by giving to others, we increase our knowledge of and belief in love.[102]

In a word, Jesus and love were poverty's only "explanation" for her. Duty or good deeds or humanity or religious experience was not a sufficient reason for voluntary poverty. "For a total Christian, the goal of duty is not needed—always prodding one to perform this or that good deed. It is not a duty to help Christ, it is a privilege." The poor are cared for: "Not for the sake of humanity. Not because it might be Christ who stays with us, comes to see us, takes up our time. Not because these people remind us of Christ, but because they are Christ."[103] According to the 1984 U.S. Census data, the number of poor in the United States is 33.7 million. This exceeds the number in 1965, the year in which President Johnson declared war on poverty.[104]

❖❖

CHAPTER VI

Discipleship and Today's Economy

The preceding chapter leaves many loose ends. This chapter will attempt to bring them together and deepen them. We will do so by concentrating on a profound twentieth-century understanding of obediential hearing, namely, that of Dietrich Bonhoeffer. His own life makes his words all the more convincing. His understanding of obediential hearing began to be known by others with the publication of the *Cost of Discipleship* in 1937. It opens up with a now famous lamentation that believes the whole Christian world has cheapened the meaning of the grace within which we are to live in Christ. The cheapening has been done by preaching and living a Christianity that is not discipleship, by which he means living in a relationship of personal obedience to Christ and to his personally extended call.

His words are still eloquent. "Cheap grace is grace without discipleship, grace without the cross, grace without Jesus Christ, living and incarnate."[1] The churches proclaim our salvation because of the grace Christ won for us but they have cheapened his act by making it into a "doctrine, a principle, a system."[2] The churches preach forgiveness of sins, furthermore, but in such a way that "the world finds a cheap covering for its sins [since] no contrition is required, still less any real desire to be delivered from

its sins."[3] By contrast, costly grace "confronts us with the gra-
cious call to follow Jesus; it comes as a word of forgiveness to the
broken spirit and the contrite heart."[4] Costly grace is treasure
hidden in the field for the sake of which a man will gladly go and
sell all he has. It is costly "because it costs a person his or her life;
it is a grace because it gives a person the only true life . . . it is
costly because it cost God the life of his Son."[5]

The cheapening of grace must be detected and detested since it
is discipleship's greatest enemy. It is such a shrewd counterfeit to
the Gospel that it draws those who have begun in discipleship off
that narrow road. Its central tenet is that salvation has already
been accomplished by the grace of God won for us by Christ.
While this is true as far as it goes, its truth becomes operative only
if it is responded to by an obediential hearing and following of the
one who saves his disciples.

The error undergirding the attraction of so many who claim to
believe in Christ Jesus yet give no evidence of being obediential
hearers of the living word lies in the widespread acceptance of a
separation of belief in Jesus from obedience to him. The two must
be kept together. "Only he who is obedient believes" is just as
certain a proposition, he insists, as "only he who believes is obedient."[6] Faith is authentic and real only "in the act of obedience."[7]
This obedience is not conformity to norms but to the ongoing,
concrete call issued by Christ to individuals who follow him. For
Bonhoeffer, this following entails a leaving of one's securities for a
new situation in which Christ is our security. It involves taking
concrete steps away from and beyond one's situation only to find
oneself in a new situation of discipleship. Only in this new situation is faith possible. The call of Jesus evokes and creates the
obedience that makes the step possible and the situation new.

Bonhoeffer disparages a Christianity that claims to believe
while persisting in hearing no word to obey or no call to follow.
For those in this condition, he argued, "the step of obedience must
be taken before faith becomes possible."[8] Again this is because
"only the obedient believe. If we are to believe, we must obey a
concrete command . . . Everything depends on this first step."[9]
As a result of this first stepping forth one begins to be a disciple.

This first step is only possible because Christ has called the

person forth first of all to baptism, which is essentially passive, as
he would see it. One *suffers* the call of Christ.[10] Before there was a
baptismal step there was a history. This history had Christ invade
the realm of Satan, lay hands on his own who were in that realm,
and create for himself a Church out of those he snatched from
that realm. As a result of this rescue "we are deprived of our
direct relationship with all the God-given realities of life. Christ
the Mediator has stepped in between us and them. [The baptized's] relationship with the world is now mediated through
him."[11] As a result, there can be an exclusive attachment to his
person or as Bonhoeffer calls it, a "bondage to the person of
Christ," because of Jesus' act of rescuing his own.

Interceptors and the Mediator

The reflections Bonhoeffer makes on the up-close activity of the
Spirit that generates obedience in the disciple are quite sensitive.
The words immediacy and mediator are central to these reflections. The first stage in the process of receiving costly grace is one
of deliverance from "immediacy with the world" so that Christ
would bring us "into immediacy with himself."[12] Christ interposes
himself between us and everything in our natural life not because
he condemns that which, in fact, his hands have made but in
order that he might be the mediator to us of all that we use in this
world and all to whom we would relate in it.

The Incarnation is foundational to his being the Immediate One
whose activity in us is that of Mediator. "By virtue of his Incarnation he has come between persons and their natural life. There can
be no turning back, for Christ bars the way. He wants to be the
centre; through him alone all things shall come to pass."[13] This is
both an existential description of what happens to individuals
whom Christ calls and it is at the same time a Christological
assertion. "Since his coming persons have no immediate relationship of their own anymore to anything, neither to God nor to the
world; Christ wants to be the mediator."[14] The first thing would-
be disciples must do, therefore, is to recognize and accept this

gulf. They must also "hate" anything that purports to be immediate. This goes for things as well as human relationships. "We are separated from one another by the unbridgeable gulf of otherness and strangeness which resists all our attempts to overcome it by means of natural association or emotional or spiritual union . . . Christ stands between us, and we can only get in touch with our neighbors through him."[15]

What is at stake here is one's sense of reality and its relationship to Christ. Bonhoeffer is naming his own experiences of reality and faith with these very strong contentions. One must have recourse to one's experience and sense of faith to confirm or deny them. If we can't confirm them now, we will, he believes, when we hear the call of Jesus. Only then will we see how illusory our prior sense of reality was.

When the call of Christ is heard and obeyed people "become individuals." The call is extended to those who are part of a crowd and they only begin to realize their individuality when they follow it and him. Only then will they see the two ways they have developed to protect themselves from the call and kept themselves in a superficial and inauthentic identity. These two ways are "by merging themselves in the society of their fellows and in their material environment."[16] As a result of obedience Christ becomes immediate to the disciple and the Mediator of all he or she has and needs. He is now the experienced center of all reality which he was but was not known to be. Through him all things are new.

While he isolates all in order to win them and create obedience in them, he does so in order to unite them with the world and their brothers and sisters. "Though we all have to enter upon discipleship alone, we do not remain alone. If we take him at his word and dare to become individuals, our reward is the fellowship of the Church."[17] The experience of Church is to be the beginning of the hundredfold for those who have left all. In this period he calls the Church "the People of the Mediator" who having "left house, brothers, sisters, mother, father, children or land for my sake and for the sake of the gospel" are to receive a hundred times as many homes, and so forth. (Mark 10:29–30)

All of his assertions about individuality, Christ, immediacy, Mediator, and the Church as hundredfold correspond with the personal, social, and political circumstances in which Bonhoeffer found himself.[18] His *Cost of Discipleship*, like all of his theology, is more of a witness to God's actions in him and others, insofar as he understood these, than it is a theological text.

It is surprising what Bonhoeffer considers problematic for moving from a condition of cheap to costly grace. "Reason and conscience, responsibility and piety, law and scriptural authority" are problematic.[19] Not in themselves, of course, but depending on how they are used, they are all capable of interposing themselves between the call or the word addressed to the heart and the response of obedience to it. He sees these factors, for example, operating in the rich young man, and in others Jesus called to follow him. As with him, so with us we can delay the response by rationalizing a nonresponse along these lines: "detachment from possessions is not as important as detachment of heart, therefore keep your possessions but detach your heart from them; keep your goods, having them as if you had them not; faith is what is crucial not whether you have possessions or not."[20] While all of these points are true in the abstract they are only true existentially for those who are obedient. Without this they become sophistries used to withhold the obedience of the heart. They are excuses for remaining in a cheap-grace relationship to God. Their truth is valid for disciples, for those who have stepped away from their possessions out of obedience to Christ. They become excuses for nondisciples to remain at a distance while using the understandings articulated by disciples to justify their rationalizations.

His understandings about obedience after 1937 are as important as his articulations before then. His animus against cheap grace in the thirties became an animus against religion in the forties. He excoriates religion as he calls for and is called to a deeper faith. What sums up religion for him is unreality. This is usually entered into by dealing with only part of reality. Conversely, faith deals with reality, all of it, as it is.[21] Faith degenerates into religion whenever the faithful flee from reality in one of two directions. The most frequent escape route is from the concrete, everyday world to "the realm of God." It doesn't work. "He who runs away from the world to find God only finds himself."[22] The other escape is taken by religious secularists whose erroneous piety has them "replace the eschatological cause of God on earth with their own cause of moral and religious progress."[23] To both of these fugitives Bonhoeffer says: "He who loves God loves him as Lord of the earth, such as it is. He who loves the earth loves it as God's earth. He who loves the Kingdom of God loves it . . . as the Kingdom of God on earth."[24]

The escape from reality to God and, therefore, the whole of reality usually results in much baggage such as ideals, ideas, abstractions, programs, ideologies. These are the stuff of religion. A fall from obediential hearing into religion is a new acceptance of the snake's proposal to Adam and Eve. Before the fall they were in touch with reality but after the fall they refer everything to themselves; they put themselves at the center of reality. They are in the place where God belongs with the result that God and others are their creatures.[25] It should be obvious how Bonhoeffer's way of understanding faith is highly pertinent to our use of material goods and financial resources. It gives these an obediential frame of reference within which these matters can be discerned.

Word as Address

Bonhoeffer's thought is rich and provocative. But there is an irony about studying it in that, as he would be the first to warn the reader, all of his ideas, like all theological ideas, will be misused if they divert one from the only valid starting point of Christianity, which is not ideas but the call or address of people by God in Christ. The word of address is seen by Bonhoeffer not as a once-and-for-all event but as an ongoing repeated occurrence. There is both the belief and the experience that a personal and direct encounter can occur between the one addressed and God in Christ. In lieu of this address there must be a waiting. Otherwise it is easy to mistake an engagement with ideas about God or Christ or with objectifying thought-forms from religion or theology for an encounter. He contrasts word as address and word as idea. One can rest in the idea but "address gives birth to response and responsibility."[26]

Theology and theological ideas will be valuable only if they do justice to this foundational encounter. Theology as a trove of ideas is misused and misleading if it does not lead to or assist those who seek to reflect on their experience of encounter. Theology is the servant of such reflection. "Only because Christ is present can we make him an object of inquiry."[27]

Several things are possible as a result of the encounter. First of all the person encountered by the word of address is not in a vacuum but has a series of concerns. The encounter is not an invitation to deny or neglect one's human reality as it is represented by these concerns but to surrender the concerns to the One heard. In van Beeck's Christology, inclusion and obedience are two of the components of this surrender. If these human concerns, for example, for one's material needs or financial security are part of the surrender, they will begin to look different to the one surrendering them. They can even turn into discernments of Christ while retaining their footing in the everyday world of human beings. They will, however, now be under Christ. He must take their measure, not they the measure of him. "His presidency must remain the yardstick of the concerns and of the discernments that represent the concerns."[28]

The Christology that is at the core of this volume, van Beeck's, was inspired in part by Bonhoeffer. Since van Beeck has extended Bonhoeffer's analysis beyond where the latter took it, a brief excursus on van Beeck's insights is helpful here. He contends that Christological discernments will have two reality referents, the one being Christ and the other the human concerns operating in the person addressed by Christ. Christological discernments "are attempts at cognitive structuring in the interest of being articulate about who and what Jesus Christ is . . . . Each discernment must be viewed in the context of such concerns and attitudes if their true meaning is to be realized."[29] These discernments will or should mature into titles of Christ. Since they retain their two referents, such discernments will develop metaphors to become titles of Christ.[30] For example, if the concern is about hunger, he can be "bread"; (John 6:35) if hostilities, he will be "the peace"; (Eph. 2:14) if death, he is "the resurrection and the life." (John 11:25) NAB The grist for the theological reflection and, in turn, for the Christological naming will come from actual human concerns as they are handled in faith and obedience by believers. Christology must not grow apart from these reality referents.

In the light of these contentions, it is interesting to observe the number of places in the New Testament that have a double referent, one to Christ and the Gospel he proclaimed, the other to material goods and financial resources. These texts hint at the depth and breadth of the obediential hearing going on in the first communities. To cite only a few of these:

"His son whom he appointed heir of all things." (Heb. 1:2)

"Guided by the Spirit of God . . . we are children then we are heirs, heirs of God and joint heirs with Christ." (Rom. 8:14–17)

"My God will fulfill all your needs out of the riches of his glory in Christ Jesus." (Phil. 4:19)

"But what were once my assets I now through Christ Jesus count as losses." (Phil. 3:7)

"Life to me, of course, is Christ, but then death would be a positive gain." (Phil. 1:21)

"This hoard of yours, whose will it be then? . . . [grow] rich in the sight of God." (Luke 12:20–21)

"He has filled the starving with good things, sent the rich away empty." (Luke 1:53)

"The kingdom of Heaven is like treasure hidden in a field . . . one [pearl] of great value." (Matt. 13:44–46)

"Although he was rich, he became poor for your sake, so that you should become rich through his poverty." (2 Cor. 8:9)

"With Christ [God] . . . raised us up . . . to show for all ages to come . . . how extraordinarily rich he is in grace." (Eph. 2:6–7)

"I have been made the servant of that gospel by a gift of grace from God . . . proclaiming to the Gentiles the unfathomable treasure of Christ." (Eph. 3:7–8)

These are Christological discernments that bear witness to the fidelity of the first Christians to the action of the Spirit operating in them.[31] By these acts of inclusion they brought their human concerns about security, the future, material resources, and financial needs and firmly lodged them in Christ. There is then a double fidelity here; one to their own needs in this world, the

other to Christ himself. The placing of "all things under his feet,"
(1 Cor. 15:27) therefore, or the making of all things subject to
Christ, is not a miraculous, end-time, once-and-for-all project of
the One who is to come. It is as much our project as Christ's, a
responsibility exercised by the everyday activities of inclusion and
obedience. These are the ways available to us to "abolish every
principality, every ruling force and power" (1 Cor. 15:24) we have
any connections with, thus enabling Christ to hand over the Kingdom to his Father "so that God may be all in all." (1 Cor. 15:28)[32]
Jesus assumes a sovereignty "not when the present invokes its
demand before Christ, but when the present stands before the
demand of Christ."[33]

One should be able to appreciate, therefore, the invaluable character of human concerns. First, they are the stuff of Christology,
the very matter that can keep Christology healthy. Second, they
are what grounds the reign of Christ in the world. Third, these
ongoing concerns named in terms of Christ carry to subsequent
generations evidence of the fidelity of present and past generations. Fourth, the very weight of human concerns can make the
word as address more sought for. He comes to those who labor
and are heavy burdened. Therefore, rather than looking on our
everyday worries and problems as inevitably counterproductive or
as unfortunate distractions, human concerns can be occasions for
the growing reign of Christ in the world as well as occasions for
the encounter of people by God in Christ. It should be obvious,
therefore, that the encounters we are referring to here are seldom
if ever mystical. They are more likely to occur because of the
sheer weight of life than because of a facility at prayer. The
heavier the concerns the greater the need to find a way to carry
them. This is why "the poor" is such an important category in the
Christian experience, as we saw in the last chapter.

Both Bonhoeffer and van Beeck have noted the impact on the
personal identity of those who experience and appropriate these
words as address. "True identity is not an achievement; it is a gift
resulting from the encounter with God . . . [which results in] a
responsive identity."[34] Therefore, "it is not in self-reflection but in
his active relationship to God that a person understands himself."[35] Therefore, a deeper identity appropriation accompanies

these Christological discernments. Encounter places one in the truth of himself or herself. The discernments serve to locate one in Christ and Christ in the world at the same time. While this value to the individual person is being noted, let us not overlook the value to others of such fidelity, and theirs to us. What is being created in this whole process of naming Christ through and in terms of our concerns is an alternative way of being in the world, another way of seeing the world in terms of Christ. This is "how Christ takes form in the world."

Bonhoeffer's further elaborations on the subject of obedience, written from 1939 till his death in 1944, deepen his reflections on the role of ethics and norms in obeying Christ and finally on the form Christ takes in the world through the obedience of his disciples.

Obedience 1939–44

Ethics, Bonhoeffer's major theological work, written in notes and first drafts from 1939 to 1944 and never completed, is primarily concerned with the union of God and the world in Christ through the obedience of Christ's disciples.[36] What is to be obeyed by the disciple is the word of address, or as he prefers in this volume, "the commandments of God."[37] Bonhoeffer's "commandment of God" category as well as his word-as-address describes my understanding of what the heart obeys. Although these commandments of God are in continuity with the Ten Commandments, they are different because they are personal, concrete, and specific. Since they are communicated to people, furthermore, one does not relate to a "commandment of God" the way one relates to ethical principles or even to the Ten Commandments. In these latter instances one has to "deduce the definite from the indefinite, the application from the principle, the temporal from the timeless."[38] By contrast, "God's commandment is the concrete speech of God to concrete men . . . leaving no room for application or interpretation. It leaves room only for obedience or disobedience. God's commandment can only be heard in a local and temporal context. If God's commandment is not clear, definite and concrete to the last detail, then it is not God's commandment."[39]

The reader has to ask how his or her experience fits in with these descriptions. Certainly the experience of Bonhoeffer is the explanation of his line of thought. Only a life of union with God, and actions submitted to the prompting heard in his heart had him concoct such a category. His experience enabled him to both personalize and/or Christologize the ethical. He did not see the "commandment of God" as a specification of the ethical. He insisted that it is the other way around. Ethical principles and moral laws must be understood in the light of these.[40] It is not the law or the principle or even the Ten Commandments that comes first in the experience of the disciples, rather it is this "commandment of God that is the original factor, with its concrete contents and with the liberty it makes possible; from its own resources it fixes the boundaries and creates the spaces within which it [the ethical] can be heard and understood . . . The law is comprised within the commandment; it arises from it; and it must be understood by reference to it."[41]

These "commandments of God" are issued to people not out of the blue but through the structures of the world. Another way of saying this is that these "commandments" come through what he calls the mandates.[42] These mandates are four different structures in reality that make demands on Christ's disciples. These structures are labor, marriage, government, and Church. The commandments of God come from these structures to the disciples who are immersed in some or all of them. Since Christ is already present in these four structures the demands made on disciples by these structures are also the most frequent source of "the commandments of God" that Christ would have his disciples obey.[43] Their obedience hears reality through Christ's presence in these structures. The commandments, therefore, are not issued in a mystical manner but come through these worldly structures.

A comment is called for here about the meaning of "worldly" in Bonhoeffer. One of the most frequent mistakes made by his readers is to impress their notions of secularization on his frequently used term "worldliness." For him God is worldly. Faith is worldly. Religion is other-worldly. "Worldliness is the characteristic of the God of the Bible."[44] Christianity is worldly because in Christ, God and the world are one. Worldliness and reality are virtually synonymous in his writings. What makes reality reality is Christ. What makes the world palatable is Christ. It is the world that grounds our obedience. It is from the everyday reality that impinges itself on the would-be disciple, especially family life, work life, the civil structures, and one's church that the stuff of obedience comes.[45] Certainly it seems that most if not all of our use of material and financial resources are related to these structures.

A subsequent description in the *Ethics* to formulate the context of the disciple's obedience is as compelling as that of the mandates. Bonhoeffer saw obedience to Christ coming through "the structures of responsible life," two of which are particularly worth noting. There is first of all "correspondence with reality."[46] One's obedience to Christ must be in touch with the givens of the situation. To be in Christ means to participate in the reality of the world. To follow Christ in obedience brings one into the center of everyday life and the worldliness of the world.

Bonhoeffer's emphasis sets the would-be disciple free so that things, situations, and people are able to bespeak their own reality. What he is wary of is the disciple who has a "principle at his disposal which possesses absolute validity and which he has to put into effect, fanatically overcoming all the resistance which is offered to it by reality." Instead the true disciple's methodology "sees in the given situation what is necessary and right for him to grasp and to do."[47] And in the same vein: "Correspondence with reality lies neither in a servility owed the factual nor yet in a principle of opposition to the factual, a principle of revolt against the factual in the name of some higher reality."[48] His optimism about disciples obeying in a world whose sinful structures he was as aware of as anyone derives from his conviction that Christ has already arrived at the worldliest part of the world and has reconciled it to God. "In Jesus Christ the world is loved, condemned and reconciled by God. No one has the mission to overleap the world and make it into the Kingdom of God."[49]

He was optimistic about obedience's likelihood because "there is in every thing its own law of being" and this "law" can be known.[50] He has in mind not only the law of being in each of the things of nature but human constructs as well, not only products, but social structures and systems that exist because of human effort. Knowing the "law" in each of the things about which we must make choices is how we achieve the needed "correspondence with reality." Knowing the law of the "secular" matter, in our case the part of the economic system germane to the person's choice and, on the basis of this knowledge, taking the appropriate action (in our case financial action, or any of its subsets such as buying, investing, and so on) are essentials of Christian obedience. Furthermore, disciples go about these transactions knowing that they are "appointed to the concrete and, therefore, limited responsibility which knows the world as being created, loved, condemned and reconciled by God and which acts within the world in accordance with this knowledge. The world is thus the sphere of concrete responsibility which is given to us in and through Jesus Christ."[51]

A second "structure of the responsible life" (which is confusingly called a structure) is what Bonhoeffer calls deputyship. I say confusingly because it doesn't refer at first to "out there," an objective structure but to a posture of the subject. He sees social life having to be structured by this posture of subjects. Deputyship means taking upon oneself responsibility for others or acting on behalf of others.[52] Of course, everyone has some responsibility for others; therefore all are in some ways deputies. But there are different kinds of deputyship. The one that most closely approximates Christ's is taking another's place in order to fulfill that person's responsibility. This is, of course, what Jesus did by his Incarnation, ministry, and death. He took responsibility for us before God. Once the Christian posture of deputyship is taken, then the other or others for whom you are in a deputy relationship begin to influence what you do with your life and resources. This entails the surrender of one's life for the other.[53] At its final point, Bonhoeffer's deputyship theme developed into Christ as a-man-for-others. But the theme ran all through his writings even as early as *Act and Being* in 1931 and *Communion of Saints* in 1930.[54]

Although the issue of the use of material and financial resources is not given much direct attention in Bonhoeffer's theology of obedience, one can see how relevant his whole system, especially his insights into the structures of reality, is for the theme of this volume. They localize and specify the area of the disciple's obedience, especially this understanding of the deputy character of the One the disciple is called to follow. Jesus didn't have to take upon himself responsibility for us but he did. And once he did then all his resources were put to the service of us. He loved the Lord with his whole heart, his whole self, and all his resources. He laid down his life out of love for his Father and for those for whom he took responsibility upon himself. Hearing whom each of us is called to be responsible for is key to obedience according to Bonhoeffer.

It should be obvious that taking on responsibility for others can be done for any number of motivations, but it is best done out of love. And where there is love there is God. There is only one love and it is indivisible. "The love with which we love God and neighbor is the love of God and no other; for there is no other love; there is no love which is free or independent from the love of God. Loving God is simply the other aspect of being loved by God."[55] This indivisible love is costly. It costs our hearts, our souls, and our strength. To be for others inevitably means there is less mammon for yourself. But mammon or strength expended for others is, at the same time, gain, as we have already seen both for Bonhoeffer and in the New Testament communities.

Two things remain to be done in this chapter. The first is to inquire into the converse of this or Bonhoeffer's understanding of how not to obey. The second is to show how the obedience of disciples grows Christ, so to speak, in the world, in time, in history, in social structures, in our economy.

How Not to Obey

Bonhoeffer had a deep disdain for norm-obedience because of its effects. It mistook the following of Christ with the following of norms. By this false kind of obedience the mediator of reality thus becomes remote to us and norms substitute for our relating to him. He found too many Christian ministers norm-proclaimers, too many Christians norm-gatherers and most ethicians multipliers of norms. One of the ways he proposed in the *Ethics* to develop the difference between these two kinds of obedience was to call for Christian ethicians to refuse to go the usual route ethics and ethical analyses tended to go in the Church and academies he knew. He himself recommends that there be a curtailment of ethics to the infrequent moments when the character of the obligation of a person or group is unclear.

> "The proper delimiting of the place and time [of ethics] is of crucial importance if one is to prevent the pathological overburdening of life by the ethical, if one is to prevent that abnormal fanaticization and total moralization of life which has as its consequence that those processes of concrete life which are not properly subject to general principles are exposed to constant criticism, fault-finding admonition, correction and general interference."[56]

Limiting ethics to an articulation of obligation is necessary lest it "injure and destroy the creaturely wholeness of life."[57] "Should" can legitimately become an issue only when and where "the fellowship of a family, of a marriage, of an organization in which I work and/or own property" begin to come apart.[58]

I believe he has too narrow a category of norms. Some norms are needed for consciences to be informed. Moral choices can come from both an obedience to "the commandment of God" in a framework of immediacy and, at the same time, have moral and ethical norms that inform them both proximately and remotely. Having said this, however, I believe Bonhoeffer's main points are true and that he is right to be concerned that ethics, like religion, can be used to provide an alibi for faith, and that ethics, like "a church of the crowd" can be used to provide a shield to keep the disciple from hearing and obeying what Christ would call the person to. More specifically, he was bothered by a way of doing ethics that saw itself teaching what it thought had to be known about good and evil. For Bonhoeffer human activity was then subjected to "the glaring and fatiguing light of incessant consciousness," first by the ethicians and then by those who sought out their lore.[59]

These norm-generators were trying to deal with a real problem although they were approaching it the wrong way. The problem was an inner disunion, a category that is similar to the split consciousness of previous chapters. "Man's life is now disunion with God, with men, with things and with himself."[60] To overcome this disunion people seek out knowledge, in particular knowledge of good and evil as well as self-knowledge. This knowledge is now pursued and needed in order to attain to "relationship to oneself" . . . unfortunately resulting in "recognition in all things of oneself and of oneself in all things."[61] It didn't used to be this way. Originally there was the knowledge of God in which knowledge there was the recognition of self and all things in God and of God in all things.[62]

The archetype of the person of disunion is the Pharisee. Bonhoeffer has in mind not the Pharisee of history, but an ideal type for whom "the knowledge of good and evil has come to be of permanent importance . . . [because] every situation becomes a situation of conflict in which he has to choose between good and evil . . . with innumerable factors to be observed, guarded against and distinguished. The finer the distinctions the surer will be the correct decision."[63] While this knowledge of good and evil is pursued and accumulated the disunion remains intact. Ethics, as it is ordinarily done, only adds to the problem according to him, if the knowledge of good and evil it purports to have has been discovered, apart from God, outside of God, and without a real grasp either of our origin or destiny.[64] In Jesus, Bonhoeffer found a man in whom the original unity was achieved. In and through Jesus, Bonhoeffer was continually retrieving his own unity. Consequently his "ethics" derives from his Christology, a recommendation he strenuously advanced for all Christian ethics.

It would take us too far afield to do justice to his ethics but some of his starting points can be mentioned. Ethics can go in one of two directions. The first is an accumulation of knowledge of good and evil so that the moral dilemmas of consciences can be informed. The second direction is an attempt to assist in "the recognition of reality re-unified by God's commandment."[65] "Not man's falling apart from God, from men, from things and from himself, but rather the rediscovered unity, reconciliation, is now the basis of" the discipline of Christian ethics.[66] The task of Bonhoeffer's ethics, therefore, as André Dumas comments, "is not to launch appeals to overcome the divorce between ideal and real, but to describe God's concrete commandment in the midst of reality."[67] We have already seen that reality ordinarily carries the commandment through the structures of work, family, church, and government. Christian ethics, therefore, should attempt to show how God acts in and through these structures that are already in the world rather than become an effort to get people by their obedience to bring an absent God to the world and its structures. Recall, in this connection, the Christological reading Bonhoeffer gives to "worldly" and "reality."

Love is the main difference between the two kinds of ethics. Love "is the decisive word which marks the distinction between a person in disunion and a person in the origin."[68] Before love is something we do or choose to do, it is something God does to us. He loves us first. "Love is the reconciliation of persons with God in Jesus Christ . . . and so love is something that happens to us, something passive, something over which one does not dispose himself or herself, simply because it lies beyond their disunion," and beyond their capacity.[69] Christian ethics must steep itself in the fact that love has been "poured into our hearts by the Holy Spirit which has been given to us." (Rom. 5:5) This gift enables Christians to attain to the needed consciousness referred to in earlier chapters and the union Bonhoeffer describes here.

Perhaps the clearest tip-off to the way he contrasts ethics Christian from ethics a-Christian is the title of one of the sections in his *Ethics,* "Ethics as Formation," and in the subsection, "Conformation." Recall that what we have in this volume are notes and first drafts, not the final products of his thought—hence their paradoxical and intuitive character. Ethics, he insists, should concern itself with formation. But formation means being drawn into "the only form which has overcome the world, the form of Jesus Christ."[70] Since Jesus has overcome this world, being in the world is a good place to be as long as one is in it in the form of Christ. What this does not mean is: "the effort to become like Jesus"; "the endeavor to outgrow the man within the man, the pursuit of the heroic"; "forcing of men into the pattern of an ideal or a type or a definite picture of the human character"; or "instruction in the way in which a pious and good life is to be attained."[71] What it does mean is: "being at liberty to be the Creator's creature"; allowing oneself to be the object of God's love; allowing oneself to own his or her own humanity; allowing oneself to be transformed not into an alien form "the form of God, but into [one's] own form, the form which is essentially proper to [oneself]."[72] The transformation into the form of Christ, therefore, is transformation into one's authentic humanity. "Man becomes man because God becomes man. But man does not become God . . . It is God who changes [our] form into the form of man so that man may become not indeed God but, in the eyes of God, man."[73] In a word "to be conformed with the Incarnate—that is to be a real man. It is man's right and duty that he should be man . . . to be the man one really is. Now there is no more pretence, no more hypocrisy or self-violence, no more compulsion to be something other, better or more ideal than what one is. God loves the real man. God became a real man."[74]

As with his other themes, so also his way of seeing ethics pertains to our everyday financial and material situation. What Bonhoeffer is trying to do is to get Christians to take the concrete, limited situations they face daily in the world as the privileged locus of obedience. The very fecundity of his appreciation of the concrete could distract from his attempts to get his readers to take it seriously. He takes it seriously because it is the bearer of Christ *pro me*, Christ before my very eyes in this concrete situation. An ethics, on the other hand, which would "define that which is good once and for all has, in the nature of the case, always ended in failure. Either the proposition was asserted in such general and formal terms that it retained no significance . . . or one tried to include in it . . . every conceivable case; this led to a casuistic system so unmanageable that it could satisfy the demands neither of general validity nor of concreteness."[75]

Bonhoeffer's concreteness is redolent of Jesus' "For I was hungry and you gave me food . . ." (Matt. 25:35) In terms already used, the contents of the norm of brethrenomics is human need

and Christ. And even when half of the content is not perceived—
"When did we see you hungry? . . ." (Matt. 25:37)—obedience
to the half that is perceived wins the only glory that will satisfy
the human heart: "Come, you whom my Father has blessed!"
(Matt. 25:34)

The casuistry and abstraction Bonhoeffer railed against in his
Ethics period (1939–43) are replaced by what he sees to be two
much more pervasive diversions from authentic discipleship in his
Letters and Papers from Prison (1943–45). These are what he calls
metaphysics and inwardness. They both are ways of leaving the
concrete, the Christ before one's very eyes, for some spacy, unver-
ifiable realm where a god of one's own construction reigns su-
preme and undemanding. A metaphysical God is "an answer to
unanswerable questions . . . consigned to the outer reaches of
life, on an increasingly narrow fringe, . . . far off and insignifi-
cant."[76] What would otherwise become a cipher is given a content
rich with abstraction within which we can live as long as we want
to live abstractly rather than concretely.

A parallel to this metaphysical tendency is the tendency to "inwardness." God has lost His place, seemingly, in the world come
of age, a development Bonhoeffer does not decry since this imper-
ils only religion, not faith. But the fact that the modern world can
function "as if God were not" has many Christians "try to keep
his place secure at least in the sphere of the personal, the inner,
the private."[77] He decrys this as unbiblical. "The heart in the
biblical sense is not the inner life but the whole man in relation to
God. But as a man lives just as much from 'outwards' to 'inwards'
as from 'inwards' to 'outwards,' the view that his essential nature
can be understood only from an intimate spiritual background is
wholly erroneous."[78] Such a "smuggling of God into some last
secret place" is among other things a clerical trick, in his reading
of it, often reinforced by forays into psychotherapy or existential-
ism.[79]

Both metaphysics and inwardness miss the concrete where
Christ is, escape from the here and now where Christ is, flee the
pedestrian where Christ is, refuse to hear the word as address that
comes through daily structures where we work, spend, live, give,

receive. Bonhoeffer's Christ would meet us here, not there, now not then, where it's at, as they say, instead of where it should be.

Christ Taking Form in the World

All very well and good, but will this kind of obedience and this kind of ethics make any difference at all to the world in its operations? To answer this question is impossible without at least touching on Bonhoeffer's ecclesiology.

There is an idiosyncrasy in Bonhoeffer's thought that must be unpacked to make it easier to see why and how he understood Christ and Church as he did. This idiosyncrasy can be understood by concentrating on one word: "gestalt" and its cognates *gestaltung* and *gleichgestaltung,* meaning form or structure, formation or structuring and conformation. While Christ is ordinarily seen by Christians and theologians as a person and his impact on people and history is seen in terms of event, Bonhoeffer was much more prone to see Christ as a structure, a place, a form in the world of here and now.[80] "Gestalt" is the key concept for understanding the way Bonhoeffer develops his notions of Church, as well as formation, ethics, religion, and obedience.

In the earlier part of his ministerial/theological career his ecclesiology saw the Church as the form of Christ in the world. According to his 1933 lectures, published in 1960 as *Christ the Center,* we encounter Christ in the Church.[81] This encounter happens in three ways. First, Christ addresses us by his word. This word is Christ. This word also becomes a structure once it is received by hearers. "He is the Word in the form of living address—as address the word can only be between two persons . . . [it] leads to answer and it is answerable."[82] But this "Word as address demands a community . . . it seeks a community to bring about an encounter . . . [this] happens only in community." In the preaching of the Church, "the Word of God really enters into the humiliation of the word of man [the preacher's]."[83]

The second way Christ becomes form or structure in the world is by the sacraments. The sacraments (Eucharist and baptism) are

the God-man, the whole Christ present in the world in his exalta-
tion and humiliation.[84] "His being sacramental is not a special
property, one quality among others; this is the way he exists in the
Church. The humiliation is not an accident of his divine-human
substance, but his existence."[85]

The third way the form of Christ exists in the world is as community and in the community. "His form, indeed his only form
[for us] between the ascension and the second coming is the community."[86] Thus the community is "not only the receiver of the
Word of revelation, it is itself revelation and Word of God. Only
insofar as it is itself the Word of God can it understand the Word
of God . . . the Word wills to have the form of a created body."[87]
If these observations have no correspondence in one's experience
then they will merely be ideas. They were not ideas to Bonhoeffer
but articulations of his experience.[88]

Unfortunately, they were not his only experience. Christ who
exists "as community" is also a stumbling block.[89] The Church, in
other words, certainly became such for Bonhoeffer as it concerned
itself increasingly with itself during the darkening Hitler years. It
became increasingly "religious," other-worldly, and provincial.
But this is getting ahead of the evolution of his Christology and its
relationship to ecclesiology.

In this community of Church, Christ encounters his disciples
individually and collectively by inviting them to say who he is.
Church is possible where the question, Who do you say I am? is
posed. And Church happens where this question is answered. It is
answered by our words of address to Christ. We respond to his
invitation to say who he is for us (not *how* he is the Christ or *how*
it is that he is that way). The world is becoming Church, is becoming Christ, in fact is Christ existing as community in space
and time, where and when this question is answered.

Bonhoeffer adds depth to these themes in the *Ethics*. Here he is
more interested in the formation process by which he means "being drawn into the form of Jesus Christ," as we have seen.[90] Those
who are brought into the form of Christ become the form of
Christ in the world. It is not for those who are this form to try to
apply the teaching of Christ "directly to the world" or to live out
their ethical principles in the world.[91] Efforts to shape the world

by Christian ideas or plans or programs are also the wrong approach.[92] The right approach to being the form of Christ in the world is conformation, something that has already been seen. The process of conformation means being made one with or drawn into "the unique form of Him who was made man, was crucified, and rose again."[93] Both the individual disciple and the community are "formed in the likeness of the crucified" as well as, "conformed with the Risen One."[94]

As a result of this conformation three distinct realities—humanity, Church, and Christ—come into a kind of ontological unity. "The Church now bears the form which is in truth the proper form of all humanity . . . What takes place in her takes place as an example and substitute for all men. But it is impossible to state clearly enough that the Church, too, is not an independent form by herself side by side with the form of Christ . . . the Church is nothing but a section of humanity in which Christ has really taken form."[95]

This formulation may not satisfy. Bonhoeffer's intuition is sometimes more successful than his articulation. Again, what he is opposing is often clearer than what he is proposing. He is opposing the idea that Christ is a proclaimer of a system about what would be good for the world here and now and ever after. Furthermore Christ was not interested in the universally valid, an abstract ethic, a theory of the good.[96] "Christ does not dispense with human reality for the sake of an idea which demands realization at the expense of the real."[97]

This Christology and ecclesiology get more concrete in his *Letters and Papers from Prison.* The form of Christ existing in the world is now seen as having a very particular character that reflects the character he had in his individual historical existence. That existence was being-here-for-others. Therefore, "what it means to exist in Christ [is] to live for others."[98] Conformation has moved to this perception. Here as in his previous work, Bonhoeffer is more of a pointer signaling the direction of the following of Christ than a theologian who fully explains the theology of what he is saying.[99] Again a spatial image is involved. Transcendence is now horizontal. We encounter Christ in the other. "The beyond [of God] is not what is infinitely remote but what is nearest at hand."[100]

Bonhoeffer began in the Church and obedience took him into the world. This was also where he saw the Church being called, past religion and cheap grace, words as ideas and abstractions. He was not desolate in prison. Nor was he unhopeful about the Church, but he thought that before it would be renewed it would have to do several things. One was to shut up, stop the flow of words that poured out from its inauthenticity and begin to listen quietly to the call of Christ. What would help in this would be for the Church to sell all its holdings and for its ministers to live on the free will offerings of the people.[101] This poor Church, this silent Church, this poor clergy could then do two things. One was to practice "the arcane discipline," an undeveloped idea he expressed before his death.[102] It referred to something akin to intentional communities in which the mysteries of Christ's life are savored, celebrated, and responded to. The other activity was to simply be in the world, conformed to the Christ who lived for others. A social form that was Christ in the world existing for the sake of the world rather than for itself—this is the last known sentiment he had about obedience, Christ, and Church.[103]

Bonhoeffer's thought anticipated many of the developments within the Churches. Certainly the emphasis of Vatican II that the Church be in the world and in the service of the world is one such anticipation. Equally important, perhaps, is the development of the base communities especially in the third world in these last twenty years. But more important than these for our purposes in this chapter is the frame of reference within which he saw obedience to Christ. It is fiercely loyal to the person of Christ and yet it is reverent about the world and its structures insofar as they bear the marks of Christ's sublation of them (in my terminology). The faithful disciple names this process and reinforces it by his or her inclusion and obedience.

CHAPTER VII

❖❖

Hope and Economic Activity

The way of life that Christian faith has the power to generate will develop in still a further dimension if it is free to function. Besides healing, two directions have been described so far—inclusion and obedience. In this chapter a third direction will be described, namely, hope. Hope with respect to what? Hope with respect to all of our activities that seek to meet our financial and material needs with our assets and resources. Hope also with respect to the material and financial needs of others.

Hope is an energy. According to Catholic theology, it is a theological virtue. This means that this energy has God as its object.[1] It is infused at baptism which means it is not produced by our efforts the way moral virtues are.[2] Notwithstanding its infused character, it will only be strong if it is exercised. Important and foundational as these points are, they will not be dwelt upon here. What I will discuss is the vision the theological virtues can engender. I will contend that faith, hope, and love can supply a vision that is capable of aligning everyday material and financial transactions within its horizon.

Hope has been part of what we have been examining in the entire volume. In the instances of healing examined in the first chapter, hope was operative. When Jesus was approached by any who sought to be healed, they had already determined he had the power to heal them. They hoped to be cured by him. Christian faith, in fact, had its beginnings in the hopes the otherwise hopeless invested in Jesus. His disciples believed in him because the very needy hoped in him and were not left wanting. The faith of the Apostles, on which our faith is built, was in turn built on the hopes the needy and the sick had in Christ.

The second chapter encourages the inclusion of one's financial concerns in the mystery of Jesus. By doing this, we are also hoping in him. We are at least hoping for more than the matters included. By acts of inclusion we lodge our hopes even for our material needs in him. And, finally, by obeying the Lord into whose reality we have plunged our financial concerns, we are continuing these same hopes. By centering our finances and ourselves on a horizon that includes but transcends them, our attitudes toward our possessions and finances are likely to be kept in a proper perspective, depending, of course, on the depth of our release of these into Christ.

Hope is also a way of perceiving and is not simply discrete acts, although it entails both. The hope that is a component part of most of our actions becomes more explicit by reflection. The objects of our hopes can be secular or religious. In either case, hoping accompanies the ordinary activities of our lives. Our faith is only as strong as its ability to integrate all our lesser so-called secular hopes into our deepest hope. While our hoping can have a number of objects that promise satisfaction when possessed, these can remain separate from one another or they can be integrated into one hope. Such integration is unlikely without a more enlightened vision of what all our hopes are hoping for. "May he enlighten the eyes of your mind so that you can see what hope his call holds for you." (Eph. 1:18)

The Anatomy of Hope

There are myriad hopes that propel our everyday activities. Most have a particular and immediate object in view. We know pretty clearly, for example, why we buy this cereal, make this investment, pay the tuition for a course in school, or agree to work for this salary. There is a hope dimension to each of these activities. We hope for some satisfaction and nutrition from the cereal, an increase in our capital from the investment, to be more educated from the courses, and "to make ends meet" from the salary. These realizable and proximate hopes for this or that have a further dimension to them. This is concealed, perhaps, in the preposition "from." What we hope for from each of these choices and from the object triggering the transactions is both proximate and at the same time it is beyond the here and now. I intend not only to enjoy the cereal and feed myself, I also hope from this and similar actions and purchases to be well. I hope for well-being, to live, to live a life with loved ones, to live a full life. In all four instances I have cited it should be evident that I hope for something from each of the transactions but I seem also to hope for something beyond them which the actions themselves can lead to but do not produce.

Three prepositions—in, from, and for—suggest a way of uncovering the anatomy of our hopes. It seems there are three levels to them. One of these is the level of ultimacy. In the final analysis, all of my actions are leading somewhere, seeking for more. Here in [italics] is the operative preposition: In what or in whom am I hoping? There are also intermediate hopes—what do I hope *for* from this or that transaction? Our economic activity begins here. I hope, for example, for freedom *from* want or from insolvency. I hope for well-being, for security, for the ability to afford a way of life I value, for the capability of providing for myself and others, and so forth. Intermediate hopes are Janus-like. They look in two directions. The first is at the particular object focused on. The second is for some further good beyond the particular object. I have to hope because its realization is future and it is not certain even then. Then, third, there are more immediate hopes. It is not easy to distinguish desire and hope in this third level of immediate hopes. St. Thomas distinguishes them by observing that (the object of hope) is something arduous, attainable only with difficulty.[3] We do not speak of hoping for a trifle, for example, because it lies easily within our grasp. An act of hope differs from desire because it has for its object a future good without qualification. Also desires are more instinctively and unreflexively pursued. Our immediate hopes, on the other hand, might have the same object as our desires but are pursued reflexively. The distinction from moral theology between a human act *(actus humanus)* and an act of man *(actus hominis)* might clarify the difference. Human acts are those done by the powers that make human beings different from merely sentient or instinctual beings. An act of man, on the other hand, is done by a human being but is deficient in its deliberation. It is not yet a humanly whole act.

If faith and hope were to function only in the area of ultimacy, they would not be functioning fully. The presumption here is that faith functioning fully can and should affect not only our ultimate hopes but our intermediate and immediate hopes as well. It is possible to integrate our finance-related activities and the hopes we have in pursuing these with the hopes we have for more than these. Faith is meant to function at all the levels of our hopes. In brief, then, we hope *in* God. We hope *for more* than God, also. *From* our hopes for that which is less than God we hope for the more that, according to our beliefs, is God.

But this brings our experience of God into the analysis. The stronger the experience of God, the more these spatial and temporal terms of proximate and remote, ultimate and immediate, lose their deceptive clarity. Faith and hope are given as gifts so that God-out-there and beyond might become God-with-us, the beyond within. It is the failure to exercise these gifts of faith and hope that keeps the ultimate, ultimate, or, to put it another way, that has God more a datum of confessional faith than of experience. Active faith brings the ultimate into the realm of the proximate and makes the future present and the One hoped in "real" enough to be even more hoped in, leaned on, trusted. If that is not our own experience, it is at least that of those who have believed fully. Judging from the saints, God's sovereignty can come so near that its exercise on the particulars of our lives can become evident. God's reign can be so proximate that our many diffused hopes become few and focused.

Two parables already examined in the first chapter can be revisited to see the hope vista Christians are encouraged to aspire to and live in. "The kingdom of Heaven is like treasure hidden in a field which someone has found; he hides it again, goes off in his joy, sells everything he owns and buys the field." (Matt. 13:44) This disarmingly simple picture of the Christian's life sees the initiative of God in bringing us to become aware of treasure in the field we happen to be traversing. Its discovery is wholly unexpected. The treasure is of such enormous value that its purchase will take every bit of capital we have access to. The value of the exchange is not doubted for a second. The very discovery of the treasure, even before it is procured, makes the heart sing. The eye becomes single. Life assumes an all-consuming purpose. Other values, goals, and goods are immediately relativized and caught up into this vortex.

The reign of God is like this. This is what can happen and is meant to happen in those who hear the Gospel. The treasure that is Love impacting the heart becomes so real and yearning for God, so strong that all that is diffuse comes together and one's hopes focus on obtaining the field and its hidden treasure that can be unearthed, enjoyed, "possessed." The other goods one needs and has, one's financial situation, in particular, will become of notably lesser worth and assume their places as so many means to an end. The treasured "object" is not seen, of course. (Rom. 8:24) But it has been located and savored. It has been discovered to be of such overriding desirability that the previous degree of hope in God is now seen as pale and faint by comparison. This discovery brings hope out of the lair of a faraway lure and makes its energy exert an undeniable kind of drawing power. This development, in turn, reduces the likelihood that lesser goods will prove seductive or preoccupying. They retain their value but that value is always seen as starkly relative when weighed against this treasure. (Even more desirable, of course, would be the state of soul in which these lesser goods were seen as coming from this treasure.)

The other parable that conveys the same deck-clearing, life-rearranging effect is about a pearl. "The kingdom of heaven is like a merchant looking for fine pearls. When he finds one of great value, he goes and sells everything he owns and buys it." (Matt. 13:45–46) Again the hope-leap because of the concentration of the heart on one object that becomes an all-consuming good. Again the economics of its acquisition—many things for one thing, many negotiations in view of the pearl of really great price. One can see something else here. The merchant was searching for fine pearls because he was a pearl merchant who made a living selling pearls. But this pearl was of such beauty that it spelled the end of his pearl business. He sold all he had to acquire it.

As it did for the man with the treasure, the discovery changed everything, most of all his hopes. They were then single. This pearl could not be added to his fortunes. His fortunes had to be transformed. They then had a finality beyond themselves. There is a materiality about these parables that argues against a spiritualization of their meaning. A pearl is a pearl and material resources are put up for sale to purchase it. The kingdom of heaven is not like a discovery of a pearl of great price which is instantaneously possessed by the discoverer. Its price is the other pearls then assessed as of lesser worth. Since overriding worth is attributed to one of them, a concrete process of divestment or dispossession for the sake of possession and acquisition begins. Materiality for materiality. The tangible in exchange for the tangible. This is a very Jewish praxis—Jesus was no Hellenist.

It could be objected that this degree of hope and this emphasis on the material component is unreal. Jesus' own life is the answer to these objections. He fleshes out the word he speaks. He needed food, clothing, lodging, material means to live; but the pearl for him was not only the object of the hope he entertained, it was also the source of all the material means he required to live his life. It's not as if Jesus were preaching a transcending of material needs. Quite the opposite. His Father was not above bird food, he preached, so are not you more important than the birds whom your heavenly Father feeds? And will he not clothe you who clothes the flowers of the field in such splendor? (Matt. 6:25–29) "Your heavenly Father knows you need them all." (Matt. 6:32) The issue is not one of our transcending our needs but of how we go about meeting them. "Set your hearts on his kingdom first . . . and all these other things will be given you as well." (Matt. 6:32) These parables, like the Gospel itself, do not disdain our human material needs but describe an object of such delight and trustworthiness that the many needs we continue to have are met, so to speak, from the new place in which the heart has housed itself and is at rest.

Since we have not experienced the goodness of God in the manner and measure the parables describe, they are spoken to us to hope to experience God in this way. So if this pearl has not been found, hope to find it, the parables say. If this treasure has not been discovered, be on the lookout for it. If our lives are not as single-minded as the parables press us to be, have expectations that they will become so. Their author who is also their embodiment is the only proof they have. They were forged from his own experience of God. He did not lay expectations or burdens on others that he himself was not privy to. The reign of God was a joy and responsibility he himself had learned to carry. Its lightness and the joy it afforded him made him eager to let everyone in on his discovery.

The anatomy of hope uncovered thus far suggests that hope is a component of most of our activities. The human phenomenon of hoping can sometimes be an explicit act, but that seems to be infrequent. It seems it is more a disposition of spirit, a habit of the human spirit that allows many objects to draw it now here now there, the drawing power of one object unrelated to the other. Or it can be a habit of spirit that derives from an experience of God or from a firm conviction about God or from the need to hope in God. Whichever of these it comes from, what develops with it is an horizon to which our lesser hopes are drawn and within which they are integrated. More about this now.

Under the impact of the experience of God's presence and steadfast caring, our hopes and material needs can be situated in an horizon. Horizon implies a vista beyond the immanent, the immediate, the here and now. A faith-generated horizon can appropriate the many particularized hopes we inevitably have without disparaging or annihilating them. Within a faith-horizon the otherwise scattered hopes for things and hope in God can come together. Hope in God produces an horizon within which particular hopes are recognized for what they are. The more conscious and explicit the horizon, the more influential it will be about what is hoped in and what is hoped for from possessions and financial activities. It also provides an early warning system. Material and financial hopes that are not in alignment with one's religious faith and hope will begin to afflict persons with anxiety, a diffusion of energies, and identity turmoil.

Some of our hopes are destructive. Some lack viability. Some are crass. Some are for that which is good but insufficiently related to our other values. A faith-horizon can see these for what they are and give them the door or put them in their place. In other words, there is the corrective function that faith can play on our hopes. Its horizon can intensify the valid, unlock the narrow, and critique the false hopes harbored by believers so that the power of the Spirit can free them and their communities and finally the structures in which they play a part. Faith will correct our hopes if there is a habit of reflection on our experience. Our experiences can be positive as with the pearl merchant or negative as when we get our fingers burned by ill-advised hopes the pursuit of which bring us grief.

One important experience in this matter of hope is poverty. Poverty is a condition that makes hope more likely because with possessions few, it is needed. Hope will be meager, or nonexistent to the extent that it is unnecessary. It is unnecessary where there is satisfaction approaching satiety. Possessions and finances, therefore, are crucial to the issue of hope and whether one lives hoping or not needing to hope. But quantity is not as clearly the issue as attitude. People with virtually nothing can be very attached to that little and people with much can be quite detached from it. To say this, however, is to say the exception. The much more frequent situation is that the more laden one is with wealth and possessions, the harder it is to pass through the eye of the needle into this reign of God. Why would one need to? Things are fine. We have already examined this issue in the previous chapters.

A Direction for Our Hopes

One contention thus far is that to be worthy of the name Christian, hope must include not only hope in God but also hope for things of this world within the horizon of faith. The question in this section is whether from our faith we can develop a hope-vision that is specific enough to give direction to the whole material resources dimension of our lives? I believe we can. Furthermore, I believe the Gospel intends to supply such a horizon. There are several mysteries in the Gospels that are germane, the most important one being the mystery of Pentecost. In the Acts of Apostles, there are several very detailed scenes describing the impact Pentecost had on the followers of Jesus. Notice the relevance to our volume: "And all who shared the faith owned everything in common; they sold their goods and possessions and distributed the proceeds among themselves according to what each one needed. Each day, with one heart, they regularly went to the Temple but met in their houses for the breaking of bread; they shared their food gladly and generously; they praised God and were looked up to by everyone." (Acts 2:44–47) And in the same vein: "None of their members was ever in want, as all those who owned land or houses would sell them, and bring the money from the sale of them to present it to the apostles." (Acts 4:34–35)

As I hope to show in detail, these are parts of eschatological scenes that interpret, summarize, and idealize the historical experience that followed the coming of the Spirit upon the followers of Jesus. What I first wish to emphasize, however, is that this is a description of faith freely functioning in the wake of the outpouring of the Spirit. If our faith were to function freely now it would propel us in the directions cited here: praise of God, communal worship, care for one another materially expressed. God would be praised by a people made one in the Spirit. "The whole group of believers was united, heart and soul." (Acts 4:32) They were not only made one in the Spirit but they reinforced this unity with the attitudes the Spirit prompted in them. Their perceptions about themselves, one another, and their possessions were radically changed. "No one claimed private ownership of any possessions, as everything they owned was held in common." (Acts 4:32) They had undergone a transformation at the core of their identities. The change included a new sense of belonging to a personal reality beyond themselves. Its name was Jesus. They also ceased to be at a distance from one another as they had been before this outpouring of the Spirit. No one claimed anything as his or her own because they had each been transported into a new way of being. With a changed sense of belonging their belongings ceased to be clung to quite so tightly.

The experience is not merely interior. The external change is drastic to the degree that their interiorities were impacted. The sharing of what they have with one another is only one part of this. Their relationships with one another give evidence of having overcome the anticommunal dynamisms of comparison and competition that Jesus had found so disappointing. They could love one another now because they let in the Spirit of Love that would create a unanimity of heart and mind among them. They could also love one another because they were able to see in one another the Lord who was making them members of one another. As they remembered him, they were more and more membered to one another. Loving God with hearts filled with God's love enabled them to love themselves and one another without the calculations that had made their love of one another so deficient in their pre-Pentecost relationships.

Luke records the horizontal transcendence that the outpoured Spirit released. Their possessions feel different to each of them because they have a different finality. The awaited reign of God had arrived with the gift of the Spirit. They could become single-minded about God's reign because that reign was not now simply promised, it was also experienced. As a result they could "[not] . . . worry . . . set your hearts on his kingdom, and these other things will be given you as well." (Luke 12:29–31)

A significant series of connections are made in the Acts passages. They are not concepts but interconnections. These connections are both a description and an augur of the impact the Spirit has on those who receive it. An augur is different from a promise. A promise's realization is still in the future but an augur is something that has already gone on or is going on that also portends a further realization. In these scenes we have an augur of the way in which material needs are dealt with by those whose hearts are transformed. It suggests that the Spirit is incorrectly kept at a remove from their economic behavior by Christians. Their praise of God for His "signs and wonders" not the least of which is His all-embracing caring for them, is still another connection. His

largesse and caring "comes down from above," but it breaks in
from all sides just as surely. The text conveys this by depicting a
community of shared goods.

These texts describe a Christianity so far from our everyday
experience that we are forced to ask several questions. Why the
disparity? Is this Pentecost experience so different from our experiences of God, of one another, and of our manner of ownership of
goods because we are sinful or because it was meant to be a one-
shot event? If this event really happened, why didn't it last? Even
more pointedly: Did it really happen? Are these historical accounts? If they are, do they call into question our contemporary
Christianity because a sharing of goods is virtually unknown to
us. If they are not, what are they? What are they saying? It is
important that the nature of these Pentecost texts be understood
lest we make no demands or foolish demands on ourselves and
one another by reason of a response based on ignorance.

While several authors have argued that Pentecost is wholly a
Lukan construction sprung from his theological a priori, their
evidence for this is not convincing.[4] One of the more reflective and
convincing positions is that taken by James D. G. Dunn. Taking
into account Luke's theological concerns, Dunn concludes from
internal evidence that there is a historical event to which they
refer.[5] Dunn also mounts considerable evidence for the likelihood
of the event taking place after Jesus' death on the great pilgrim
festival of Pentecost, the Jewish feast on which the Jews celebrated their covenant renewal.[6] This is, of course, what Luke
claims. In addition, "the Jerusalem Pentecost was determinative
for the growth of Christianity as a whole."[7] He likens it to
a brushfire whose major outbreak was Jerusalem, engulfing
"smaller outbreaks which had started independently or by chance
sparks."[8] In brief, then, although Luke is making theological
points by his selection and treatment of the material, he should
not be accused of creating these out of whole cloth or independently of history or the religious experience of the first community.

Notwithstanding their historical foundation, these Pentecost
depictions are also eschatological scenes. This means something
very particular. As depictions of behavior they are closer to por-

traits than photographs, to myth than to historical narrative. In this they are like the Gospels' depictions of the person of Jesus of Nazareth. Because both the Gospels and these scenes have their roots in history, they can be trusted as approximating what happened. But they have been written from an interpretation of that experience. The fact that the experience is interpreted doesn't make it less credible or usable for the Christian community. The gift of the Spirit is both the explanation of the initial experience and of the interpretation of the experience by the Evangelist. Interpretation is what the Evangelist's charisma of inspiration is given for.[9] Inspiration guided the purposes of the Evangelist. It goes without saying that the Evangelist is not held to the canons of historiography as we require twentieth-century historians to be.[10]

Insofar as they are historical these scenes give a picture of the past. But as eschatological scenes, they give a picture of our future, of what we are being shaped by God to be. Being in Christ through the Spirit-gift means that we are already in these last days; the new age has already begun. But we are in the new eschatological age only in a seed-tall way, to mix metaphors. What the full harvest will look like will be quite unlike the present seeds. What will the seed grown to its full potential look like? That is what an eschatological scene is given to us to see. We are given these to know what is possible from within the life we have already received. Not only possible but the inexorable direction this life will grow toward if the seed is received and given room to grow. In a word, the role these eschatologized scenes are meant to play in our lives is to furnish us with a vision of what to hope for. They are more accounts about the future than they are about the past. They describe what is within reach, what we can afford to strive toward, what a faith and a hope that is allowed by our freedom to become will flower into. But more pertinently they also depict what we should allow ourselves to hope for in this whole matter of possessions and our financial condition.

These eschatological scenes are given so that we might see in what was what *will be* and from what happened, what *can* happen! It is meant to happen! They are meant to fire Christian imaginations. They are given to inspire us and to reinvigorate the quality of our relationship to God, to one another, and the role our possessions are to play in this. We are to entertain a vision that hopes for a quantum leap in the quality of these, not a leap into outer immeasurable space but one that moves our own and others' activity toward a disposition of material and financial resources that is inspired by the invasion of our spirits by the Holy Spirit.

The Symbol of Pentecost

Because of the kind of "information" a symbolic scene like Pentecost communicates, a word must be said about symbols in general and about the symbolic event of Pentecost in particular. God is not revealed to the hundred and twenty nor to the Evangelists nor is He to us without some symbol mediating that disclosure. Such knowledge does not grasp God's essence, of course. God impacts our consciousness with a symbolic knowledge of His presence. The symbolic knowledge that represents God will always come from things we know or experience directly such as wind, fire, speech, receiving, sharing. We know these things and experiences through our senses and directly. By tapping into all of these knowables the experience of the descent of the Spirit upon the Apostles and the disciples is communicated by Luke.

One of the things that is important about the symbolic character of the knowledge in question here is its inexhaustibility and its irreducibility to one meaning.[11] The same content, so to speak, can be received by many, but each can and should derive something unique from it. The event of Pentecost and the symbolic knowledge communicated by Luke are not intended for speculation or analysis, but for participation. A symbol speaks to us only insofar as it lures us to situate ourselves mentally within the universe of meaning and value that it opens to us.[12] Nathan Mitchell would be even more graphic: "A symbol is not an object to be manipulated . . . but an environment to be inhabited. Symbols are places to live, breathing spaces . . . new horizons for life, new values and motivation."[13] A symbol "does something to us, moves, shifts our center of awareness, changes our values."[14] It can influence commitments, release hidden energies, strengthen people, arouse the will. It discloses "not by presenting its meaning for inspection but by drawing us into its own movement and carrying us out of ourselves."[15]

Symbols draw us into realms of awareness much deeper than those that our discursive thought can plumb. This is because they can they are able to touch, affect, and generate aspiration, single-mindedness, and wholeheartedness in ways that ideas addressed to our reasoning seldom if ever do. They can also, according to Mircea Eliade, "reveal a perspective in which heterogeneous realities are susceptible of articulation into a whole, or even of integration into a system. In other words, the religious symbol allows man to discover a certain unity of the world and, at the same time, to disclose to himself his proper destiny as an integrating part of the world."[16]

Entry into the Pentecost symbol event, therefore, could have the effect of giving the economic/financial/possessional components of our lives a meaning that conjoins them to the "spiritual" in the hearts of believers. What would otherwise remain heterogeneous can be made a whole and generate a unitary vision that combines opposites—the Spirit and the economic order. Pentecost's perspective takes us far beyond healing and brings these two into an alignment. A substantial transformation follows the entry of the Spirit into our history and activity. Given the entry, the metaphor transubstantiation becomes apropos.

In this connection another insight Eliade has into religious symbols is germane. He notes symbols' "capacity for expressing paradoxical situations which are otherwise quite inexpressible, e.g., of passage from a profane mode of existence to a spiritual existence."[17] To live in time and in the Spirit, to live within the experience of transcendence and immanence simultaneously, to assign a spiritual worth to material possessions, to bring to material expression a spiritual experience, to transform money and property into fellowship and community—any or all of these give evidence that polarities have been bridged and that paradoxes have been integrated without reductionism. Entry into this symbol of Pentecost both contemplatively and practically can do much to bring this integration about. "Symbols have a way of

causing immediate reality as well as particular situations to burst"
out of their confines and open out to a larger, deeper meaning in a
way that concepts never can.[18] The role the Spirit plays in those
who would participate in the symbol is both to bring them into it
and to prompt responses to God through it and because of it.
Participation in the mystery shapes subsequent actions. From
mysteries entered, history is affected and changed.

Mystery entered into is a wholly different intentionality than
seeking a solution to a problem.[19] Mystery entered into affects
actions and changes behavior. These changes and actions may
affect a solution to economic problems, but this effect is not the
primary intention the participants have. What is primary is attention to the mystery and fidelity to it in living out our ordinary
lives. Constructing blueprints for behavior or deducing programs
of behavior from the mystery of the poured out Spirit is a misuse
of the mystery. Blueprints preempt the role of the Spirit. Blueprints are hatched by people who insist on making symbols have a
single referent. Pentecost can mean only one thing to such people
and the bottom line of the single meaning they have derived from
it is this or that regimen of behavior. Rather, the Spirit would
prompt unique responses in the hearts of those who undergo the
discipline needed to enter into the Pentecost mystery. The responses will be many, not one.

The New Communality

With these prior questions out of the way we can return with
greater freedom to the reflection on Pentecost. What follows is
intended not as an argument addressed to one's critical faculty but
a meditation hopefully appealing to the heart and imagination of
readers so that they might be encouraged to do the same and enter
into the mystery in their own way. It is only one way of standing
in the Pentecost experience.

The impact of the Spirit poured out on the hundred and twenty
and the onlookers was that "everyone was filled with awe; the
apostles worked many signs and miracles." (Acts 2:43) These

signs and wonders were belief, joy, praise, proclamation, communality, the sharing first of their sense of God and later their possessions with one another. "None of their members was ever in
want, as all those who owned land or houses would sell them, and
bring the money from the sale of them, to present it to the apostles; it was then distributed to any who might be in need . . . [for
example, Barnabas] owned a piece of land and he sold it and
brought the money and presented it to the apostles." (Acts 4:34–
37)

At its simplest, there is a "before" and "after" experience described here. Before "the descent of the Spirit," the relationships
among Jesus' followers are described as problematic at least at
times (e.g., Luke 22:24) After the outpouring of the Spirit-gift, a
marked difference takes place. There is a sharp decrease in the
distance between one another. "They shared their food gladly and
generously." (Acts 2:46) There is a lessening of their care of themselves and a heightening of their desire to be with and care for one
another. Their mutuality, expressed in spiritual and material
ways, shows that their senses of selfhood had undergone a transformation. All are acting as if they were one part of a larger whole
in their sense of themselves. It was as if the Spirit operated as a
centrifugal force propelling them out of themselves into a life of
proclamation and mission beyond themselves. And as a centripe-
tal force. "Each day, with one heart, they regularly went to the
Temple but met in their houses for the breaking of bread." (Acts
2:46)

The largesse of God experienced by each is complemented by
the largesse shown by the members of the community to one another. What each has comes unstuck from "me and mine" and is
made available to one another. Their dispossession was not in
function of growth in personal virtue or a personal response to a
unique call or a fidelity to a blueprint spelled out for them about
what a Pentecost people should do. It is their response to the
experience of God come close in and through neighbor. "Neighbor" now is the all-providing God enfleshed, inviting them to
accept from neighbor his providing for them. At the same time
others can rely on those who are provided for to imitate God's
providing. The material resources at their disposal become supple

in their hands and at the disposal of the new thing God is doing in their midst.

One of our common resources is speech. It is not exempt from the new degree of mutuality evident in this event. Their speech became as unstuck as their possessions. They find themselves able to use their speech in such wise that they communicate to their hearers words that are life giving, words that come from hearts filled with that which goes far beyond their prior ability to communicate just as what they say surpasses their prior understandings. A desire to be with one another seems prompted in part by the unique form of nourishment they received from those who spoke to their hearts about God come close in Christ. Just as their material possessions become instrumental for expressing a new way of being, a co-being, so to speak, so also their speech could evoke and express this same co-being. But their tongues of fire were not only for the community of believers. Many "devout Jews of every nation under heaven" who were staying in Jerusalem at the time of the downpouring of the Spirit began to hear about the marvels of God in their own tongues. Jesus' followers, filled with the Holy Spirit, "began to speak different languages as the Spirit gave them power to express themselves." (Acts 2:4) The new way of being together was not going to be limited to or inhibited by the tongues they spoke. Tongues of fire are a symbol within this symbolic event.

One of the attractions of this "love communism," as it has been called, was its spontaneity.[20] The loving kindness of God that shows up in their relationships with one another is depicted as amazing, unorganized, spontaneous. They did not decide to become a community and issue rules of behavior. They were made one abruptly in a way that startled them. Their new behavior toward one another bears a profound similarity to Jesus' behavior toward them and his relaxed attitude toward possessions. And why should it have been otherwise since the Spirit they had received was the Spirit of Jesus?

There are any number of experiences latent in this mystery of Pentecost. It can be entered and become

- an experience of the promised Spirit.
- an experience of Jesus present anew in and as Spirit.

- an experience of the covenant care Jesus promises to those who await and yield to God's reign over them.
- an experience of a community in which many leave their isolated individualized selves and become members of a new person, one body, the new creation in the midst of the old.
- an experience of being moved by a complementary power not their own, yet one in which each remains free to be moved.
- an experience of what had been awaited happening now, materializing before their very eyes; in surprising ways yet, upon reflection, according to what was promised.

Hopeless Christianity

There are several ways of misusing this mystery. The most pervasive misuse of Pentecost by Christians is a nonuse of it. Certainly, acknowledging the outpouring of the Spirit once a year on the feast Pentecost is an insufficient entering of this mystery. So also is any acknowledgment that merely sees it as a once and long-ago event. Most Christians are too passive and unexpectant about the degree of power they could be enjoying and exercising. One piece of evidence that the mystery of Pentecost is not being entered and releasing its power into our history is the infrequency and superficiality of sharing both our faith and our material goods with one another. Where are the notable among Christians? The etiquette we have come to accept in most congregational relationships hardly does justice to our being members of one another in the power of the Spirit. Is our co-being, which is an apt description of life in Christ, something we expect to experience in any tangible way? Do Pentecost, the Spirit-Gift, and what follows from it tend to be sealed up in a separate sphere, a spiritual world, rather than an energy released in this world of flesh and blood, money and goods, assets and debits, experience and community?

Modern Christians' hopes are too small. The "divine wind" of Pentecost is the same force that operated over the formless wasteland of Genesis. (Gen. 1:2) That "divine wind" (Gen. 1:2) put form where there was formlessness and order where there was chaos. What was transformed in this myth was everything. What is to be transformed by the same Pneuma is eventually everything. But between now and then it would enable those who allow themselves to be caught by it to situate and maintain economic life in its rightful place, rather than one that allows the economy to grow into a behemoth that we servilely serve. The Spirit can assist in establishing this new order if it is expected and "allowed" to function in the areas where it has for too long been unexpected or unwanted. We must allow the scope of our hopes to be the same that God has for us. Pentecost, an event between creation and the *eschaton,* unveils the width and depth of hopes we have been given to hope. These should include hope about our economic systems. These alternately tempt us to assert our own autonomy or despair. They easily make fools of us by exercising more and more of a sovereignty over us, or we make fools of ourselves by our autonomous opportunism with respect to them.

The Church is to provide the world with a raison d'être for hoping. The world needs to hope its systems and resources can be brought to the point where they will be harnessed to serve human purposes and needs. It needs believers who are hopers, who have hope for this world. Our hope is not merely for the world of nature and its resources but also for human ingenuity, integrity, and for what is necessary to develop mature and peaceful societies and just social systems. Our hope is both in God and in human beings in whom God acts. Our hope includes history and social systems in its purview because the Incarnation and the reconciling act of the Cross took place in our history and became foundational for all human history. Jesus' victory is continually swallowing up the worst shot nature deals to us, namely, death, and the worst blow that we deliver to God's plan for us, namely, sin. Christian hope informed by the doctrines of creation, redemption, Pentecost, and the resurrection of the dead can suffuse those who appropriate them with hope.

Two acts against hope, which we could also call acts of near-despair, have been practiced for so long in Christianity that they are not even seen to be contrary to our faith and hope. The one is an act that mistakes the subpar degree of power experienced by most Christians and their congregations as par. It wrongly judges that this meager energy is what we should expect at present from faith and from God come close to us in Christ and the Spirit. The circularity here moves from meager expectation to meager power and from meager power to the belief that this is as it should be. It often goes on to theologize on this, contending that any greater degree of power is to be expected in the "not yet" time of the Parousia. In the "already," the now, what you see is what you get and ought to expect from faith, Pentecost and Spirit.

But this is a pre-Pentecost faith! It is a reversion to an Israel-awaiting-the-promises level of power. Should we not enjoy and insist that we experience the promised experience? Pentecost is not a future mystery. It is the Father and Jesus sending the Spirit now into the hearts of those who ask, seek, knock. "If you then, evil as you are, know how to give your children what is good, how much more will the heavenly Father give the Holy Spirit to those who ask him!" (Luke 11:13) The mistake here is about power, the power of faith. It is not expected to be power. We are of course talking about degrees of power and about the social effects we should expect and hold one another to because of our faith, and because God has and would continue to come close in Christ through the Spirit. We do ourselves and God and the world considerable disservice by observing the pathetically slight impact the Church has on the world and the enormously strong impact the world has on the Church and concluding that is all we can expect, that this is the best we can do until the definitive rearrangement is brought about by God when Christ comes in glory.

The mistake here is about hope, what to hope for and when to hope for it and how much power to hope for from hope. If the Gospel says anything, it says that the One who was to come has come and through and in the Spirit would be power now for us and through us. What Israel awaited and what the Apostles after the Ascension of Jesus hunkered down to receive has arrived. When it did, what was "not yet" moved over to the "already" side of the ledger. What is still in the not-yet side is the fullness of this power. But it is a serious mistake to simply await that final fullness, since God means to give power now through the gift of the Spirit, power meant to be transforming of people, relationships, congregations, communities, neighborhoods, and nations. This transformation is to have begun already, affecting people and the transactions people have with one another, among which are buying and selling, working and consuming, saving and financing. If this power is of no relevance to and exercises no influence on relationships and these everyday transactions now, how will this Spirit transform the human enterprise definitively? We are already in the economy of the bestowed Spirit. The act of near despair we are massively guilty of is to wait for mysteries to happen that have already happened.

When the Baptist wondered whether Jesus on whom the Spirit had already descended was the one whom he and Israel had awaited, Jesus asked him to answer his own question by what his eyes could see and ears record about the presence of power affecting a healing of the maladies by which people had been disfigured. (Luke 7:18–23) Jesus recommended a unique kind of empiricism to John, paraphrasing Luke 4:18–21: "What you were awaiting was power, John. Do you see the world we both grew up in being transformed? If you do, then realize the Spirit of God has anointed me. If you don't, then keep waiting." Translated for our purposes: if our everyday actions of buying, selling, consuming, furnishing, clothing ourselves, and so forth are swayed only by wants or the power of the interests or by the fads, the consumerism, the avarice of our age, then the Spirit is either no power at all, or it has been misconstrued as a spiritualistic power meant for souls only, or it is an entropic phenomenon that operated a long time ago but has run down to a faint vestige of itself, or it is an energy that is wholly future to us. But it is different from any of the above, therefore . . .

The Gospel of Luke and the Acts of the Apostles are perhaps the most pointed reflections on this in the Scriptures. In the first of these two books, there is Jesus who in his Spirit-embued-flesh makes his way to Jerusalem there to suffer, die, and be raised from the dead. This is followed by the second age, that of the Spirit of Jesus in his members. It is an age of power. (Acts 1:8) Those who receive it begin to journey outward from Jerusalem to the ends of the earth. Pentecost is the mystery that begins this second, final age. But we are in this second age, the age of the Spirit which would propel those receiving it to witness to Jesus in every nation and level of society and in every social system of every nation. One system that it would impact in particular, at least for Luke, is that of buying and selling, distribution and consumption. In modern terminology, the economy.

This brings me to the second act against hope I've mentioned. It is another low-grade form of despair that pervades Christianity and it pertains to the vehicle the Spirit would use to witness to Jesus and the Father. The vehicles the Spirit would bring into being and, in turn, use to witness to the truth and viability of that which is being proclaimed are people in communities who become the behavioral evidence that something is coming "from above" and really is impacting the humanity of the receivers. This can be seen by the way they act with one another. This peculiar behavior was to be that they loved one another.

One of the preoccupations of Luke was the loss of fervor of the communities that were contemporary to him. As I have mentioned, the evidence of this was the apparently widespread retention of surplus goods and monies by the wealthier members of the communities who left the needs of the less fortunate members of the congregation insufficiently attended to.[21] Luke saw and foresaw growing trouble because the cultures they were situated in were dictating to Christians and their use of their material and financial resources. Luke says, as Paul did before him (1 Cor. 11:17–34), that if the culture succeeds in dictating to the faith of the Christians then the faith and the faithful will become more and more accommodating to the culture rather than the other way around.[22] To forge a new way was why the Spirit was sent. It was a power that could transform old cultures or create a new culture from the old ones. But before it affected whole cultures it was a power that made many one in their local situations.

If the modern Christian is left unaware of the degree of communality the Spirit would bring about, then he or she is likely to overlook this Lukan emphasis in Acts on the sharing of goods with others or dismiss it as something that was peculiar to Luke's own time or to his theological preoccupation. Some sharing of goods is an intrinsic part of the outpouring of the Spirit, not a nice addition that can be taken or left, as one sees fit. Absent it, and the world's capacity to dictate to Christians' identities and shred the power of the faith remains unchecked by contrary behavior. What is born from above is a human community whose human transactions assume a new form. The members are not a series of born-again individuals who become individually more religious while their day-to-day transactions continue on irrespective of the new community. The proclamation of the Gospel is credible where there is evidence of the social change that faith in Christ and the power of the Spirit are bringing about. Luke is protesting against those who choose to await what has already come into history. He is also protesting against a Christianity whose followers follow Jesus one by one. He is protesting, as John the Evangelist did, against a Christianity that is happy to believe in Jesus but doesn't care to drink of the Holy Spirit in such measure that living waters would flow both into and from those who have drunk so that others may see and hear and repent and be saved. (John 7:37–39)

In brief, several points are being underscored here:

1. The outpouring of the Spirit at Pentecost is not an event for the first disciples but one in which all generations of Jesus' disciples are to participate.

2. Nor is it to be merely associated with the definitive future but with the present and with power received now.

3. This power is, among its other effects, community making.

4. These communities are to be among the marvels God is accomplishing in the world.

5. One of these marvels is an abundance. "Everyone who has left houses, brothers, sisters, father, mother, children or land for the sake of my name will receive a hundred times as much, and also inherit eternal life." (Matt. 19:29)

6. The hope believers have in God now is given tangibility and reinforcement in the community. (Hope in God and the sharing of goods ground each other.)

The Trinity and the Sharing of Goods

A pregnant concept in which to further root this Pentecost narrative in the theme of this book is that of "koinonia." The community is described as being "faithful to the teachings of the apostles, to the brotherhood [koinonia], to the breaking of bread and to the prayers." (Acts 2:42) This is a richly suggestive detail since the full panoply of the notion of koinonia spans both the life of the Trinity and mundane monetary transactions. Its cognate is *koinos,* common (things), things belonging to several.[23]

"All who shared the faith owned everything in common [koina]." (Acts 2:44)

Luke didn't invent the word "koinonia." Previously it had been used in Greek philosophy to describe a degree of friendship that included the mutual sharing of material goods.[24] Qumran also used the word to convey the notion of the surrender of property by the community's members to the community. By rule, members did not own anything of their own.[25] Its usage in other places in the New Testament sheds further light on its use in Acts. In 1 John 1:3 the author explains that the purpose of his writing is "so that you too may share life [koinonia] with us. Our life [koinonia] is shared with the Father and with his Son, Jesus Christ." Here koinonia conveys the communion of Father with the Son in the Godhead in which the writer and his readers participate. The reader-become-believer is brought into the same koinonia the writer has with the Father and the Son.

Paul's koinonia usages are also enlightening. "You can rely on God, who has called you to be partners with [koinonia] his Son Jesus Christ our Lord." (1 Cor. 1:9) God is the initiator of the bonding that obtains between His Son and believers. For Paul, koinonia begins in the Godhead. Those who are drawn into this koinonia of God in Christ have power available to them which is to be converted into human expressions of communality. Koinonia for Paul becomes diakonia when what is received is acted on in human relationships.[26] Diakonia is koinonia converted into the concrete service of others. Diakonia can be of many different varieties. The one we are emphasizing here is care for the material needs of others with goods, monies, and the resources one has at one's own disposal.

The first community described in Acts by its sharing of all things in common witnessed to this diakonal dimension of the mystery of God come close in Christ. Its response is described as steep, abrupt, total. Subsequent generations of Christians, including the second generation described by Paul, received the same Spirit and call but their execution of that identical call was not apparently a once-and-for-all act of dispossession but an ongoing discernment made from within circumstances of need, both their own and others'. Their model in this was to be Christ who "although he was rich, became poor for your sake." (2 Cor. 8:9) Their gradual dispossession was to be motivated by love of him who embraced poverty so that he could clothe them with himself. Their concrete follow-through resulted in communities that reproduced in a human way the character of Trinitarian koinonia. They gave of their goods, services, and finances.

To say this is not to know specifically or ahead of time what any one person, family, or congregation did then or should do, give or receive now. (God save us from quantifiers who are all too ready to reduce love to measurements!) The purpose of stating the connection is to invite Christians to see the drastically changed finality of their goods, possessions, investments, and finances since they no longer belong to themselves. Widespread and long-ingrained reluctance to hear this side of what it means to be "in Christ" prolongs the imbalance, the maldistribution, and the inequality where "there should be a fair balance." (2 Cor. 8:13)[27] Insofar as a congregation is not rooted in koinonia, it will be wanting in its witness and cohesiveness. And once diakonia is not rooted in koinonia, the faith is ethicalized at best or, more often, the care of members for members is spiritualized. Then the ordinary way of evoking a response to needs is by obligation and the ordinary dodge is by referral to civil institutions and welfare agencies.

One of the functions of faith is to generate and purify hope. One of the functions of Pentecost is to supply Christians with a unitary vision of the place of possessions in the new life they are given to live. One of the great values of the depiction of Pentecost as we have it in Acts is its summary quality and its merely quasi-historical character. The value of its having some historical basis is its ability to show us the direction the Spirit-gift took the Church in its pristine, birth moments. The value of its being only quasi-historical is its ability to haze history into a symbolic event. The scenario it conveys does not call for a quantified response or to a literalism that would seek to reproduce the Acts community. Its idealization suggests the direction the Spirit would take the Christian enterprise. Reducing Pentecost to rules or directives misuses it. Opening up to the Spirit-gift with all its ramifications, especially to the diakonal finality of possessions, roots economics in the heart where all that merits the name Christian belongs and rightly takes its start. The very fact that the Spirit is given as the explanation of the event and the new behavior it inaugurates should give rise to much hope, since this same energy is still available to those who believe in Jesus. The seemingly intractable, imperious, impervious world of economics will not succeed in retaining its autonomy any more than the simpler structures, political and economic, did in the first century. Not, at least, if the Spirit we embrace is as Semitic as that which was poured out at Pentecost. This Spirit is given not to remove those who receive it from the world but to animate them in the world of everyday things, thus enabling them to become an augur of the new order, the new creation.

Growing in Hope and Seeing Less

There is an ironic point in this matter of faith and hope. Growth in hope does not mean that the shape of the future will become clearer and clearer. One of the ironies about hope is that the stronger it becomes the less it knows. The stronger hope becomes the more certainly the hoper will be able to say with the Psalmist, "You are my hope, O Lord." (Ps. 71:5) To be privy to a unitary vision does not mean one comes to greater clarity about its details. An immature hope hopes in the vision or in what one sees. Both Johannes Metz and Walter Kasper make the point that as believers grow in hope for the world they know less and less about the form this future will take.[28] Faith fully functioning develops in us a growing confidence not about what we can see about the future but about what we can't see. "Faith can guarantee the blessings that we hope for." (Heb. 11:1) It is a growing conviction about "the existence of realities that are unseen." (Heb. 11:1) Christian faith does not grow in its ability to see the object of its hope. "Hope, not visibly present, or we should not be hoping —nobody goes on hoping for something which he can already see." (Rom. 8:24) The measure of growth in hope, then, is not sight but hope itself, both hope for the world and hope in One who loves the world as God does and as God's Spirit gives them to love the world.

Generating hope is the ironic function of faith because, on the one hand, we are given a vision that gives our scattered, economically related hopes a unitary direction, and on the other, as this hope grows there is a lessening of detail in the vision. How can these two points be made simultaneously without being contradictory? Christian hoping does not go in the direction of becoming sight or possession but in the direction of accepting God's incomprehensibility. Even in our beatific state when we will see God face to face, God will be always greater—*Deus semper major.* The formal object of the beatific vision is not God known and seen but God incomprehensible, according to Karl Rahner and St. Thomas Aquinas.[29] In his way Paul says something similar when he notes that hope is one of three powers that will "remain," rather than a power that will drop us onto the shores of eternity and then cease to be necessary. (1 Cor. 13:13)

While we grow in acceptance of God's incomprehensibility we need not make a virtue out of incomprehension of everything else that is less than God. Comprehending all we can know about our finances and material resources as well as the role they have in relationship to God and social order is essential to coming to terms with a large part of life as it is here and now. Development in comprehension of this aspect of our lives is a must. This development can simultaneously remain open to God being "always greater" and finally incomprehensible. If we mix these two up we could end up by knowing too much about God and our future and too little about the present and its systems. Or we could end up esteeming ignorance about everything that isn't God.

On the one hand, this chapter says that it is urgent that we have a vision of a future, the shape of which includes God, goods, and one another in a unity and continuity forged by Spirit. On the other hand, we cannot come to a vision that has us hope in it rather than in God. This has often happened in Christian history. It is important to distance ourselves from three ways of misconstruing our future. Each of these presumes to see too much, hence each is an unacceptable way for Christians to move in concept, aspiration, or behavior from "is" to "will be."

The first of these unacceptable ways of trying to move from present to future is by conjuring up utopias. Utopias are and have no where, literally.[30] Nor do they have any chance of coming about. They fascinate precisely because they do not deal with the here and now. But at the same time, their attraction is in their being able to account for all the desiderata our little hearts desire.[31] Since these utopias usually have many of the elements of Christianity, they have often proved dangerous to the living out of Christian faith because they invite those who accept them to live in an unreality that does not give an account of history or of the effect in history of Christ in any of his three moments present, past, or future. Nor do they face facts squarely, especially society's injustices, the maldistribution of goods, hunger, and indigence. The major difference between a Christian vision of our world and a utopian vision that claims to be Christian is that the first sees the transcendent already operating in the immanent while the second transcends the immanent, or even more accurately transcendentalizes the immanent, disconnecting it from what it can't handle in the reality we all see and fret over.[32]

The second form or conceptual vehicle which, like utopia, Christians have a special weakness for because it absorbs so many features of the dream God has given Christians to dream, is utopian socialism. I am referring here to the ideologies that purport to give a full account of human nature and society and the requisite economic and political systems that will deliver this ideal future. One of their central tenets is the need for state and/or collective ownership.[33] Utopian socialism, which began in earnest

in nineteenth-century Europe and is alive today, takes the dysfunctional features of society into account and proffers a solution
for them. This solution involves a series of political and economic
moves.[34] These might be called for and valid enough in themselves, but the schemes of utopian socialism, which would get us
from the present to the ideal future, fail to pass muster at the bar
of authentic Christianity because the construct of the ideal future
is wholly immanent in its conception. If utopias won't work because they disconnect what is from what is to come, utopian socialisms won't work and, in fact, haven't worked because they are
rearranged projections of the present; they are projections that are
unconnected with the transcendent powers that operate in the
present order, the chief of which are the theological virtues of
faith, hope, and love. As a result, utopian socialisms have attempted to get from the present to the ideal future by coercion
and its violent concomitants. Furthermore, they give no clear account of the transcendentality of humans. And finally they give no
clear account of "what hope his call holds for you." (Eph. 1:18)
Instead they hold out immanentized small hopes in political and
economic terms, which turn out to be rearrangements of the same
elements that are the problem and, hence, will hardly deliver the
solution.[35]

The third unacceptable form that would move us from "is" to
"will be" is Christian apocalypticism.[36] Christian hope to be true
to its doctrinal, scriptural, and symbolic foundations must know
the difference between apocalyptic hoping and eschatological hoping. Apocalyptic hoping is irresponsible about human concerns
while eschatological hoping will be responsible about them.[37]

Apocalyptic as a literary genre developed in Israel after her
exile and in a context of profound disillusionment, both political
and religious. Because the salvation they had hoped would take
place in the social and political processes of history receded further and further from realization, a generation of apocalypticists
developed who hoped in God *solo* rather than in God and *for* the
world. Apocalyptic contended that God's intervention will bring
about an end to history and the world.[38] All human attempts to
make things better will go for naught even though these efforts
will be taken into account in a final judgment, but only to reward

the virtue they manifested. "The apocalypticist thinks in terms of a radical dichotomy between earth and heaven."[39] Although it had precedents, the flowering of the genre awaits the Maccabean period and the persecution of the Jews under Antiochus Epiphanes IV (167–164 B.C.).[40]

In the time of Jesus, apocalyptic thinking was flourishing. Christian eschatology borrows from the themes of apocalyptic but reworks them in a remarkable way. Jesus turns out to be the future that apocalypticism had awaited. He who was to come has come, and what will be will somehow be him and of him. To be in him is to participate in the new aeon while living in the old. His passion, death, and resurrection spell the end of history as we had perceived it and the beginning of the new history, a history which has Jesus as its Alpha and Omega. He is the "reason" history has meaning now but he is also the only way it will have any future meaning. Our efforts to improve systems and structures in the world have meaning and he is the ground of that meaning. He is the reason creation and the *creata* with which it teems "might be freed from its slavery to corruption and brought into the same glorious freedom as the children of God." (Rom. 8:21) Jesus is why "wood hath hope."

Although in eschatological hoping there is a discontinuity between history as well as the world as we know these and "the new heavens and the new earth," that discontinuity will not be a repudiation of these. Nor is it an invitation to hope less or to hope for less or to hope in God *solo*. It is an invitation to hope in a way that leaves us free not of concerns but free of being alone in dealing with them. Christian eschatology deals with the world through him, with him, and in him who is the new age, the final times, and the future of God and our humanity together.

Correcting Our Hopes

A striking exemplification of how a false vision of the future misleads the followers of Jesus can be found in the Emmaus story in Luke 24:13–35. Here we have a vision, even a Christological vision, of how Israel would be set free. We also have enormous hopes invested in Jesus by two of Jesus' followers. But they had attached their hopes to their vision of him. Furthermore, their superficial form of inclusion was not followed up by an obedience to him or to the Word of God. As a result, they wanted him to conform to their vision and hopes. Jesus, who catches up with them in their flight from Jerusalem is patient with their concerns. He does not preside over these "at some safe, clinical, judgmental distance" but brings them into his own person.[41] In the course of making their concerns his own, however, he changes them substantially. This was ever the case in his earthly ministry as it is also here in his Risen ministry.

As a result of their changed vision, they saw things differently: him, themselves, their concern about Israel and how to handle it. As it is changed, their relationship to him changes as does his relationship to them. The story as it unfolds suggests how Jesus "does justice to our concerns in our surrender to him and his presence-in-the-Spirit to us."[42] The concern is now located in the Risen Jesus but it is not by being placed there either displaced or transcended. Nor is it solved in its problematic status. Israel still had to be set free. Yet it is yielded up. It is "placed" in a new reality. The concern changes in those who embrace it in its new *situs.*

Placing one's concerns in the Risen Christ present in the Spirit, into whose communion (koinonia) we have been drawn together with others, dramatically changes the way we handle our concerns as we have seen. As the Emmaus story represents it, the hopes we entertain about our concerns when they are purified by the Risen Lord present in the Spirit go in the direction of he-is-our-hope. This involves a process of purification of our concerns, not a denuding or denial of them. One's changed hope-vista continues to include concern for a free Israel, as we see here, except that the Spirit's action begins to compose into one: he, we, Israel, and free. In the same way it can compose: he, we, need, and wealth. The Spirit's composition joins and orders, subordinating to Jesus what "flesh and blood" had confusedly fused or left disjoined.

Emmaus also exemplifies how not to hope, obey, include. It is as if Cleopas and his companion (Luke 24:18) had said, "We were hoping he would accomplish the task we put on him to do and do so in the manner in which we envisioned him doing it. Since he didn't, we removed ourselves from the way, the site, and the community within which we had nurtured our hopes." Cleopas and his companion were selective about the hopes they projected onto him, factoring out what they did not choose to hear from Jesus' lips. The Risen Jesus, present in the Spirit, succeeds where the pre-Easter Jesus failed. He brings them from hoping in their hopes about their concerns to hoping in him about them as he accounts for his seeming failure by making them face all what the prophets (and he) had announced about the Messiah having to undergo what he did in order to enter into his glory. (Luke 24:25–27)

A hope whose object is seen is usually generated by a god of our own construction. Such a hope and such a construction usually tries to go straightway to solution, possession, glory, without passing through the disillusioning paschal moments of darkness and surrender. Such hoping will end up either dashed or momentarily realized but with a self-generated, partial realization that will not last or satisfy. By contrast, hopes that are prepared to cling to him in whom they have been placed, all through the stripping down of their earth-boundedness, can enter into a boundlessness and peace and come to taste the limitless hopes God has for us even in time.

Even though Jesus' own efforts resulted in death and burial, nevertheless "he is the one who was not abandoned to Hades, and whose body did not see corruption. God raised this man Jesus to life, and of that we are all witnesses." (Acts 2:31–32) Exalted at God's right hand, he who in time had received the promised Holy Spirit from the Father, now poured this Spirit out on his followers. This is "what you see and hear." (Acts 2:34) His hopes in God were not mocked nor was what he hoped for—for his disciples, Israel, the other sheep I have who are not of this fold, those coming from east to west to the banquet, the nations, and so forth. His risen body bears the marks of continuity with history and discontinuity—they testify to his efforts at the amelioration of the human condition. The wounds testify to his failure and, made glorious, they constitute an eloquent sign of the completion of his efforts. An apocalyptic Easter would have disconnects at all the points at which Christian Easter has connects: with creation, concerns, flesh, blood, history, effort, and so on. The appearances of the Risen Jesus depict one who is attuned to his followers' concerns. Mary Magdalene's loneliness, the Apostles' fear, the Emmaus disciples' disappointment, Thomas' doubt, the fisherman's search for fish—he appears in the midst of their concerns, disparaging none of them, taking upon himself each of these, transforming all of them.

In the symbol event of Easter, the Risen Jesus is still concerned about human concerns. They are met by him, not ignored or disparaged as trivial. He is the way he was before Easter, not too tall for humanity in its ordinariness. He bears all the marks of one who reverences his own and others' humanity, not one who has departed it. An apocalyptic resurrection would not have been of the body. An apocalyptic resurrection would encourage irresponsibility about the world and all that concerns us in it. It would symbolize a hoist away and apart from human life, the body, concerns, political and economic systems. At best it would foster a he-will-eventually-bring-about-the-new-order split consciousness about the world. The Easter symbol, instead, takes history, Jesus' and ours, seriously. It takes Jesus' efforts and ours seriously. His wounds are made glorious, not obliterated, in the Resurrection.

The mysteries of Resurrection and Pentecost could have a freeing effect on those who would steep themselves in them. Both are immensely assuring and encouraging while they are innocent of strategy, tactics, and blueprints. They should leave us capable of living in an assurance that God takes our own history seriously as well as our efforts to affect the world no less than He did Jesus' history and efforts. One of the effects the energy of hope infused at baptism should develop in us is the ability to live in the symbols of Pentecost and the Resurrection, thus enabling us to perform with hope the never-ceasing activity of trying to finance and supply the wherewithal for our lives, homes, families, and goals. By attending to these, we also learn to hope for this aspect of the world and enable it to do the same. By steeping ourselves in the mysteries of Christ, we develop a conviction that history, our own and others', has a point to it. They bring together the hopes we have in God with the hopes we have for that which is less than God, namely, hope for this world, and our activity in it including our economic activity.

❖❖

CHAPTER VIII

That Christ
May Be My Wealth

In the second chapter, I contended that Christ's intentions for the temporal order, the economy in particular, might best be seen in terms of sublation. His sublation of the economy goes on whenever and insofar as the economy in its particular functioning is being made to serve human beings, their valid purposes, and needs. In a word, seeking to bring about economic justice (micro and macro) coincides with the sublating intentions of Christ.

But affecting the economy, trying to make its parts just and healthy is a tall order, one that is seldom effectively undertaken directly because of the obscurity and complexity of the tasks. Given this, what I set out to do, therefore, was to show what individuals and microeconomic units could do in an indirect way in bringing about this transformation. Examining their power in terms of faith, I uncovered four of the functions faith could perform that would affect their economic behavior. Explicit reflection on these teaches people of faith a language, among other things, by which they can speak to money. The evidence that they are learning the language they need to speak to money is very much related to the image and the names they have for Christ.

A farseeing Christology formulated by Franz Jozef van Beeck has provided an overall framework within which we have examined the relationship between Christ and the specific concern of this volume, our finances and possessions and the system for which these are stand-ins. A healthy Christology develops, according to van Beeck, whenever the everyday things that matter to Christians are *in via* to becoming the titles by which Christians name Jesus.[1] His study traces the passage from concern, interest, or worry to entitlement. These entitlements show that the Lord is presiding over these concerns. An unhealthy Christology, on the other hand, is one that is out of touch with the things that concern Christians. He is only entitled by names Christians have been taught to call him instead of by names that indicate they are handling their concerns by relating and surrendering them to him.

Jesus can be found in and would preside over all human concerns, for he is Lord.[2] Our concerns concern him. In him we learn to handle them. Through believers he begins to subject them and the social systems to which they are linked to himself. Through the Spirit we learn to name these concerns in terms of him. They begin to lose their self-assertiveness, their autonomy, their potential for making exaggerated claims on our attention and diffusing our loyalty.

To understand how the Spirit works to make human concerns grist for the mill of worship and come under the presidency of Jesus, we need to know more about the process of metaphor making. To accurately perceive things we have to allow them to speak their reality to us. As always in the act of perception, as the object speaks its reality to us, a constitutive part of the act of perceiving is the word or name we give to what it is we perceive. This other-than-us is encountered, worded, or named by us.[3] By naming something, we conjoin what we perceive with the word that appears most appropriate to the reality in question. In the case of metaphors, however, we conjoin what is ordinarily not linked to the reality perceived. A metaphor conjoins what is not usually joined to the reality by ordinary speech or perception.[4] For example, wealth or wealthy would usually be used of a large amount of money and of a person who had a superabundance of it or of material resources. But to say that "someone is my wealth" brings us into the strange world of metaphor because of the conjoining of different realities whose link is not immediately evident. It's in terms of wealth that Paul named Jesus. "I have accounted all else rubbish so that Christ may be my wealth." (Phil. 3:8) (NAB)

Metaphors arise out of concerns. "The material for metaphors is taken from significant areas of human experience, from things people find important."[5] Whatever matters to us will end up as at least potential for metaphors. Since our concerns are many and are bound to bump into one another, we can see at times how we deal with our many concerns by the ways in which our metaphors signal the conjoining of what is disparate. The more important concerns control the less important. Any overview of the New Testament will show "the wide range of metaphors used by the Christians of the New Testament to address themselves to Christ. They bear witness to the fact that Jesus Christ is their preeminent concern and inclusive of all other concerns."[6]

By saying that Christ is his wealth, Paul is naming the reality of his relationship to Christ and Christ's to him. He is indicating how he has come to handle his concern about his own material needs, resources, and future. "We think in words but we handle reality in names."[7] Christians who can say with Paul either that they want Christ to be their wealth or that he actually is are handling two realities with one name. They are expressing a unitary consciousness. Or they are enhancing the possibility that their own consciousness will be unitary by so naming him. The process is not logical nor is it the result of reasoning. Christological metaphors "function as names and in doing so they convey the believer's responsive act of surrender which cannot be reduced to cognition."[8] A Christological metaphor like any metaphor exceeds the cognitive meaning of the words used.

Such metaphors can become subject to reflection, objectivity, nonsituational cognition, and conceptualization. They are capable of being considered in themselves, examined for their own logic, their relationship to other titles, and so forth. This is a valid, even a necessary process. It becomes counterproductive, however, if one forgets or ignores or disdains the living encounters from which the metaphoric title takes it truth, meaning, life. Just as the metaphors by which Jesus is entitled must not forget the difficult situations in which they had their beginnings and continue to have their real purpose, so also they must not be allowed to grow apart from the shared human concerns that give them currency. "The full meaning of the metaphor is dependent on the realization of its bond with human concerns."[9] By naming him with that which represents our concerns "he becomes at once the one who presides over and does justice to them."[10] The metaphor both clarifies the existential reality we are in and evokes continuing commitment.

Underlying this approach to metaphor is van Beeck's basic insight into Christology. It is only secondarily "a coherent system of thought."[11] It is primarily a rhetoric. "Rhetoric is the sum of all those elements and aspects of language which show that language is primarily an activity in situations and only on that basis a cognitive act."[12] "Christological statements," therefore, "are primarily expressions of dialogue among persons in dialectical response both to the Risen Lord and to the concerns of their culture."[13] Christology is culturally irrelevant if it loses touch with the concerns of the culture. It is functioning for its own sake. Christology that is in touch with a culture's concerns will be relevant to that culture. The faithful's acts of inclusion, obedience, and hope have created a sacred tradition or a record of human concerns that were brought into the mystery of Christ. "Established Christological discernments are the memorials of the Church's thoughtful compassion extended to human concerns in the past."[14] Christology must, therefore, remain hospitable to new discernments. New discernments about the mystery of Christ will derive from the present Church's hospitality to "new human concerns—concerns that must be assumed into the humanity of Christ if the Church is to do justice to the *totus Christus* as well as to all of humanity."[15]

In this way the Body of Christ would continue to be the way Jesus was in his humanity. The Gospels record his patience with and acceptance of human concerns. The Evangelists record his concern to lose nothing of that which was brought to him. "I will certainly not reject anyone who comes to me, because I have come from heaven, not to do my will but to do the will of him who sent me. Now the will of him who sent me is that I should lose nothing of all that he has given to me, but that I should raise it up on the last day." (John 6:37–39) Instead of functioning like this, however, believers and their Church too often made Christology "the family ideology."[16] Normative Christology became frozen, contenting itself with much repetition and slight refinements over the years. "In insisting on the glory of Jesus, traditional Christology often involved itself in self-glorification."[17] Christianity then became "neurotically committed to the defense of the divinity of a man who did not consider equality with God a matter for snatching."[18] It "traded in the assurance that comes from hope, for the impenetrability that comes from complicity with a prestigious thought system."[19] The result was that "it could piously, without getting involved in conflict, leave a world caught in misery and violence to its own ethical devices."[20] Van Beeck observes that the Church's teaching office often tended to prefer "the denunciation of the errors of the ideologies produced by the struggle" about concerns to taking responsibility for encouraging and endorsing patient and compassionate Christological discernment of them.[21] Such a Christology has lost its way, "and the cries of the poor and the suffering and the searching go unheeded."[22] The main argument for a patient, human-concerns type of Christology in contrast to an immobile, intolerant one is simply the fact that it is more like Jesus.

From these insights it should be obvious that an unhealthy economy, one that is not being brought under human values or made instrumental for meeting human needs or implementing human rights, must have some relationship to an unhealthy Christology. The one could more easily develop a life of its own because the other developed a life of its own. Both Christology and the economy would be healthier if those who participated in each were to disallow the distance and separation between them to continue. One contributes to the health of Christology by continually submitting one's material and financial means, as also one's needs and the needs of others, to Christ as the single source of one's well-being, one's material and financial well-being included. In the case of the economy, health comes much more slowly since its structures are far more intractable. But since social structures are very much in a continuity with human hearts at their best and worst, hearts can affect systems even though it would take so much longer for the economy to be healthy than for Christology to be healthy.

It seems that Christ would have his followers join him in his purposes to have the economy exist for human beings rather than human beings for the economy. One could participate in this endeavor by taking direct action on the economy in all the places and ways in which it operates harshly, unjustly, ineptly. This kind of participation presumes both accurate knowledge of the problem, a solution to it, a strategy to achieve it, and the power with others to pull this off. Since these are not often at hand, a second way, one that is more accessible and universal, is needed to participate in Christ's sublation of the economy. This volume maps out this second way. It is not indifferent to the economy; it in fact seeks to affect it by the kind of integrity such a spirituality and regimen can generate. At the core of this regimen is the process of naming Christ while functioning actively within the economy. It seems to me Paul the Apostle is a model in living this way.

Gain Reassessed

Paul loved to mull and savor financial metaphors in appreciating the mystery of Christ and being one with him. For example Christ was treasure possessed in earthen vessels. (2 Cor. 4:7) "Although he was rich, he became poor for your sake, so that you should become rich through his poverty." (2 Cor. 8:9)

His reflections from prison when he wrote his letters to the Philippians are quite relevant. Paul had good reason to reflect on his life at the time he wrote this epistle because he was in prison and the outcome of his trial was uncertain. By A.D. 61–63, the likely years of the letter, he could claim, "Life to me, of course, is Christ, but then death would be a positive gain." (Phil. 1:21) He had time and reason to reflect on what he had going for him, his resources material, relational, and religious. He recalls the times he had been in great want and hungry as well as those in which he was well provided for. "I know how to live modestly, and I know how to live luxuriously too . . . There is nothing I cannot do in the One who strengthens me." (Phil. 4:12–13) He contrasts his present condition with the "support systems" and resources which "were once my assets"—circumcision, being of the stock of Israel and the tribe of Benjamin, a Hebrew, a Pharisee, above reproach when it came to observance. All of them "I now through Christ Jesus count as losses." (Phil. 3:5–8) He counts them all as rubbish by comparison. His forfeiture of all of these supports was "for his sake," and in order that he "may be my wealth." (Phil. 3:8) NAB

"I have counted all else rubbish so that Christ may be my wealth." (Phil. 3:8) NAB This sentiment in particular is a terse summation of what I have been attempting to explain throughout this volume. By naming Christ as the wealth he would have is the evidence that Paul had become a participant in Christ's sublation of the temporal order contemporary with him.

A dramatic transposition had taken place from one way of seeing himself, God, Israel, his material needs, and his security—to another way of seeing these same realities. What he had going for him most of all before Damascus was a "justice of my own based on observance of the law." (Phil. 3:9) NAB This was the immaterial root of his personal sense of security, value, and purpose. After Damascus and as a result of his fidelity to what began to be disclosed there, Paul could explain with simplicity that his material and immaterial well-being were then all wrapped up with someone who seemed to be more who Paul was than he was to himself. "Life to me, of course, is Christ." (Phil. 1:21) The initiative in this transposition was God's. The response was Paul's. "It has its origin in God and is based on faith." (Phil. 3:9) NAB The Christian faith Paul had was both the same as and different from his Jewish faith. It was the same insofar as it was faith in God, the God of Abraham, Isaac, and Jacob. It was different at the same time because while his whole heart, soul, mind, and strength were still opened out to God, he was now faced into a horizon filled with a person who invited response. The person of Christ grasped Paul's heart and whole purpose for being. Christ became the form of his belief, hope, and love. He and faith in him became the measure of all things for Paul. All choices and labors were done in him and with him and for him. Just as he had tried to become

wealthy by amassing a fortune in righteousness through observance of God's law, the form of his wealth now was Jesus. The
way to the acquisition of this treasure was not possession but
dispossession of his own autonomy by clinging to this new form of
wealth and uprightness. "The uprightness I have gained . . .
[comes] through faith in Christ." (Phil. 3:9) Jesus was Paul's uprightness, not to mention his wisdom, holiness, salvation; in a
word, his wealth. (1 Cor. 1:30)

These sentiments of Paul are descriptive both of his experience
and also of his yearning. Because of the love he already experienced he couldn't get enough, so to speak, of the beloved. He
desired passionately to know Christ "and the power of his resurrection." (Phil. 3:10) He knew a little of this and the effect of this
little was to yearn for more. His faith and love intensified his hope
rather than left him either bereft or with a sense of possession or
comprehension. That hope had a *finis* to it: His hope left him
"striving toward the goal of resurrection from the dead" (Phil.
3:11), since such a condition of existence would enable him to be
wholly one with the one who had become his life. "I want to be
gone and to be with Christ." (Phil. 1:23)

As we have seen, the Christ who is now Paul's wealth is not
simply the individual person of the Risen Christ with whom Paul
longs to be one but is also the Christ who is present in the world,
inextricably one with his members. In moving from living in and
for themselves to living in such a way that he becomes their life
and wealth, these members pass through the paschal way of being
made new, undergoing what Christ experienced, and hence come
to know him through the pattern of the death he suffered.

The members of Christ's own body were part of Paul's wealth.
"Every time I pray for you all, I always pray with joy for your
partnership in the gospel from the very first day up to the present." (Phil. 1:3–5) The "first day" was approximately A.D. 50
when Paul and Luke announced the Gospel in Philippi. "God will
testify for me how much I long for you all with the warm longing
of Christ Jesus." (Phil. 1:8) He loved them as Christ loved them.
He loved them because they were Christ to him. You are "my joy
and my crown." (Phil. 4:1) His affection for them seems to have
been met by theirs for him. Their affection for him showed itself

in very concrete ways. "You have all shared together in the grace that has been mine, both my chains and my work defending and establishing the gospel." (Phil. 1:7) They had sent one of their number, Epaphroditus, to him to take care of his needs. (Phil. 2:25) He risked "his life to do the duty to me which you could not do yourselves." (Phil. 2:30) Their care for Paul included material goods. While in prison in the place where he was writing he received things from them which "I needed." (Phil. 4:16) Acknowledging their generosity as "a fragrant offering, a sacrifice acceptable and pleasing to God," Paul prays that God "will supply your needs fully, in a way worthy of his magnificent riches in Christ Jesus." (Phil. 4:18–19) NAB

When Paul says, therefore, that Christ is his wealth, he is saying that the person of the Risen Lord is his wealth and that the community which has been made one in the Spirit is also this wealth since it is no less Christ for Paul. (1 Cor. 12:12) Likewise, through its members, it mediates the love Jesus has for him. It is also the recipient of the love of God which the Spirit poured out into Paul's heart. (Rom. 5:5) The community is both Christ and on the way to being Christ's.

The Apostle at the same time seeks "to know him and the power of his resurrection, and partake of [koinonia] his sufferings by being molded to the pattern of his death." (Phil. 3:10) How interesting that koinonia should show up again in this connection! Paul sees an unbroken continuity between the action of God which brings us into and gives us a share in the fellowship or communion of Father, Son, and Spirit and actions done by us that have us bring Christ to the fullest stature possible within each of our lifetimes by our sharing in his sufferings. The same word, "koinonia," is used of both of these. We have koinonia or communion with Christ Risen and communion here and now with his suffering. Note, this is not just suffering of people but *his* suffering. "I wish to know how to share in his suffering." (Phil. 3:10) NAB The Risen Lord cannot be the one referred to here since he has already suffered. Yet the suffering referred to here is both his and it is present suffering. The problem is solved if one accepts what Paul says here and in other places about the mystery of Christ, namely, that the community of believers made one in the Spirit are who he is and is now. He presented himself to Paul in this manner from the outset. "Saul, Saul, why are you persecuting me? Who are you, Lord?" he asked, and the answer came, "I am Jesus whom you are persecuting." (Acts 9:4–5) Jesus then was suffering in his members at Saul's hands. Now Paul who suffered shipwreck and famine and scourging and every kind of affliction for Jesus sought to have an even greater share in and a deeper participation in this one Christ, both through the power of the Resurrection flowing into him and through the community which by its members' sufferings was being transformed along with Paul into the pattern of his death.

Christians, therefore, can live vision-thin about their futures and the future forms of society in contrast to the vision-thick utopians or utopian socialists or the world-despairing apocalyptists because we are supplied with an in-depth vision of the meaning of the present, and present suffering in particular. This vision sees a convergence between Jesus' embrace of the poor and suffering and the believers' embrace of Jesus in these. Since he would come to fuller stature now through them, they have plenty to occupy them here and now. How their ministry will cash out in the future is, therefore, unnecessary to speculate about in detail, since serving him in these "least" is already koinonia with him. Attempts at implementing a detailed blueprint can also easily miss his presence in the poor. He is both risen and drawing us into his fullness and at the same time suffering and calling out to us to bring him to the degree of fullness our love and our material/financial resources make possible. A societal vision of the future will be counterproductive if it instrumentalizes people, making each a means to the implementation of an extrinsic end-time vision. On the other hand, having a share in (the koinonia of) his suffering as that is being experienced in the present will be part of the future communion.

One of the greatest sufferings Paul and the community had to endure came from those who had been members but who then mutilated the body of Christ. (Phil. 3:2) By relating to the Lord and the members from a posture of acquisition rather than a self-emptying one (Phil. 2:5–11), they showed that "their god is the stomach . . . their minds are set on earthly things." (Phil. 3:18–

19) They had become believers up to a point but in the course of this they attempted to add Christ to their acquisitions and appetites. Their wealth was still in and of the world.

To see Christ as one's wealth is the result of considerable activity on the part of the Holy Spirit working on the affections of the one who comes to make such a statement. It is also the result of fidelity on the part of the one impacted by the Spirit's activity. This fidelity will show itself by consistency in acts of inclusion, obedience, and hope.

An Urgency

Christ is our wealth! There is an urgency that he be so named. The urgency is considerable for many reasons. There is first of all the confusion that comes to all of us in our pursuit of things, and the hoping that the accumulation of monies is the wealth that will satisfy. A culture built from this activity deranges human beings. There is also the strain put on relationships among people from this mistaken identification of what will constitute their security and their satisfaction. The strain shows itself in many ways and with many degrees of severity: domestic tension, international exploitation, third world poverty, first world disparity of opportunity, slums, class hatred, trade wars, abuse, neglect, disease, standards of life that must be preserved, and so forth. The rhetoric of the title—he is our wealth—does not disparage the yearning for wealth or for a fullness that will complete our humanity. But faith gives wisdom to the yearning. It roots the material form of that yearning in immortality, purifying and ordering our concerns about it. It gives our yearning a perspective within which the ongoing concerns are occasions for both worship and witness.

This perspective is nothing other than Christ the person, the many-membered reality and an unfinished reality that is being built up by each of us who are members of him "until we all reach unity in faith and knowledge of the Son of God and form the perfect Man fully mature with the fullness of Christ himself." (Eph. 4:13) This perfect collective person is what the Spirit is forming in the world "so that a perfect offering may be made to the glory of [God's] name." By being faithful over a few things, the things we have, the things we dispose of and the things we forgo, the things we give away, we grow this Christ and this Christ grows in our moment in history.

The process of inclusion, obedience, and hope not only affects our concerns and us, it also is completing Jesus. What he embraces comes under his sovereignty in an active and explicit way through the behavior of believers. As the members who are a constitutive part of the mystery of Jesus join what they touch and what touches them to him, he increases while they decrease in their own isolation from one another and isolation from this source of their life. By leaving in his hands what we're inclined to take into our own, he, we, and our concerns all change and conjoin in the Spirit.

"A theology that grows out of critical sympathy with the world and turns humanity into the stuff of worship and witness is reenacting, in an intellectual fashion, God's love of the whole world in the person of the *Logos* Incarnate, the way of Jesus Christ in obedience to the Father's will and the hope that comes from the presence of Christ alive."[23] Naming Christ from ever greater depths of surrender from hearts immersed in the universal human condition makes him universally credible.

There is, in brief, considerable significance in Paul's way of naming his relationship to Christ for our following of Christ, for the integration of our religious values with our material and financial resources, and for bringing economic activity within reach of and under the influence of religious faith.

Notes

Chapter I   Naming and Healing the Illness

[1] These terms are defined somewhat differently by different authors. See Tibor Scitovsky, *Money and the Balance of Payments* (Chicago: Rand McNally & Co., 1969), ch. 2.

[2] On the relationship between faith and values, see Bernard Lonergan, *Method in Theology* (New York: Herder and Herder, 1972), p. 116.

[3] Walter Brueggemann, *The Prophetic Imagination* (Philadelphia: Fortress Press, 1978), ch. 3.

[4] Ibid., p. 30.

[5] Ibid., p. 31.

[6] Ibid., p. 31.

[7] Ibid., p. 30.

[8] Ibid., p. 42.

[9] Ibid., p. 35.

[10] Ibid., p. 41.

[11] Ibid., p. 41.

[12] Robert J. Karris, "Poor and Rich: The Lukan Sitz im Leben," in *Perspectives on Luke—Acts,* ed. Chas. Talbert (Edinburgh: T. & T. Clark, Ltd., 1978), pp. 112–24. Also Luke T. Johnson, *The Literary Function of Possessions in Luke—Acts,* Society of Biblical Literature Dissertation Series 30 (Missoula: Scholars Press, 1977), esp. chs. 2 and 3.

[13] Davis L. Mealand, *Poverty and Expectation in the Gospels* (London: Society for the Promotion of Christian Knowledge, 1980), ch. 2.

[14] Joseph A. Fitzmyer, S.J., *The Gospel According to Luke (I–IX),* Anchor Bible, vol. 28 (Garden City, N.Y.: Doubleday & Co., Inc., 1981), pp. 35–62.

[15] Ibid., ch. 7 *passim.*

[16] Bruce Malina, *The New Testament World; Insights from Cultural Anthropology* (Atlanta: John Knox Press, 1981), chs. 1 and 3.

[17] Gnosticism was one of the earliest thought systems used by Christians to construe their faith in a disembodied way. See "Gnosis," by Robert Haardt in *Sacramentum Mundi,* ed. Karl Rahner, S.J. (New York: Herder and Herder, 1969), vol. 2, pp. 377–79.

[18] Richard J. Cassidy, *Jesus, Politics and Society, A Study in Luke's Gospel* (Maryknoll: Orbis Books, 1978), esp. pp. 20–33.

[19] Norman Perrin, *The Kingdom of God in the Teaching of Jesus* (London: S.C.M. Press, 1963), pp. 158–90.

[20] Fitzmyer, *Luke,* p. 222.

[21] Joseph A. Fitzmyer, S.J., *Essays on the Semitic Background of the New Testament* (London: Geoffrey Chapman, 1971), p. 170.

[22] Brueggemann, *Imagination,* p. 60.

[23] An excellent example of the traditional discomfort Christians have felt about money in connection with their faith has been researched by Lester K. Little, *Religious Poverty and the Profit Economy in Medieval Europe* (Ithaca, N.Y.: Cornell University Press, 1978), *passim.*

[24] Joachim Jeremias, *Jerusalem in the Time of Jesus* (Philadelphia: Fortress Press, 1969), pp. 95–99 and 147–221.

[25] Jeremias would not scale the taxes this high. Ibid., pp. 124–26.

[26] The situation is far too complex to settle for this formulation of it. Sadducees can be taken broadly or narrowly; also they go through different periods of ascendency and descendency. See ibid., pp. 222–32. Also *Jerome Biblical Commentary,* ed. Raymond Brown, Joseph Fitzmyer & Roland Murphy (Englewood Cliffs, N.J.: Prentice-Hall, 1968), index on Sadducees.

[27] One of the classical understandings of the linkage is, of course, the *Spiritual Exercises of St. Ignatius.* For more recent understandings, see Arturo Paoli, *Meditations on St. Luke* (Maryknoll: Orbis Books, 1972), ch. 2.

[28] Fitzmyer, *Luke,* pp. 509–10.

[29] Fitzmyer, *Luke,* p. 511.

[30] Samuel Taylor Coleridge, *Biographia Literaria,* ed. J. Shawcross (London: Oxford University Press, 1907), vol. 1, p. 202.

[31] Walter Brueggemann, "The Book of Jeremiah," *Interpretation* 37 (April 1983): 135.

[32] Ibid.

[33] Avery Dulles, "Fundamental Theology and the Dynamics of Conversion," *The Thomist* 45 (1981): 135.

[34] William F. Lynch, S.J., *Images of Hope* (Baltimore: Helicon Press, 1965), p. 243.

[35] The whole development of hermeneutics has sensitized us to this development. For the role of texts in this process, see Hans George Gadamer, *Truth and Method* (New York: Seabury Press, 1975), e.g. pp. 330–41.

[36] John Dominic Crossan, *In Parables* (New York: Harper & Row, 1973), pp. 12–13.

[37] Fitzmyer, *Essays,* p. 175.

[38] Joachim Jeremias, *The Parables of Jesus* (New York: Charles Scribner's Sons, 1963), p. 59.

[39] Madonna Kolbenschlag, "The American Economy, Religious Values and a New Moral Imperative," *Cross Currents* 34 (Summer 1984): 153.

[40] Ibid., p. 154.

[41] Harvey H. Guthrie, Jr., *Theology as Thanksgiving* (New York: Seabury Press, 1981), pp. 31–70.

[42] Modern scholars have uncovered a more profound relationship between Jesus and Phariseaism than had been previously appreciated. For example, John Pawlikowski, *Christ in the Light of the Christian-Jewish Dialogue* (New York: Paulist Press, 1982), esp. ch. 4.

[43] Jeremias, *Parables,* pp. 144–45.

[44] John R. Donahue, S.J., "Tax Collectors and Sinners: An Attempt at Identification," *Catholic Biblical Quarterly* 33 (1971): 39–61.

[45] Ibid.

[46] Fitzmyer, *Luke,* pp. 470–71.

[47] I am unable to retrieve the origin of this quotation.

[48] Fitzmyer, *Luke,* p. 234.

[49] See footnote to Matt. 19:13ff. in *New American Bible* (New York: Catholic Book Pub. Co., 1970), p. 28.

[50] This remark will become clearer in Chapters IV and V when the three classes of men are analyzed.

[51] Fitzmyer, *Luke,* p. 739.

[52] Sandra Schneiders, I.H.M., "The Paschal Imagination: Objectivity and Subjectivity in N.T. Interpretation," *Theological Studies* 43 (March 1982): 52ff.

[53] This conflation of the two horizons is the specific area of analysis in Gadamer, *Truth and Method,* pp. 269–74.

[54] Sandra Schneiders, I.H.M., "Faith, Hermeneutics and the Literal Sense of Scripture," *Theological Studies* 39 (December 1978): 34–36.

Chapter II The Sublation of the Economy

[1] For example, "Dogmatic Constitution on Divine Revelation," in *The Documents of Vatican II,* ed. Walter M. Abbot, S.J. (New York: Herder and Herder, 1966), pp. 116–17.

[2] This term is used differently by different authors. I am not indebted to anyone's rendering of it.

[3] Michael J. Petry, *Hegel's Philosophy of Subjective Spirit* (Dordrecht: Reidel Publishing Co., 1978), vol. 1, pp. 28–31.

[4] Its etymology implies a removal of something from its previous situation; see *Harper's New Latin Dictionary,* p. 1876.

[5] See Council of Chalcedon in Denziger's *Enchiridion Symbolorum* (Freiburg: Verlag Herder, 1963), p. 108.

[6] A good overview of the development of the soteriological principle can be found in John Carmody and Thomas E. Clarke's *Word and Redeemer* (New York: Paulist Press, 1965), pp. 53–60.

[7] This soteriological principle of the patristic age is used by many theologians, for example, by Wolfhart Pannenberg, *Jesus—God and Man* (Philadelphia: The Westminster Press, 1968), p. 40.

[8] Abbot, *Vatican II,* p. 495.

[9] Ibid., p. 497.

[10] Ibid., p. 497.

[11] Ibid., p. 497.

[12] Ibid., p. 495.

[13] Ibid., p. 497.

[14] The council's two major documents on the church were "The Dogmatic Constitution on the Church" and "The Pastoral Constitution on the Church in the Modern World," Abbot, *Vatican II,* p. 14ff; p. 199ff.

[15] Raymond Brown, *The Gospel According to John (I–XII),* Anchor Bible, vol. 29 (Garden City, N.Y.: Doubleday & Co., Inc., 1966), p. 468. Brown notes an alternative reading in an early manuscript, a neuter plural, which suggests that more than people are being drawn to Christ.

[16] Abbot, *Vatican II,* p. 27.

[17] William Warner, *Beautiful Swimmers* (Boston: Atlantic Monthly Press, 1976).

[18] This comment is rooted in the notion of covenant, see Chapter IV.

[19] Abbot, *Vatican II,* pp. 233, 240, and 262.

[20] Brown, *John,* pp. 477–78; see also comment on footnote 15.

[21] Hans George Gadamer, *Truth and Method* (New York: Seabury Press, 1975), p. 264.

[22] "While Christ is indeed head over the whole world, only the Church is his body." Eduard Schweizer, *The Letter to the Ephesians* (Minneapolis: Angsburg Pub. House, 1982), p. 163.

[23] Schweizer gives a brief historical overview of the development of the doctrine of the "real redemption" of the universe." Ibid., pp. 266–76.

[24] Pannenberg, *Jesus,* pp. 33–37.

[25] Ibid.

[26] David Hollenbach, S.J., *Claims in Conflict* (New York: Paulist Press, 1979), p. 145.

[27] Ibid., p. 146.

[28] Ibid., p. 146.

[29] Ibid., p. 151.

[30] Ibid., pp. 149–50.

[31] Ibid., p. 147.

[32] Ibid., p. 147.

[33] *Origins,* November 15, 1984, vol. 14, nos. 22–23, pp. 338–83; and October 10, 1985, vol. 15, no. 17, pp. 258–96.

[34] Synod of Bishops, Second General Assembly (1971) "Justice in the World," in *The Gospel of Peace and Justice,* ed. Joseph Gremillion (Maryknoll: Orbis Books, 1976), p. 514.

[35] One of the earliest and more successful efforts in this discipline: Karl Polanyi's *The Great Transformation* (Boston: Beacon Press, 1957).

[36] Bernard Lonergan, *Method in Theology* (New York: Herder and Herder, 1972), p. 85.

[37] Ibid., p. 82.

[38] Ibid.

[39] A good overview of developments before the eighteenth century can be found in Joseph Spengler's *Origins of Economic Thought and Justice* (London: Feffer & Simmons, 1980), esp. ch. 6.

[40] Lonergan, *Method,* pp. 114–15.

[41] Ibid., p. 85

[42] Ibid., p. 259

[43] See Albert O. Hirschmann, *The Passions And The Interests* (Princeton: Princeton University Press, 1977), *passim.*

[44] Abbot, *Vatican II,* p. 495.

[45] Ibid., p. 495.

Chapter III   Inclusion

[1] Ernst Kasemann, *Commentary on Romans* (Grand Rapids: Eerdmans Publishing Co., 1980), p. 327.

[2] Ibid., p. 328.

[3] Ibid., p. 327.

[4] Ibid., p. 301.

[5] Ibid., p. 330.

[6] Vatican II notes that the baptized "are assigned to the apostolate by the Lord himself." Walter M. Abbot, S.J., ed., *The Documents of Vatican II* (New York: Herder and Herder, 1966), p. 492.

[7] Raimundo Panikkar, *Worship and Secular Man* (Maryknoll: Orbis Books, 1973), p. 1.

[8] Ibid., p. 48.

⁹ Ibid., p. 1.

¹⁰ Ibid., p. 34.

¹¹ Ibid., p. 6.

¹² Wolfhart Pannenberg, *Jesus—God and Man* (Philadelphia: The Westminster Press, 1968), p. 232.

¹³ Joseph A. Fitzmyer, S.J., *The Gospel According to Luke (I–IX)*, Anchor Bible, vol. 28 (Garden City, N.Y.: Doubleday & Co., Inc., 1981), p. 517.

¹⁴ This question of disordered wants is more a question of obedience, hence, matter for the next chapter.

¹⁵ Louis J. Puhl, S.J., ed., *The Spiritual Exercises of St. Ignatius* (Chicago: Loyola University Press, 1951), p. 60.

¹⁶ Ibid.

¹⁷ Franz Jozef van Beeck, S.J., *Christ Proclaimed* (Ramsey: Paulist Press, 1979), pp. 121–22.

¹⁸ Ibid., p. 108.

¹⁹ Ibid., p. 146.

²⁰ The Gospel itself is the best evidence for this comment.

²¹ Raymond Brown, *The Gospel According to John (I–XII)*, Anchor Bible, vol. 29 (Garden City, N.Y.: Doubleday & Co., Inc., 1966), p. cx.

²² Ibid., pp. cxvi–cxxi.

²³ Ibid., p. 284.

²⁴ Ibid., p. 271.

²⁵ Therefore, what is united with Him is redeemed or healed.

²⁶ Van Beeck, *Christ,* p. 394.

²⁷ Ibid., pp. 182 and 424.

²⁸ Ibid. A divine Personkern means "an inner space devoid of humanity at the center of Jesus." Ibid., p. 423.

²⁹ Ibid., p. 423.

³⁰ Ibid., p. 159.

³¹ Jon Sobrino, S.J., *Christology at the Crossroads* (Maryknoll: Orbis Books, 1978), p. 80.

³² Ibid., p. 80.

³³ Ibid., p. 81.

³⁴ Ibid., p. 82.

³⁵ Van Beeck, *Christ,* p. 513.

³⁶ Ibid., pp. 139–40 and 510.

³⁷ Ibid., p. 141.

³⁸ Ibid., p. 574.

³⁹ Jean Hering, *The Epistle to the Hebrews* (London: Epworth Press, 1970), p. 39.

[40] Ibid., p. 40.

[41] Raymond Brown, *Christ Above All: The Message of the Hebrews* (Downers Grove: Ill.: Inter Varsity Press, 1982), p. 101.

[42] David Peterson, *Hebrews and Perfection; An Examination of the Concept of Perfection in Hebrews* (Cambridge: Cambridge University Press, 1982), Society for New Testament Monograph #47, p. 12.

[43] Ibid., p. 169.

[44] Ibid., p. 171.

[45] Ibid., p. 171.

[46] A. Cody, "The Conception of Offering in Hebrews," *New Testament Studies* 9 (1962): 199.

[47] Brown, *Christ Above All*, p. 135.

[48] Peterson, *Hebrews*, p. 173.

[49] Brown, *Christ Above All*, p. 135.

[50] Peterson, *Hebrews*, pp. 186–87.

[51] Ibid., p. 139.

[52] Ibid., p. 146.

[53] Ibid., p. 262.

[54] Bo Reicke, *The Epistles of James, Peter and Jude*, Anchor Bible, vol. 37 (Garden City, N.Y.: Doubleday & Co., Inc., 1964), pp. XXII–XXIII.

[55] Abbot, *Vatican II*, p. 27.

[56] Ibid., p. 27.

[57] Ibid., p. 27.

[58] Abbot, *Vatican II*, p. 60.

[59] The notion of sublation in the second chapter is a first step in systematizing this theology of secularity.

[60] Van Beeck, *Christ*, p. 165.

[61] Ibid., p. 165.

[62] Edward Schillebeeckx, *Christ: The Experience of Jesus as Lord* (New York: The Seabury Press, 1980), p. 269.

[63] Ralph Lerner, "Commerce and Character: The Anglo-American as New-Model Man," *The William and Mary Quarterly* 36 (January 1979): 1–26.

[64] Contradictory views on self-interest go back to the beginnings of economics as a science. See Milton Myers, *The Soul of Modern Economic Man; Ideas of Self-Interest: Hobbes to Adam Smith* (Chicago: University of Chicago Press, 1983), esp. chs. 1 and 4.

[65] This piece of logic has not impressed every savant since Smith. See Albert Hirschman's "Rival Interpretations of Market Society," *Journal of Economic Literature* 20 (December 1982): 1463ff.

[66] Alexis de Tocqueville, *Democracy in America* (London: Oxford University Press/Galaxy, 1947), p. 334.

[67] Ibid., p. 311.

[68] Ibid., p. 312.

[69] Ibid., p. 313.

[70] Bernard Lonergan, unpublished 1976 Questionnaire quoted by Tim Lilburn, S.J., "Bernard Lonergan and the Feeling of Powerlessness," *Review for Religious* 43 (March–April 1984): 249.

[71] Ibid.

[72] Waldermar Molinski, "Integralism," in *Sacramentum Mundi,* ed. Karl Rahner et al., vol. 3 (New York: Herder and Herder, 1969), p. 151.

[73] Ibid.

[74] Ibid.

[75] Gabriel Daly, O.S.A., *Transcendence and Immanence, A Study in Catholic Modernism and Integralism* (Oxford: Clarendon Press, 1980), pp. 187–88.

[76] Abbot, *Vatican II,* p. 233.

[77] Ibid.

[78] Ibid., p. 234.

[79] Ibid., p. 261.

[80] Ibid., p. 271.

[81] Bernard Lonergan, *Method in Theology* (New York: Herder and Herder, 1972), p. 241.

[82] Tim Lilburn, "Lonergan," p. 247.

[83] Bernard Lonergan, "Theology and Praxis," in *Catholic Theological Society Proceedings, 32nd Annual Convention,* ed. Luke Solm, F.S.C. (Bronx: Manhattan College, 1977), p. 7.

Chapter IV   Obedient Hearing—The Third Function of Faith

[1] Walter Brueggemann, "Covenant as Subversive Paradigm," *Christian Century* 97 (1980): 1096.

[2] John Bright, *Covenant and Promise* (Philadelphia: The Westminster Press, 1976), pp. 31–43.

[3] Birger Gerhardsson, *The Ethos of the Bible* (Philadelphia: Fortress Press, 1981), p. 29. Also Gerhardsson's "The Hermeneutic Program in Mt. 22, 37–40" in *Jews, Greeks and Christians,* a W. D. Davies Festschrift, ed. by Robert Hamerton-Kelly (Leiden: E. J. Brill, 1976), pp. 129–50.

[4] G. Ernest Wright, "The Book of Deuteronomy," *Interpreter's Bible,*

ed. George Arthur Buttrick (New York: Abingdon Cokesbury Press, 1953), vol. 2, p. 372.

5 Gerhardsson, *Ethos,* p. 29.

6 Ibid., p. 30.

7 *Interpreter's Bible,* p. 380.

8 Ibid., p. 356.

9 Gerhardsson, *Ethos,* p. 30.

10 Gerhard Kittel, *Theological Dictionary of the New Testament* (Grand Rapids: Eerdmans Pub. Co., 1964), vol. 4, S.V. "Mamonas," p. 389.

11 Gerhardsson, *Ethos,* pp. 38–39.

12 Ibid., p. 41.

13 Ibid., p. 48.

14 The most recent and thorough biography of Ignatius Loyola is Candido de Dalmases, S.J., *Ignatius of Loyola, Founder of the Jesuits* (St. Louis: The Institute of Jesuit Sources, 1985).

15 For the transition from Ignatius' former desires to his mature desires, see E. Edward Kinerk, S.J., "Eliciting Great Desires: Their Place in the Spirituality of the Society of Jesus," *Studies in the Spirituality of Jesuits* 16 (November 1984): 5–9.

16 Louis J. Puhl, S.J., ed., *Spiritual Exercises of St. Ignatius* (Chicago: Loyola University Press, 1951), p. 12.

17 Ibid., p. 6.

18 Ibid., p. 3.

19 Ibid., p. 44.

20 Ibid., p. 45.

21 These are called "A Meditation on Two Standards" and "Three Classes of Men." Ibid., pp. 60–63 and 64–65.

22 Ibid., p. 65.

23 Ibid., p. 71.

24 Ibid., p. 64.

25 Ibid., p. 64.

26 Ibid., p. 65.

27 Ibid., p. 81.

28 Ibid., p. 101.

29 Ibid., p. 101.

30 Ibid., p. 102.

31 Ibid., p. 102.

32 Ibid., p. 103.

33 Ibid., pp. 141–50.

34 Karl Rahner, "The Logic of Concrete, Individual Knowledge in Ig-

natius Loyola," in *The Dynamic Element in the Church,* ed. Karl Rahner (New York: Herder and Herder, 1964), ch. 2, p. 158.

[35] Ibid.

[36] Ibid., p. 155.

[37] I have already noted the importance of theory in Lonergan in the second chapter. Also valuable in this regard is Harvey Egan, S.J., *The Spiritual Exercises and the Ignatian Mystical Horizon* (St. Louis: Institute of Jesuit Sources, 1976), *passim.*

[38] Lonergan, *Method,* pp. 238–41.

[39] Ibid., p. 240.

[40] Ibid., p. 240.

[41] Ibid., p. 119.

[42] Ibid., p. 119.

[43] Ibid., p. 240.

[44] Ibid., p. 242.

[45] Mary Douglas and Baron Isherwood, *The World of Goods* (New York: Basic Books, Inc., 1979), p. 57.

[46] Ibid., p. 5.

[47] Ibid., p. 10.

[48] Ibid., p. 12.

[49] Christopher Lasch, *The Minimal Self: Psychic Survival in Troubled Times* (New York: W. W. Norton & Co., 1984), pp. 27–29.

[50] Ibid., p. 27.

[51] Ibid., p. 33.

[52] Ibid., p. 34.

[53] Ibid., p. 30.

[54] Lonergan, *Method,* p. 105.

[55] Ibid., pp. 84–85 and 257.

[56] Ibid., p. 303.

[57] Ibid., p. 82.

[58] Ibid., p. 258.

[59] Ibid., p. 258.

[60] Ibid., p. 83.

[61] Ibid., p. 84.

[62] Ibid., p. 15.

[63] Ibid., p. 15.

[64] Ibid., p. 15.

[65] Ibid., p. 84.

[66] Ibid., p. 105.

[67] Ibid., p. 112.

[68] Ibid., p. 113.

[69] Ibid., p. 105.

[70] Ibid.

[71] The phrase is Eric Voegelin's whose interest about consciousness was similar to Lonergan's. For a good introduction to his thought on this subject, see John Carmody, "Voegelin's Noetic Differentiations: Religious Implications," *Horizons* 8 (1981): 223ff.

Chapter V Extending the Tent Poles

[1] In my own volume *The Conspiracy of God* (Garden City, N.Y.: Doubleday & Co., Inc., 1973), esp. ch. 5. See also my "Hindsight Prayer," chapter 7 in *Living With Apocalypse; Spiritual Resources for Social Compassion,"* ed. Tilden Edwards (San Francisco: Harper & Row, 1984).

[2] The key teleological principles in one of their classical expressions are found in the Principle and Foundation of the Spiritual Exercises. Louis J. Puhl, S.J. ed., *Spiritual Exercises of St. Ignatius* (Chicago: Loyola University Press, 1951), p. 16.

[3] Ibid., p. 33. The Exercises assume and reinforce a call ethic.

[4] Conspicuous consumption means something different to an economist than to a layman. Roger Mason, *Conspicuous Consumption* (New York: St. Martin's Press, 1981), esp. ch. 1.

[5] We will go into this again in the next chapter on Bonhoeffer.

[6] Karl Rahner, "On the Question of a Formal Existential Ethics," *Theological Investigations* (Baltimore: Helicon Press, 1964), vol. 2, p. 227.

[7] This is fundamental to Christian spirituality. The many traditions of Christian spirituality and asceticism are in function of being able to discern this.

[8] This is the reason for Ignatius' emphasis on what he calls indifference.

[9] Rahner, "Question," p. 227.

[10] Ibid., p. 229.

[11] Puhl, *Spiritual Exercises,* p. 102.

[12] Rahner, "Question," p. 232.

[13] From a volume on Christian faith and the U.S. economy by Shantilal P. Bhagot, *What Does It Profit . . . ?* (Elgin, Ill.: The Brethren Press, 1983), ch. 4.

[14] Gerhard Kittel, *Theological Dictionary of the New Testament* (Grand Rapids: Eerdmans Pub. Co., 1964), vol. 2, article on "Eleemosune" by Rudolf Bultmann, who also notes that it is often difficult to distinguish between almsgiving and acts of benevolence in the New Testament, p. 486.

[15] L. William Countryman, *The Rich Christian in the Church of the Early Empire* (Toronto: The Edwin Mellen Press, 1980), p. 103.

[16] Ibid., p. 109.

[17] Ibid., p. 110.

[18] Ibid., pp. 118–19.

[19] Keith Fullerton Nickle, *The Collection: A Study in Paul's Strategy* (Studies in Biblical Theology #48) (Naperville, Ill.: Alec R. Allenson, 1966), esp. ch. 4.

[20] Ibid., p. 70.

[21] Walter Pilgrim, *Good News to the Poor* (Minneapolis: Augsburg Press, 1981), p. 31.

[22] The reasons for the attraction may not be evident until the person has gone beyond the limitations of time. For example, Matthew 25:37, "Lord, when did we see you hungry . . . ?"

[23] This idea of social location determining perception is a constant in liberation theology. One of the more perceptive treatments of it is John B. Libanio, *Spiritual Discernment and Politics* (Maryknoll: Orbis Books, 1982), esp. chs. 1 and 2.

[24] Monika Hellwig, "Good News to the Poor: Do They Understand It Better?" in *Tracing the Spirit,* ed. James Hug, S.J. (Ramsey: The Paulist Press, 1983), p. 135.

[25] Ibid.

[26] Ibid., p. 145.

[27] Donal Dorr, *Option for the Poor* (Maryknoll: Orbis Books, 1983), p. 253.

[28] Ibid., p. 254.

[29] Ibid., p. 257.

[30] Ibid., p. 257.

[31] Ibid., pp. 165–66.

[32] Ibid., p. 200.

[33] Ibid., p. 201.

[34] Ibid., p. 202.

[35] Ibid., p. 203.

[36] Ibid., p. 210.

[37] Ibid., p. 213.

[38] Ibid., p. 212.

[39] Ibid., pp. 220–21.

[40] Ibid., p. 222.

[41] Ibid., p. 222.

[42] Ibid., p. 227.

[43] Ibid., p. 229.

[44] Ibid., p. 230.

[45] Ibid., p. 233.

[46] John Paul II, *Origins* 14, no. 6 (4 October 1984): 246.

[47] Ibid., p. 246.

[48] Ibid., p. 247.

[49] To be "artisans and authors" of our cultures, we need to develop a discriminating sense of this. Walter M. Abbot, S.J., ed. *The Documents of Vatican II* (New York: Herder and Herder, 1966), p. 261.

[50] Marcello Azevedo, S.J., *Inculturation and the Challenges of Modernity* (Rome: Gregorian University Press, 1982), p. 7.

[51] Abbot, *Vatican II*, p. 264.

[52] Azevedo, *Inculturation*, p. 31.

[53] Ibid., pp. 30–36.

[54] Ibid., p. 32.

[55] Ibid., p. 46.

[56] Louis Dumont and Karl Polanyi were already cited in this connection. See also Wolfgang Schlichter, *The Rise of Western Rationalism* (Berkeley: University of California Press, 1981), esp. ch. 2.

[57] Herman E. Daly, *Steady State Economics* (San Francisco: W. H. Freeman & Co., 1977), p. 20.

[58] Anthony J. Tambasco, *The Bible for Ethics: Juan-Luis Segundo and First-World Ethics* (Lanham: University Press of America, 1981), pp. 92–93.

[59] Libanio, *Spiritual Discernment*, p. 23.

[60] Gustavo Gutierrez, *The Power of the Poor in History* (Maryknoll: Orbis Books, 1983), p. 12.

[61] Ibid., p. 50.

[62] Ibid., p. 65.

[63] Ibid., p. 202.

[64] Ibid., p. 211.

[65] Ibid., p. 210.

[66] Ibid., p. 211.

[67] Ibid., p. 212.

[68] Ibid., p. 212.

[69] See ibid., p. 129.

[70] See the Congregation's: "Instruction on Certain Aspects of the Theology of Liberation," *Origins* 14, no. 13 (13 September 1984); and John Paul II, "One Church, Many Cultures," *Origins* 14, no. 30 (10 January 1985).

[71] Congregation, "Instruction," p. 200.

[72] Ibid., p. 202.

[73] Ibid., p. 203.

[74] Margaret Quigley and Michael Garvey, *The Dorothy Day Book* (Springfield, Ill.: Templegate Publishers, 1982), p. 70.

[75] Dorothy Day, *Loaves and Fishes* (New York: Harper & Row, 1963), p. 79.

[76] Quigley and Garvey, *Dorothy Day*, p. 11.

[77] George Higgins, "Dorothy Day: A Sign for the Times," *Origins* 10, no. 3 (12 February 1981): 547.

[78] Ibid., p. 549.

[79] Ibid., p. 546.

[80] William D. Miller, *Dorothy Day: A Biography* (San Francisco: Harper & Row, 1982), p. 12.

[81] Ibid., p. 226.

[82] Ibid., p. 226.

[83] Marc H. Ellis, *Peter Maurin: Prophet in the 20th Century* (Ramsey: The Paulist Press, 1981), p. 40.

[84] Ibid., p. 42.

[85] Ibid., p. 35.

[86] Ibid., p. 35.

[87] Ibid., p. 50.

[88] Ibid., p. 49.

[89] Ibid., p. 49.

[90] Ibid., p. 46.

[91] Ibid., p. 53.

[92] Ibid., pp. 69–70.

[93] Peter Maurin, *Easy Essays* (Chicago: Franciscan Herald Press, 1961), pp. 123 and 105.

[94] Ibid., p. 37.

[95] Ibid., p. 38.

[96] Dorothy Day, *Loaves and Fishes*, p. 81.

[97] Ibid., pp. 82 and 89.

[98] Ibid., p. 245.

[99] Ibid., p. 202.

[100] Quigley and Garvey, *Dorothy Day*, p. 53.

[101] Ibid., p. 54.

[102] Dorothy Day, *On Pilgrimage* (New York: Curtis Books, 1972), p. 170.

[103] Dorothy Day, *By Little and By Little, The Selective Writings of Dorothy Day* (New York: Knopf, 1983), p. 97.

[104] U.S. Bureau of the Census, Current Population Reports Series P-60, no. 149, "Money, Income and Poverty Status of Families in the United

States: 1984" (Washington, D.C.: U.S. Government Printing Office, 1985).

Chapter VI   Discipleship and Today's Economy

[1] Dietrich Bonhoeffer, *The Cost of Discipleship* (New York: Macmillan, 1963), p. 36.

[2] Ibid., p. 35.

[3] Ibid., p. 35.

[4] Ibid., p. 37.

[5] Ibid., p. 37.

[6] Ibid., p. 54.

[7] Ibid., p. 54.

[8] Ibid., p. 55.

[9] Ibid., p. 206.

[10] Ibid., p. 206.

[11] Ibid., p. 207.

[12] Ibid., p. 84.

[13] Ibid., p. 85.

[14] Ibid., p. 86.

[15] Ibid., pp. 87–88.

[16] Ibid., p. 84.

[17] Ibid., p. 90.

[18] Eberhard Bethge, *Dietrich Bonhoeffer* (New York: Harper & Row, 1977), p. 379.

[19] Bonhoeffer, *Discipleship*, p. 69.

[20] Ibid.

[21] André Dumas, "Religion and Reality in the Work of Bonhoeffer," in *A Bonhoeffer Legacy*, ed. by A. J. Klassen (Grand Rapids: Eerdmans Publishing Co., 1981), pp. 258–67.

[22] Quoted by Dumas in "Religion," p. 260.

[23] Ibid., p. 260.

[24] Ibid., p. 261.

[25] Ibid., p. 261.

[26] Bonhoeffer, *Discipleship*, p. 70.

[27] Dietrich Bonhoeffer, *Christ the Center* (New York: Harper & Row, 1966), p. 43.

[28] Franz Jozef van Beeck, *Christ Proclaimed* (Ramsey: Paulist Press, 1979), p. 239.

[29] Van Beeck, *Christ*, p. 141.

[30] I will treat this in greater depth in the last chapter.

[31] Van Beeck, *Christ*, p. 233.

[32] Our attitude about "destroying sovereignties" is established in Chapter II.

[33] Bonhoeffer, *Christ*, p. 80.

[34] Van Beeck, *Christ*, p. 246.

[35] Ibid., p. 246.

[36] Dietrich Bonhoeffer, *Ethics* (New York: Macmillan, 1967).

[37] Ibid., p. 277.

[38] Ibid., p. 277.

[39] Ibid., p. 278.

[40] Ibid., p. 285.

[41] Ibid., p. 285.

[42] Ibid., p. 207.

[43] Ibid., p. 207.

[44] The worldliness *(Weltkirchlichkeit)* of God in Bonhoeffer is analyzed by André Dumas, *Dietrich Bonhoeffer, Theologian of Reality* (New York: Macmillan, 1968), chs. 6 and 10.

[45] Dumas, "Religion," p. 265.

[46] Bonhoeffer, *Ethics*, p. 227.

[47] Ibid., p. 227.

[48] Ibid., p. 228.

[49] Ibid., p. 232.

[50] Ibid., pp. 236 and 327–28.

[51] Ibid., p. 233.

[52] Ibid., pp. 224–25.

[53] Ibid., p. 226.

[54] Both of these manuscripts were published much later—1954 and 1956, respectively.

[55] Bonhoeffer, *Ethics*, p. 53.

[56] Ibid., p. 265.

[57] Ibid., p. 265.

[58] Ibid., p. 266.

[59] Ibid., p. 283.

[60] Ibid., p. 20.

[61] Ibid., p. 25.

[62] Ibid., p. 17.

[63] Ibid., pp. 26–27.

[64] Ibid., pp. 17–18.

[65] Ibid., p. 301.

[66] Ibid., p. 286.

[67] Dumas, *Bonhoeffer*, p. 156.

[68] Bonhoeffer, *Ethics,* p. 49.

[69] Ibid., p. 52.

[70] Ibid., p. 80.

[71] Ibid., pp. 80–81.

[72] Ibid., p. 82.

[73] Ibid., p. 82.

[74] Ibid., p. 81.

[75] Ibid., p. 264.

[76] Dietrich Bonhoeffer, *Letters and Papers from Prison,* ed. Eberhard Bethge (New York: Macmillan, 1972), pp. 360–61.

[77] Ibid., p. 344.

[78] Ibid., p. 346.

[79] Ibid., pp. 344–46.

[80] I believe André Dumas has seen this best. See his *Bonhoeffer,* ch. 8.

[81] Bonhoeffer, *Christ,* pp. 59–60.

[82] Ibid., pp. 50–51.

[83] Ibid., p. 52.

[84] Ibid., p. 55.

[85] Ibid., p. 58.

[86] Ibid., p. 60.

[87] Ibid., p. 60.

[88] Bethge, *Bonhoeffer,* pp. 379 and 387–88.

[89] Bonhoeffer, *Christ,* p. 60.

[90] Bonhoeffer, *Ethics,* p. 80.

[91] Ibid., p. 80.

[92] Ibid., p. 80.

[93] Ibid., p. 81.

[94] Ibid., p. 81.

[95] Ibid., p. 83.

[96] Ibid., p. 85.

[97] Ibid., p. 85.

[98] Bonhoeffer, *Prison,* p. 381.

[99] Most of his writings were notes written with a view to eventually publishing complete works on the topics broached by him.

[100] Ibid., p. 282.

[101] Ibid., p. 382.

[102] Ibid., p. 281.

[103] Ibid., pp. 382–83.

Chapter VII   Hope and Economic Activity

[1] See "Virtue," *Sacramentum Mundi* (New York: Herder and Herder, 1970), vol. 6, entry by Karl Rahner, pp. 337–38.

[2] "Hope," Ibid., vol. 3, entry by F. Kerstiens, pp. 61–65.

[3] James L. Muyskens, *The Sufficiency of Hope,* The Conceptual Foundations of Religion (Philadelphia: Temple University Press, 1979), p. 18.

[4] Haenchen gives a good overview of the literature on this question in the Acts of the Apostles in general and the Pentecost miracle in particular. See Ernst Haenchen, *The Acts of the Apostles, A Commentary* (Philadelphia: The Westminster Press, 1971), intro. and pp. 166–75.

[5] James D. G. Dunn, *Christ and the Spirit* (Philadelphia: The Westminster Press, 1975), pp. 136–52.

[6] Ibid., p. 142.

[7] Ibid., p. 154.

[8] Ibid., p. 139.

[9] See "Inspiration," *Sacramentum Mundi,* vol. 3, entry by Luis Alonso-Schokel, pp. 145–50.

[10] See Joseph A. Fitzmyer, S.J., *The Gospel According to Luke (I–IX)* Anchor Bible, vol. 28 (Garden City, N.Y.: Doubleday & Co., Inc., 1981), pp. 14–17.

[11] Philip Wheelwright, *Metaphor and Reality* (Bloomington, Ind.: Indiana University Press, 1962), pp. 94–96 for his distinction between tensive and steno symbols.

[12] Avery Dulles, *Models of Revelation* (Garden City, N.Y.: Doubleday & Co., Inc., 1983), pp. 132–33.

[13] Nathan Mitchell, "Symbols Are Actions, Not Objects," *Living Worship* 13, no. 2 (February 1977): 1–2.

[14] Victor White, a disciple of Carl Jung, quoted by Dulles in *Models,* p. 136.

[15] Ibid., p. 137. He attributes this idea to Michael Polanyi.

[16] Mircea Eliade, "Methodological Remarks on the Study of Religious Symbolism," in *The History of Religions,* ed. Mircea Eliade and Joseph M. Kitagawa (Chicago: University of Chicago Press, 1959), pp. 99–100.

[17] Mircea Eliade, *Patterns in Comparative Religion* (New York: Sheed and Ward, 1958), p. 456.

[18] Ibid., p. 419.

[19] Gabriel Marcel, *The Mystery of Being* (London: The Harvill Press, 1950), ch. 10.

[20] Martin Hengel, *Property and Riches in the Early Church* (Philadel-

phia: Fortress Press, 1974), p. 88. This term, "love communism," was probably coined by the sociologist of religion, Ernst Troeltsch.

[21] Esp. Karris' "Poor and Rich: The Lukan *Sitz im Leben,*" in *Perspectives on Luke-Acts,* ed. Chas. Talbert (Edinburgh: T. & T. Clark, Ltd., 1978), pp. 122–23.

[22] See my "Eucharist in Corinth: You Are the Christ," in *Above Every Name: The Lordship of Christ and Social Systems,* ed. Thomas E. Clarke (Ramsey, N.J.: Paulist Press, 1980).

[23] Cf. "koinos," art. by Hauck in Gerhard Kittel's *Theological Dictionary of the New Testament* (Grand Rapids: Eerdmans Pub. Co., 1964), vol. 3, pp. 789 and 809.

[24] Hauck, *Theol. Dictionary,* p. 798.

[25] Hauck, *Theol. Dictionary,* pp. 790, 796, 803.

[26] Cf. "diakonia," article by Beyer in Kittel, *Theological Dictionary,* vol. 2, pp. 87–93.

[27] Keith Fullerton Nickle, *The Collection, A Study in Paul's Strategy* (Studies in Biblical Theology #48 (Naperville, Ill.: Alec R. Allenson, 1966), p. 180.

[28] Walter Kasper, *Faith and the Future* (New York: Crossroads Pub. Co., 1982), p. 9.

[29] Karl Rahner, "An Investigation of the Incomprehensibility of God in Thomas Aquinas," in *Theological Investigations,* ed. Karl Rahner (New York: The Seabury Press, 1979), vol. 16, p. 246.

[30] Karl Mannheim, *Ideology and Utopia* (New York: Harcourt, Brace and Co., 1960), p. 173.

[31] Ibid., pp. 184–90.

[32] Ibid., pp. 174–83.

[33] Paul Ricoeur, *Politics and Social Essays* (Athens, Oh.: Ohio University Press, 1974), ch. 12.

[34] Mihailo Markovic, *Democratic Socialism* (New York: St. Martin's Press, 1982). This volume advocates a nonutopian socialism, esp. ch. 1.

[35] See my "Individualism and Rights in Karl Marx," in *Human Rights in the Americas: Struggle for Consensus,* ed. Alfred Hennelly and John Langan (Washington, D.C.: Georgetown University Press, 1982), ch. 5.

[36] Robert W. Funk, *Apocalypticism; An Historical and Theological Problem* (New York: Herder and Herder, 1969), pp. 175–91.

[37] Ted Peters, *Futures Human and Divine* (Atlanta: John Knox Press, 1978), pp. 46–47.

[38] George W. MacRae, S.J., "Eschatology," *Chicago Studies* 17, no. 1 (Spring 1978): 62.

[39] Ibid., p. 62.

[40] Ibid., pp. 63–64.

[41] Franz Jozef van Beeck, *Christ Proclaimed* (Ramsey: Paulist Press, 1979), p. 155.

[42] Ibid., p. 153.

Chapter VIII   That Christ May Be My Wealth

[1] Franz Jozef van Beeck, *Christ Proclaimed* (Ramsey: Paulist Press, 1979), p. 238.

[2] Ibid., p. 122.

[3] Ibid., p. 91.

[4] Ibid., p. 92.

[5] Ibid., p. 122.

[6] Ibid., p. 123.

[7] Ibid., p. 139.

[8] Ibid., p. 127.

[9] Ibid., p. 141.

[10] Ibid., p. 140.

[11] Ibid., p. 114.

[12] Ibid., p. 101.

[13] Ibid., p. 108.

[14] Ibid., p. 509.

[15] Ibid., p. 509.

[16] Ibid., p. 513.

[17] Ibid., p. 511.

[18] Ibid., p. 511.

[19] Ibid., p. 512.

[20] Ibid., p. 512.

[21] Ibid., p. 513.

[22] Ibid., p. 513.

[23] Ibid., p. 573.

Index

Abba, 18, 19
Ablutions (handwashing), 33, 34, 147
Abraham, 13, 39, 89, 108, 164, 240
Acid rain, 65
Act and Being (Bonhoeffer), 189
Acts of the Apostles, 7, 78, 146, 148, 208–9, 214–15, 216, 220, 221, 223, 224, 225, 231
Addiction (addictive behavior), viii, 142, 144
Affections: Spiritual Exercises and schooling of, 119–30
Alienation, 131
Almsgiving, 33–34, 36, 38, 146–49
Anawim, 40, 150
Anomie, 162
Antiochus Epiphanes IV, 229
Anxiety, 8–9, 10, 12
Apocalypticism, 228–29, 231–32
Aristotle, 102
Assets (goods, resources), 8, 184; Christ as one's wealth and, 234–45; covenant and, 113, 114–16; hope and sharing and, 200–33 (see also Hope; Sharing); mammon illness and (see Mammon illness); obediential hearing and (see Obedience); Spiritual Exercises and, 120–30. *See also* Money; Possessions
Attachment(s), 120–39; detachment and, 120–39; Spiritual Exercises and, 120–30. *See also* specific aspects, kinds
Augurs, 209, 225
Autonomy, 57, 65, 77, 84, 85, 90, 102, 103–4, 106, 218, 225, 235; as

antithesis of inclusion, 85. *See also* Faith
Avarice. *See* Greed

Banks, viii
Baptism, vii, 71, 72, 75, 95, 147, 179, 196–97, 200; and inclusion, 75 (see also Inclusion); meaning of, 75–76
Beatitudes, 22–23, 158
"Bodies as a living sacrifice," 70–72, 75–76, 78
Body of Christ, 71, 148–49, 154, 166, 237; almsgiving and, 148–49
Bonhoeffer, Dietrich, 177–99
Bread, 183, 208, 215, 223; and wine, Eucharist and, vii–viii, 75–76 (see also Eucharist)
Brethrenomics, 146–49, 153, 194–95
Brueggemann, Walter, 3–4, 23

Call (call ethic), 127–30; discipleship and, 178–79, 180; obediential hearing and, 141, 153, 154, 178–79, 180; Spiritual Exercises and, 127–30
Cappadocian Gregorys, 54
Care (caring), 8, 118; Christ as one's wealth and, 237–45; hope and sharing and, 209–10, 215, 217
Catholic Worker (newspaper), 171
Catholic Worker Movement, 168–76
Chalcedon: Council of, 54, 87
Charity, 90, 95, 150, 176. *See also* Almsgiving
Childlikeness, 40
Christ. *See* Jesus (Jesus Christ)
Christology, ix, 177–79; Bonhoeffer's, 177–99; Christ as one's wealth and, 234–45; inclusion and, 81–88, 183,

185–86, 187, 197–99; soteriological principle of, 54; Van Beeck's (see Van Beeck, Franz Jozef). See also specific aspects, concepts, individuals

Christ Proclaimed (Van Beeck), ix, 252

Christ the Center (Bonhoeffer), 196–97

Church (Roman Catholic Church). See Roman Catholic Church

Cleopas, 231

Coleridge, Samuel Taylor, 23

Collection(s), 147–48; at liturgical services, 53

Colossians, Letter to the, 59

Commitment, 57, 145, 158, 164

Common sense, 62–63, 65, 135, 136, 138, 139

Communion. See Koinonia

Communion of Spirits (Bonhoeffer), 189

Community (communality), ix, 1, 2, 26–27, 45, 107–8, 117, 118, 141, 146, 147–48, 151–52, 163, 165, 172, 175; Christ as, 197–99, 242–43; new, hope and sharing and, 208, 214–33

Commutative justice, 60–61

Compassion, ix, 1, 2, 4, 8, 12–13, 14, 22, 34, 66, 237, 238; almsgiving and, 146–48; God's, 122; Jesus', 44

Competition (competitiveness), 149, 153

Conscience, 93, 144, 169, 191

Consciousness: human, 62–68, 86, 94, 130–39, 149, 165, 191–92; differentiated, 62, 63–68, 135, 136–37; modernity and, 162–64; split, 14–17, 48–49, 65–68, 113; technology and, 161–62; transcendence and, 130–39; undifferentiated, 62–63, 64, 65, 66–67, 135, 136–37; unitary, 20–21, 22, 28, 47, 48–49, 236

Consolation: desolation and, 128–30

Consumption (consumerism), xi, 52, 54, 133–35, 139, 142, 143, 152, 161–64, 220; conspicuous, 143

Contemplation, 121, 123

Contracts: commutative justice and, 61

Conversion, 31, 40, 46, 74, 100, 130–33; healing and, 31, 40, 46–49; imagination and, 23–25; intellectual and moral, 130–33; option for the poor and, 156, 157, 158

Co-optation: image of Christ vis-à-vis the economic system and, 52, 53

Corinthians, Letters to the, 52, 53, 56, 148–49, 184, 185, 223, 224, 239, 241

Cost of Discipleship (Bonhoeffer), 177–86

Covenant, 105–19; New, 109–19

Creation, 59, 218, 225; new, 225

Cross, 115

Culture, 244; faith and enculturation and, 142, 143, 149, 159–64, 221, 237, 244; and growth ethic, Maurin on, 173–74; and mammon illness, 1–49 (see also Mammon illness). See also specific aspects, developments

Day, Dorothy, 167–76

Death, 183, 218, 231, 239, 241–43; and resurrection (see Resurrection)

Demons. See Devil (demons)

Despair, 218, 221

Deuteronomy, Book of, 107, 108, 111, 112, 114, 150

Devil (demons), 20, 43–45, 79. See also Lucifer; Satan

Diakonia, 223–25

Dignity: justice and, 56, 61, 103, 165

Discipleship, 177–79; Bonhoeffer on, 177–99; today's economy and, 177–99

Distributive justice, 60, 61

Domitian, Emperor, 94

Dorr, Donal, 154–55

Douglas, Mary, 133

Dumas, André, 193

Dunn, James D. G., 210

Easter, 231–32

Economic anthropology, 46–49, 62, 64

Economic rationality: development of, 162–64

Election, 128–30

Eliade, Mircea, 213–14

Elitism, 45, 100–1
Emmaus, 229–31
Epaphroditus, 242
Ephesians, Letter to the, 58–59, 183, 184, 201, 228, 244
Equipoise (singleness of heart), 141, 142–45, 146, 151, 153. *See also* Indifference
Ethics, 61–62, 64, 72, 75, 191–96, 197–99; obediential hearing and, 186–90 *(see also* Obedience). *See also* Morals
Ethics (Bonhoeffer), 186–90, 191–96, 197–99
Eucharist, vii–viii, 75–76, 84, 99, 196–97
Evangelii Nuntiandi (Paul VI, 1975), 156, 157
Exegesis: historical-critical, eisegesis versus, 45
Exodus, Book of, 107
Ezekiel, Book of, 109

Faith, viii, ix–x, 1–49, 50–68, 200, 240, 244–45; and culture, 1, 69, 142, 149, 159–64, 221 *(see also* Culture); discipleship and, 178–99; ethics and, 186–99; healing powers of, 21–36, 219, 221, 222; hope and, 200–33 *(see also* Hope); inclusion as the second function of, 69–104 *(see also* Inclusion); obediential hearing as the third function of, 105–39, 140–76, 178 *(see also* Obedience); Spiritual Exercises and, 119–30; sublation of the economic system and *(see* Sublation); values and, 66–68 *(see also* Values)
Fathers of the Church, 147
Finances (financial activities). *See* Money; specific aspects, concepts
Food and drink symbolism, 83, 84
Fools (folly), 34–36, 218
Francis of Assisi, St., 171–72
Freedom, ix, 47–48, 56, 64, 122, 137, 140–41, 144, 145, 165, 188; hope and, 200, 202, 229. *See also* Autonomy
Freire, Paolo, 164

Genesis, Book of, 96, 217–18

Gentiles, 73
Gerasenes, 43–44, 48
Gestalt, 196
God, 3–6, 7–10; and covenant, 105–19; faith in and sublation of the economy as His intention, 50–68, 69–104 *(see also* Faith; Sublation); hope and, 200–33; inclusion in *(see* Inclusion); Kingdom of *(see* Kingdom of God); obediential hearing and, 105–39 *(see also* Obedience); Spiritual Exercises and, 119–30. *See also* specific aspects, concepts, developments
Good News, 58, 153, 156, 160. *See also* Resurrection
Good Samaritan: parable of, 13–14
Gospel(s), x–xi, 5–6, 53, 78, 143, 147, 204, 208, 211, 219, 222, 237, 242; obediential hearing and, 143, 147, 153, 178 *(see also* Obedience); and the poor, 152, 153, 163–64, 166, 173 *(see also* Poverty; specific aspects). *See also* specific aspects, individuals, problems
Grace, 143, 177–78, 242; Bonhoeffer on discipleship and, 177–82, 199; Spiritual Exercises and, 120, 121, 122, 126–27
Greed (avarice, rapaciousness), 33, 81, 152, 220
Gregorys of Cappadocia, 54
Growth ethic, 173–74. *See also* "Making it"; Profit
Gutierrez, Gustavo, 164–67

Handwashing (ablutions), 33, 34, 147
Headship image (Godhead), 58–60, 82, 223
Healing (cure): mammon illness and, 3, 5, 9–10, 15–16, 17, 21–49; conversion and, 31, 40, 46–49; faith and, 200–1, 220; hope and, 200–1, 213; parables and, 24, 25–36, 42, 46; sublation of the economic system and, 69–104 *(see also* Sublation)
Health of the economy, 46–49, 62, 64, 238–39; characteristics of, 47–49, 139

Hebrews, Letter to the, 20, 25, 86, 88–89, 90–94, 96, 184, 226
Hegel, Georg Wilhelm Friedrich, 51
Hellwig, Monika, 152–53
Helplessness, 68, 134
Higgins, Monsignor George, 168
Holy Spirit, 75, 244. *See also* Spirit
Hope (hoping): economic activity and, 200–33, 237, 238, 244–45; anatomy of, 201–7; correcting, 229–33; differs from desire, 202–3; direction for, 207–12; as an energy, 200; eschatological, 228–29; faith and, 200–33 *(see also* Faith); hopeless Christianity and, 217–22; new communality and, 214–17; Pentecost and sharing and, 212–22, 223; seeing less and growing in, 225–29; Trinity and sharing of goods and, 223–24
Hosea, Book of, 109
Hostility: image of Christ's posture toward the economy as, 52, 53
Hunger march (Washington, D.C., 1932), 168–69

Identity (self-identity), 162, 221, 244; authentic, obediential hearing and, 180, 182, 185–86, 192; Pentecost and, 215
Ideology, 162–63, 182, 227, 238; enculturated faith and, 162–64, 182, 227, 238
Idolatry, 112
Ignatius Loyola, 79–80, 119–30, 157; Rules for the Discernment of Spirits of, 128–30; Spiritual Exercises of, 119–30
Illness, 1–49, 69; faith and, 3–49 *(see also* Faith); healing, 21–49, 200–1, 220 *(see also* Healing); hope and, 200–1, 220 *(see also* Hope); mammon, 10–49 *(see also* Mammon illness). *See also* Health; specific aspects, concepts, developments, problems
Imagination, 211–12; healing powers of, 22–25, 211–12
Incarnation, 53, 54, 179, 189, 194, 245
Inclusion, 69–104, 183, 201, 230–31,

237, 244–45; and Christology, 81–88, 183, 185–86, 187, 197–99; clarifying, objections to, 97–104; as the second function of faith, 69–104; a way of life, 78–81
Indifference, 52, 53, 125, 131, 142–45, 163. *See also* Equipoise
Individualism, 64, 98, 142
Individuation, 64. *See also* Self-appropriation
Injustice(s), 53, 98–99, 166, 227. *See also* Justice; specific aspects, kinds, problems
Integralism, 102, 104, 131
Interiority, 64–65, 66–67, 135, 136–39, 142, 143, 160, 161, 209
International Synod of Bishops: "Justice in the World" of (1971), 62
Irenaeus, 147
Isaiah, 188
Israel (Israelites), 4–6, 11–36, 51, 60, 89, 93, 240; and almsgiving, 146–48; and covenant, 106–19. *See also* Jews (Judaism)

Jeremiah, Book of, 72, 109
Jerusalem, 18–19, 29, 37, 148–49, 210, 220, 230
Jesus (Jesus Christ): Christology and *(see* Christology); and faith, 50–68, 69–104 *(see also* Faith); and healing, 200–1 *(see also* Healing); historical, 85–88, 92; hope and, 200–33 *(see also* Hope); humanity (human concerns) of, 85–88, 89, 91, 92, 93, 96, 206, 237–38 *(see also* specific aspects, kinds); inclusion and, 69–104 *(see also* Inclusion); the Mediator, 179–80, 242; ministry of, 78–96, 115, 189, 206, 230; mystery of, 71, 74, 75, 86, 91, 105, 237, 242–45; New Covenant and, 110, 113–19; obediential hearing of *(see* Obedience); perfection of, 91–93; presence in the poor of, 243 *(see also* Poverty; specific aspects); priesthood of, 88–96, 99, 105; Spiritual Exercises and, 120–30; sublating intentions to the economic system of, 50–68, 69–104 *(see also* Sublation); titles (metaphors) for,

81–82, 87–88, 183, 235–44. *See also* specific aspects

Jews (Judaism), 88–89, 90–94, 96, 205, 210, 216, 229, 240; and almsgiving, 146–48; and covenant, 106–19. *See also* Israel

John, St. (the Evangelist), Gospel of, 37, 44, 56, 58, 71, 77, 82, 83, 84–85, 183, 222, 223, 237

John XXIII, Pope, 155

John Paul II, Pope, 156–59, 161, 166–67

Johnson, Lyndon B.: and war on poverty, 176

John the Baptist, 37, 220

Joshua, Book of, 106, 107

Jubilee ordinance, 108

Jung, Carl, 64

Justice, 1, 3, 4, 34, 36, 60–62, 66, 81, 99, 152, 176, 230, 234, 237, 240; commutative, 60–61; distributive, 60, 61; hope and, 218; social, 60, 61. *See also* Injustice(s)

Kasemann, Ernst, 71

Kasper, Walter, 225–26

Kingdom of God (Kingdom of Heaven), 7, 11–12, 22–36, 40–41, 42, 43, 166, 184, 188; hope and, 204–10

Kings, Book(s) of, 3, 5

Koinonia, 223–25, 230, 242–44

Lasch, Christopher, 134

Latin American Church, 155–57, 164–67

Lazarus, 12–13, 37, 44, 145–46, 158, 159

Leo XIII, Pope, 154–55

Letters and Papers from Prison (Bonhoeffer), 195, 198

Leviticus, Book of, 108

Liberation theology, 157, 167

Lonergan, Bernard, 60, 62, 64–65, 100, 104, 130–39, 143, 156

Love, 1, 2, 8, 34, 36, 40–41, 42, 49, 116–19, 126–27, 133, 145, 190, 200, 209, 243; ethics and, 193–95; of God, 36, 41, 42, 67, 73, 112–13, 114, 115–16, 118, 125, 137–38, 145, 204, 209, 240, 241; God's, for man

and the world, 57–58, 72, 78, 112, 113, 137–38, 188, 189, 190, 193, 226, 241; obediential hearing and, 112, 113, 114–19, 137–38, 139, 143, 190, 193; of one another, 114–19, 190, 209, 221, 228; Spiritual Exercises and, 120–21, 123, 126–27; unconditional, 115–19

Lucifer, 123–24. *See also* Devil; Satan

Luke, Gospel of, 4, 7–10, 11, 12, 13, 14–15, 17, 18, 19–20, 21, 22, 23, 25–26, 27–28, 29, 30–31, 33–35, 36–40, 41–42, 43–44, 52, 79, 80, 81, 90, 91, 101, 126, 143–44, 146–47, 184, 209, 210, 212, 215, 219, 220–22, 229–30, 231

Lynch, William, 23

"Making it," 16, 22–23. *See also* Growth ethic

Mammon illness, 10–49, 79, 113, 116, 117, 118, 124; cure (healing), 21–49, 79 *(see also* Healing; specific aspects); faith and, 3–49 *(see also* Faith); sublation of the economy and *(see* Sublation). *See also* Illness; specific aspects, concepts, developments

Mark, Gospel of, 57, 82, 118, 180

Marriage, 124, 187

Martha and Mary episode, 80

Mater et Magistra (encyclical, John XXIII), 155

Matthew, Gospel of, 9, 113–16, 118, 146, 147, 150, 160, 194, 195, 204, 205, 222

Maurin, Peter, 169–76

Medellin: document of the Latin American bishops at (1968), 155–56, 157

Meditation, ix, 120–21, 123–25

Metz, Johannes, 225–26

Mitchell, Nathan, 212–13

Modernity, 161–64; traits of, 161–64

Money (finances), 2, 52, 54, 68, 80, 114, 120, 125; Christ as one's wealth and, 234–45; faith and sublation of the economy and, 52–68, 69–104, 234–45 *(see also* Faith; Sublation); hope and sharing and, 203–33; obediential hearing and *(see*

Obedience). *See also* Assets;
Possessions; specific aspects
Money changers, 52
Monotheism, 112
Morals (moral choices, moral criteria
and goals), 60, 61–62, 64, 72, 74,
75, 131–39, 140–76 *passim,* 177–99;
norms, 144–45, 186, 190 *(see also*
Ethics); obedience and, 131–39,
186–90 *(see also* Obedience); and
self-transcendence *(see*
Transcendence)
"Morning Offering syndrome," 70
Moses, 4, 5, 107, 165
Mystery (mysteries), 71, 74, 86, 214,
217, 220, 232–33; of Jesus, 71, 74,
78, 86, 91, 105, 232–33, 237, 242–
45; of Pentecost, 208, 214–22, 232;
of voluntary poverty, 176

Neighbors, 215–16, 219; hope and
sharing and, 215–16 *(see also*
Sharing); and love of one another,
114–19 *(see also under* Love)
Nicea: Christological formulas of, 87
Nuclear weapons, 65
Numbness, 12–13, 14, 22, 25, 28

Obedience (obediential hearing), 105–
39, 140–76, 177–99, 201, 237, 244–
45; false, 190–96; as function of
faith, 105–39, 140–76; new, 113–19;
norms, 117–18; to reality, oneself,
and God, 130–39, 140–76 *passim,*
177–99, 237, 244–45; self-
transcendence and, 130–39 *(see also*
Transcendence); Spiritual Exercises
and, 119–30
O'Brien, David, 168
Octogesima Adveniens (encyclical,
Paul VI, 1971), 156
Offertory, 75–76
On Pilgrimage: The Sixties (Day), 176
Option for the Poor (Dorr), 154–55
Origen, 147

Panikkar, Raimundo, 76–77
Parables, 113–15, 145–46; healing
and, 24, 25–36, 42, 46; hope and,
203–6. *See also* specific parables

Pascendi dominici gregis (encyclical,
Pius X, 1907), 102
Paul, Apostle, St., 52, 70–71, 72–74,
76, 77, 147–49, 221, 223–24, 226,
236, 239–44
Paul VI, Pope, 155, 156
Peace, ix, 129, 183, 231
Pearl of great price parable, 24, 204–6
Pentecost, 208–22, 223–25; mystery
of, 208, 214–22, 232; symbolism of,
212–14, 232
Peter, Apostle, St.: Letter of, 41, 94–
95
Peterson, David, 92
Pharisees, 15, 30–31, 32–34, 114, 147,
192
Philippians, Letter to the, 184, 239–
44
Philosophy and science: split between,
65
Pius X, Pope, 102
Pius XI, Pope, 155
Pluralism, 161–62
Populorum Progressio (encyclical, Paul
VI), 155
Possessions (goods): Christ as one's
wealth and, 235–45; hope and
sharing of, 200–33 *(see also* Hope;
Sharing); obediential hearing and
use of, 114–39, 140–76, 177–99
passim; Spiritual Exercises and,
120–30. *See also* Assets; Money
Poverty (the poor), x, 1, 9, 12–13, 33,
39, 61, 107–8, 140–76 *passim,* 224;
almsgiving and, 146–49; Christ as
one's wealth and caring for, 238–
45; hope and sharing and, 207, 224;
(see also Hope; Sharing); option for,
relation of the Church to, 150–76;
Spiritual Exercises and, 118, 121,
123, 124; U.S. Census data (1984),
176
Power: faith and Spirit and, 219–22,
223–24
Prayer, 32, 45–46, 95, 99, 120, 169,
185, 223, 241, 242; Spiritual
Exercises and, 120–27
Privatism, 98, 99–100, 132, 153
Profit (gain, profit motive), 72, 77–98,
160–64; reassessed, Christ as one's

wealth and, 239–45. *See also*
Growth ethic; "Making it"
Prophets, 108, 114, 150, 231
Promises, 61, 209; commutative
justice and, 61; differs from augurs,
209
Proverbs, Book of, 147
Psalms, Book of, 111, 225
Puebla Conference, 166
Purse image: in Luke, 12, 17–18

Quadragesimo Anno (encyclical, Pius
XI, 1931), 155, 169

Rahner, Karl, 129, 226
Reality (realities), 162–64, 198–99,
201, 208–9, 213, 214, 226, 230;
Christ's titles and, 235–37, 244–45;
obediential hearing and, 179, 180–
86, 187–90, 192–96; symbols and,
213
Redemption, 59–60, 67–68, 99, 153,
218; almsgiving and, 147
Redemptor Hominis (encyclical, John
Paul II), 157–58
"Renewed mind" ("transformed
mind"), 71, 72, 74, 75
Repentance, 222
Rerum Novarum (encyclical, Leo
XIII, 1891), 154–55, 169
Responsibility (obligations), 74;
obedience and, 188, 189, 190, 191
Resurrection (Risen Christ), 40, 53,
58, 59, 60, 81, 92, 93, 183, 191,
218, 220, 229, 230–32, 241–43;
mystery of, 232–33
Retreat (retreatants): Spiritual
Exercises and, 119–30
Rich man parable, 25–29, 34–36,
145–46, 158, 159
Ricoeur, Paul, 23
Robinson, John, 86
Roman Catholic Church (Roman
Catholicism), vii–xi, 60–62, 72–104
passim; and Christ as one's wealth,
237–45; hope and sharing and,
200–33; and the poor, 154–76 *(see
also* Poverty); social mission of,
154–56. *See also* specific aspects,
concepts, developments, individuals
Romans, Letter to the, 70–71, 72, 73,
75, 89, 101, 138, 184, 193, 204,
206, 229, 242
Rome (Romans), 18–19, 37
Running after things: as a symptom
of mammon illness, 11, 79

Sabbath, 57, 96, 108, 115
Sacraments, vii, viii, 105, 196–97. *See
also* specific sacraments
Sacrifice, 70–72, 75–76, 78, 108, 242
Sadducees, 18–19
Salvation, 9, 12–13, 14, 38–39, 41, 54,
67–68, 144, 153; obediential hearing
and, 92–93, 121, 122, 126, 144,
177–78
Samaritan woman, 77, 83. *See also*
Good Samaritan parable
Satan, 179; as the master of mammon,
19–20. *See also* Devil; Lucifer
Schneiders, Sandra, 45–46
Schooenberg, Piet, 86
Science and philosophy: split between,
65
Second Vatican. *See* Vatican Council
II
Secularity (secularization), 57, 76,
162, 187, 201. *See also* specific
aspects, developments, problems
Self-appropriation, 64–65, 70, 136–37,
161
Self-immersion, 98; transcendence
and, 132–33. *See also*
Transcendence
Self-interest, 97–98, 149, 160–64, 175;
consequences of, 97–98. *See also*
Growth ethic; Mammon illness;
Profit; specific aspects
Self-provision, 108, 110
Self-transcendence. *See* Transcendence
Sharing, 27, 150–54; hope and, 208–
33. *See also* specific aspects
Shechem, 106
Shema: obedience to, 110–13
Sickness. *See* Illness
Sin (sinning), 10, 33, 60, 91, 145, 188;
almsgiving and remission of, 147;
forgiveness of, 147, 177–78;
Spiritual Exercises and, 122, 126
Slums (urban blight), 65, 244
Smith, Adam, 63, 97–98
Sobrino, Jon, 86

Social justice, 60, 61
Solomon, King, 3–6, 11
Soteriological principle of Christology, 54
Sower parable, 113
Speech (tongues): Pentecost and, 216
Spirit, 71–72, 73, 74, 75, 77, 82–95, 101, 235, 242–44; baptism and, 71; discipleship and, 179, 184; hope and sharing and, 208–33 passim; Pentecost and, 208–22. See also Holy Spirit
Split consciousness. See under Consciousness
Stewardship, 25–30, 32, 35, 90
Sublation (sublating intentions of Christ), 50–68, 69–104, 199, 234–45; Christ as one's wealth and, 234–45; meaning and use of term, 54. See also specific aspects, concepts
Suffering, 242–44
Symbols (symbolism), 212–14, 232–33; Pentecostal, 212–14

Tax collectors, 17, 18–19, 30–32, 33, 36–39
Technology (technetronics), 161–62
Temptations, 19–21, 78–79
Ten Commandments, 141, 186–87
Thanksgiving, 31, 32–33, 90, 95
Theories: development of, 63–65, 66, 135–36, 138, 162–63
Thomas, St., 102, 202
Thomas Aquinas, St., 87, 226
Tithe (tithing), 31, 90, 150
Tocqueville, Alexis Clérel de, 97, 98
Torah, 150
Transcendence (self-transcendence), 62, 63, 65, 100, 129, 130–39, 160–61, 162, 198–99; hope and sharing and, 201, 205, 209, 213, 227; and immanence, 23, 227, 228; and morals, 130–39; and obediential hearing, 129, 130–39
Transubstantiation: as a metaphor, vii–ix, 50, 83, 213. See also Eucharist
Trinity, and sharing of goods, 223–25
Triumphalism, 53

U.S. Catholic Bishops: "Catholic Social Teaching and the U.S. Economy" drafts of, 61–62
Urban blight (slums), 65, 244
Utopias, 227; utopian socialism, 227–28

Values (valuing), xi, 2–3, 16, 25, 41, 45, 55–57, 66, 72, 78, 102, 132–33, 139, 204, 238; enculturated faith and, 160–64; faith and sublation of the economy and, 66–68, 70–104, 142, 245; obediential hearing and, ix, 132–33, 139, 140–76 (see also Obedience); transvaluation and, 26–27
Van Beeck, Franz Jozef, ix, 81, 86, 87, 183, 185, 234–39
Vatican Council II, 55–56, 57, 67, 95, 102–4, 160, 199
Vine and its branches symbolism, 85

Wealth (the rich), xi, 26–29, 34, 81, 100–1, 118, 121, 143–44, 145–54, 207, 235–45; brethrenomics and, 146–49, 153, 194–95; Christ as one's wealth and, 235–45; faith mediated by, xi (see also Faith; specific aspects); and healing of mammon illness, 12–14, 26–49 passim, 211 (see also Healing; Mammon illness). See also Assets; Money; Poverty; Profit; specific aspects, concepts, developments, problems
Wealth of Nations (Smith), 63, 97–98
Will: God's, 71, 75, 144, 237, 245; obediential hearing and, 119, 121, 123, 127, 129, 139
Word of God, 196, 197
Worship, 70–77, 78–79, 111, 208, 235, 244, 245; authentic, 77; communal, 208; meaning of, 77
Worship and Secular Man (Panikkar), 76–77

Yahweh, 3–6, 17, 19, 20, 21, 147; and covenant with Israel, 106–19

Zacchaeus, 36–39